Turn it Up!

How To Perform At Your Highest Level For A Lifetime

DR. JEFFREY SPENCER | LIFE COACH TO THE STARS

Health Communications, Inc.
Deerfield Beach, Florida

www.hcibooks.com

Library of Congress Cataloging-in-Publication Data

Spencer, Jeffrey, Dr.
    Turn it up! / Jeffrey Spencer.
        p. cm.
    Includes index.
    ISBN-13: 978-0-7573-0618-1 (trade paper)
    ISBN-10: 0-7573-0618-7 (trade paper)
  1. Success—Psychological aspects.   I. Title.
    BF637.S8S65 2008
    158—dc22   2008008841

Publisher: Health Communications, Inc.
        3201 S.W. 15th Street
        Deerfield Beach, FL 33442-8190

Cover design by Justin Rotkowitz
Interior design by Lawna Patterson Oldfield
Interior formatting by Dawn Von Strolley Grove

CONTENTS

INTRODUCTION

We're All Born Winners

Success, as I see it, is a result, not a goal.

—Gustave Flaubert

One of my earliest recollections is being asked by my dad to help him pour a small concrete decorative disk in our front yard. Just the thought of palling up with my dad to create something together was about as good as it got for me at the time. In anticipation of the pour, I could barely restrain my overwhelming impulse to jump in and help him mix the concrete, even though I was such a young child. In the end, my help amounted to not much more than dragging an oversized shovel in the dirt alongside my dad as he pushed the cement-laden wheelbarrow to the pour site. And, once hardened, the perfectly formed disk instilled in me an overwhelming sense of pride and accomplishment that I had not previously experienced. And I liked what I felt: competent, capable, empowered, acknowledged, enthusiastic, and optimistic—so much so that I wanted more of the same.

As the years passed, I became more and more conscious of the fact that to be human is to desire and that desire and achievement are ever-present, indelible parts of the human experience and something to be embraced; not shied away from. And, if what people are telling me is true and represents a cross section of humanity, then desiring a more fulfilling and successful life is at the top of our wish list, something I wholeheartedly endorse and encourage everyone to pursue with a vengeance. I believe that with true success comes fulfillment, security, optimism, service to humanity, and goodwill, and these important signatures of success are as tangible as the material acquisitions that accompany them.

Most people have a well-defined sense of what circumstances they believe will bring them success, happiness, and fulfillment. Conceiving that list is perhaps the easiest part of the entire success process. The challenge to success is seldom a matter of enthusiasm or motivation, but, more specifically, in knowing exactly how to create it.

"What do I need to do to become more successful?" is, by far, the most frequent question I get asked as a coach and advisor to athletic teams, businesspeople, artists, entertainers, and array of others in varying disciplines. Finding and implementing the answer to this question is what separates those who "could have been something" from those who "are something." In *Turn It Up!*, I teach through illustrative examples and practical approaches what you can do to answer this question for yourself and make the difference.

The good news is you can create your own personal success system following the guidelines set down in this book. To develop your talents, mindset, and knowledge base to build the infrastructure needed to create your success only takes time and effort. That's it! That's what makes the difference between those who "do" and those who "don't." And, it never takes as much time and effort as we think. Devoting a little time to its creation on a regular basis will get you there in the least time. And, once your infrastructure is in place, your talents can then be applied toward achieving your specific goals with confidence. However, developing a proven template for success that is workable and sustainable and makes sense for your own life is definitely easier said than done.

Witnessing this major challenge throughout my years of consulting, training, counseling, and speaking, I've developed a plan to incorporate the mental and the physical, fusing them together for a fail-proof personal success system that builds and maintains the necessary infrastructure. Even though most people want an easy life and think it will give them the life fulfillment they seek, my experience tells me that the happiest people are those who perpetually seek goals and whose lives are appropriately challenged, so they remain alert and focused on moving forward toward a better future. Your picking up this book is living proof that this is true.

Having been in the success game for years, my conclusion is that *we're all born winners* and have the capacity to live abundantly successful lives. "Yeah, right," you might say. Is this statement a stretch? To some, yes. But not because it is; only because they think it is. My experience tells me it's so. We may not believe it, have learned it, trusted it, or have experienced it. Yet, it's indisputable that each of us has our own special innate talents and unique life perspective that makes us a distinct entity among the 6-plus billion people on the planet at this moment. Think about that. This means that in all of human history—past, present, and future—there's only one of us. This distinctness uniquely qualifies each of us to do some great things in life.

We all have the raw human resources to become successful. The secret to a passionate, productive, purposeful, and prosperous life is to identify and refine our talents into highly productive assets enabling us to conceive of and parlay our efforts into goals accomplished. Successful people know that talent and will aren't enough, so they focus their time and effort on honing their skills sufficiently to manifest their aspirations and then place them within well-constructed plans. They just keep applying the same strategy and churning out successes one after another. It simply becomes an exercise of connecting the dots and playing by the success rules—something we can all do with the correct knowledge and application. That's what the "U2s," "Lance Armstrongs," and other perpetual successes of the world have done, and this is the framework that I provide you in this book.

Correctly connecting the dots is, of course, more challenging than it appears. Otherwise we'd all be leading utopian lives perpetually basking in the fruits of our passions and labor. Certainly, it takes time and effort to refine our raw talent and polish our planning and execution skills to the point where they enable us to reach our goals consistently. But it's virtually never as time and energy intensive as originally believed. Ask any successful person and they'll tell you that the biggest challenge to initiating action to pursue a goal is overcoming the intimidation of how big and difficult we make the process to be in our minds. This exaggeration often dissuades many from ever even attempting a goal. Even the ultra-successful have encountered this very same defeatist challenge en route to their first significant success. They overcame it, just as we all can, by continually refining their mental, physical, and technical skills by devoting daily time to each, even if just for a few minutes a day. And then *presto!*, one day their efforts hit critical mass and they pull off that pivotal success that begins their life transformation to become a full-blown, full-time success dynamo.

I personally know from firsthand experience that everyone is born with the innate capacity to succeed. While growing up, so many of the risk factors foretelling a life gone wrong applied to me that I could have been the poster child for the harbingers of a troubled life: welfare household; alcoholism; divorce; rat-infested, dilapidated home; no money; poor nutrition; raised by a single mom.

Thankfully, my life was redirected through committed mentors who selflessly taught me how to set and achieve goals, and mostly to help me understand that my destiny was not preordained by my genetics or dictated by my circumstantial developmental influences, but, by what I *did*. They taught me to combine my innate tenacity, talents, and passions with the self-sufficiency they instilled in me to focus and finish the job and maintain a positive life outlook. It was with this invaluable guidance that I could plan and execute tasks that would bring forth and optimize my positive potential rather than fulfilling the prophecy of my adverse early-life circumstances.

Having been taught and forced to use my self-sufficiency skills by my mentors, I was able to precisely direct my energies toward and complete the plans that enabled me to make the 1972 United States Olympic Team as a sprint and tandem cyclist, receive my bachelor's and master's degrees *cum laude* from the University of Southern California, write books, present seminars, travel the world, work with some of the most talented and accomplished people on the planet, be happily married, have a successful chiropractic practice, show my art-glass sculptures in the best galleries, and believe my best work is still in front of me. For certain, my own cleverness didn't create these outcomes; they were the product of solid mentorship at the correct time from selfless people who cared enough about me to share their wisdom. My part was easy. All I did was show up for duty and implement their sagely advice. I want to pass this on to you, and through reading *Turn It Up!*, you will acquire the skills to focus, plan, and utilize your confidence to consistently complete your success plans.

The Backbone of This Book

Thirty years ago, I began my professional success outreach, working with learning-disabled children and teens as an educational therapist, teaching them how to learn and become successful despite their challenges. This experience gave me several critical insights into the nature of success and failure. In addition to the mechanics of developing better technical learning skills and brain-data processing connections, I observed that there were common self-perception beliefs and attitudes that dramatically influenced the extent to which the students either overcame or further succumbed to their liabilities.

The common mindset deterring the children and teens was that they did not believe they were capable of success. They saw others as winners but not themselves, feared failure, had a reluctance to risk, lacked confidence in decision making, were unable and apprehensive about thinking outside the box, were unfocused and unable to create coherent plans, and were prone to illness.

Of all of these factors, the student's biggest roadblock to their learning, by far, was their mistaken belief that to be capable and deserving of success, they had to be perfect students or "like everybody else." The expectation of remembering *everything* was so burdensome to them that their fear of not remembering *anything*, literally, put so much pressure on them they often couldn't recall even the simplest facts on a test that they could easily recall in normal conversation. This incapacity, in turn, pummeled their self-confidence, compounding their belief that they weren't born winners capable of success, compelling them to fulfill that prophecy by continuing to fail and ultimately adopting the attitude that since they couldn't perform up to anticipated standards anyway, why even try.

Without question, the biggest factor that improved the students' confidence, learning, and retention was shifting their focus toward understanding their material within the context of real-life experience rather than memorizing facts associated with examination questions just for the sake of getting perfect test scores. With this "pressure off" orientation, they learned and retained much more information, had fun learning it, performed better on examinations, were much more optimistic, and consequently perceived themselves as—and became—capable of learning and applying the skills to become independent learners and self-directed "winners."

The most gratifying part of that chapter of my life was hearing the magic words that the students "no longer required my services" because they were performing up to their capacity in and out of school. This meant that they had become independent learners confident in their skills and ability to learn and apply their knowledge toward constructive problem solving. Few rewards are greater than that in life.

Several years later, I transitioned to working with American Honda's factory motorcycle racing team, developing their athletes' physical-conditioning programs. The team management decided at the end of the previous year to completely revamp their racing program by hiring relatively unknown, but accomplished, athletes and brought me in to develop and maximize their athletes' physical condition so the team could again become the dominant force in motorcycle racing they had previously been. Though I was originally contracted to oversee the athletes' physical-training regimens, I quickly found myself spending more and more time mentoring the athletes, developing their mentalities, and shaping their life structures to become more prolific successes.

Despite their incredible physical talents and exacting technical knowledge of their discipline, my first impression of the athletes was that they noticeably lacked the conviction and belief that they were winners. Most seemed preoccupied, subtlety distracted. Eye contact was sparse. Spoken sentences were choppy and uncommitted and devoid of power and authority. Their body language and mannerisms had a taint of suppressed irritability, discontent, and restlessness of spirit about them. I'd seen this collection of behaviors many times and knew it was indicative of people who doubted their abilities to succeed.

During my subsequent one-on-one conversations with them, the athletes most expressed to me that they were acutely aware that they were capable of better performances, but were frustrated by an unidentifiable *something* that was holding them back from attaining it. This unresolved breech between what the athletes' performances *were* and what they *could be* was clearly the reason for the preoccupation and subtle disconnect I felt with them. I considered this a good thing, as it meant the athletes wanted better results than they were getting and were willing to do what it took to get them.

The "something" the athletes were missing was not a *single* piece of the success puzzle but a *system* to develop, harness, and apply their talents to achieve specific goals consistent with their talents and skill sets. Their ambiguity in identifying the precise nature of the illusive "something" they lacked was obscured by the fact that the "something" was not an isolated, single "it" but several, perhaps seemingly insignificant, "its" bundled together. The "something" itself was buried in the larger collection of influences constituting their life's bigger picture. And the very good news about this is that all the "somethings" constituting the "it" that were preventing their success were completely modifiable. Combining this fact with their explicit willingness to do everything needed to acquire the assets to reach their goals made it very easy to make the adjustments necessary for the team to start to realize their talents and belief as winners, thus, improving their results.

Interestingly, the blocks to the underperforming team members preventing them from attaining their full potential were mostly identical to those seen with the learning-disabled students: not believing they were capable of success, the fear of failure, not wanting to risk a chance on success, not confident in choice making, inability to think outside the box, easily distracted, unable to create coherent plans to complete tasks, not knowing how to re-create the successes they experience, and getting sick too often.

Their biggest fault, also seen with the students, but with a slightly different twist, was their trying so hard to be so perfect with their physical and mental fitness. Believing that this would bring them the success they craved so badly, they overtaxed their minds and overtrained their bodies to the point of burnout. Unfortunately, all that did was reduce their physical and mental capacity and caused them to get sick more often, be less able to respond to opportunity, diminish their enthusiasm, create mental chaos, perform poorly, and erode their resiliency. Other challenges seen with the athletes were their inability to know when or how to say no, not giving themselves permission to succeed, poorly balancing their physical efforts with recovery, not trusting their abilities and preparation when it came time to perform, not having a deliberate protocol for creating and maintaining health, and having no clue how to develop and execute a long-term sustainable life success plan that would extend their careers.

Fortunately, these obstacles were modifiable and the athletes only needed to be properly guided in their preparation to have more success in competition. This responsibility was very important to me for several reasons. First, it was part of my obligation to pay respect to my mentors who gave me the gift of direction so I could experience greater success. Second, to help the athletes build the self-sufficiency to have prosperous lives after their athletic careers were over. Third, as an Olympian, I fully understood that the fittest athletes on the planet couldn't become top champions if they didn't consistently make the correct life decisions and properly pace themselves to perform at their highest level over an entire season and career. Finally, knowing my advice would play a direct role in the athletes' destinies, I wanted to honor the trust they placed in me by providing them the framework and tools to be self-governing in creating repetitive success in their lives.

My tenure with the team was four years. The first year was a year of implementing and adapting to the new training system and developing relationships. I made sure we didn't get ahead of ourselves by trying to do too much too quickly or aspiring to achieve unrealistic goals, knowing that's usually what happens when major changes in policy occur. Most often, this only creates chaos and disappointment because the unrealistic expectations aren't met. The team won one out of the four possible championships that year. That was a great confirmation that our system was working. The following year we added another championship, and the team was beginning to fully experience and appreciate the power of having a structured system in place that optimized everyone's success potential. Our third and fourth years saw complete dominance, as the team won most of the championships, thus, reestablishing the team's dominance in the sport and setting the stage for what would become a sports dynasty.

Having completed my tenure with the Team Honda, I began consulting individual athletes and teams in other sports doing what I did for Team Honda, creating winners by building their mental, tactical, and physical talents within a personalized success structure that would enable them to perform consistently at their best.

To enhance the breadth of my services to my clients at that juncture in my career, I investigated the world of sports injuries. Athletes get injured, and how fast and well they heal plays a vital role in how successful their seasons and careers will be. My experience as an athlete mirrored what I was seeing with my clients. They had no injury-prevention strategy in place and when injured they took too long to heal and often healed incorrectly. To fill that void, I enrolled in chiropractic college so I could speed my clients' injury recovery and address their comprehensive healthcare needs while concurrently developing their physical conditioning and personal-management programs.

Having obtained my chiropractic license, I began treating my clients' injuries, providing wellness care, prescribing diets and supplements to them while continuing to develop their fitness programs, build their success mentalities and create workable life strategies to help them balance the demands of their professional and daily lives. In essence, I became a one-stop shopping center able to provide my clients with everything necessary to build their capacity to consistently perform at their best, which, in turn, would lead to long and prosperous careers.

Because of this diversity, I started receiving inquires from people in different sports and disciplines, such as business and entertainment, to assist them in improving their physical and mental performance. Like Team Honda, most people's interest was in improving their physical performance but inevitably the personal development side became equal to, if not more important than, their attaining their goals, especially since the mind and body profoundly influence one another. As I became more familiar with the other disciplines, I saw the same challenges, but with a slightly different spin, that prevented the students and athletes from performing at their best, impacting the others: general restlessness about life, frustrated at not reaching goals, questioning whether continued success is possible, fearing the best of life had come and gone, working too hard or too often without better results, not saying no when prudent, an unbalanced social life, poor concentration, wondering if bouncing back is possible, lack of belief in talents and preparation, sub-par health, diminished enthusiasm, and complete bewilderment about how to develop, adapt, and execute a personalized life success plan to enhance and extend careers. And, same as before, all the impediments getting to and remaining on the success bandwagon were completely resolvable. Likewise, the prescription of having the knowledge, belief, commitment, and persistence and implementing a proven success system applied. There was nothing magic to it; same rules, just a different game.

Eventually, my practice evolved, and a full spectrum of people began seeking my assistance on a variety of issues all dealing in some measure with their desire to becoming more successful, which, I knew from previous experience, goes far beyond their initial goals. Typical requests I'd get were for improved mental and physical fitness, proactive wellness care, better nutrition, life coaching, career planning, professional referral, enhanced recovery, improved biomechanics, injury prevention, injury management, or any combination of the above. In reality, however, each of these specific areas are part of a larger life picture composed of several elements that when cohesively tied together in proper proportion create a highly personalized success system that produces constant wins throughout life. And, it is this observation that is the basis for my success system and for this book.

Living Proof

The origin of my success philosophy began at age nineteen when I was training for a birth on the United States Olympic Cycling Team. My coach taught me that my cycling success would be based solely on how well I minimized my mental and physical weaknesses and maximized their strengths—on and off the track. He was emphatic that being brilliant in one area alone would not enable me to make an Olympic Team, but, rather, a combination of highly refined skills in a variety of areas would. His comprehensive coaching style and meticulous mentorship enabled me to make the 1972 United States Olympic Cycling Team, and I competed in the Munich Olympics. I completely credit my coach and others' support for that achievement. It never would have happened without them.

Almost two and half decades after I began my success outreach helping individuals and teams become top performers, I was privileged to have had the opportunity to use my entire arsenal of skills developed during that time supporting Lance Armstrong and the United States Postal Service and Discovery Channel Professional Cycling Teams win seven consecutive Tours de France. It was a phenomenal seven-plus-year experience being buried at the deepest level in the day-to-day operations of the team, mending minds and bodies during the Tour. The incredible success the team had illustrates what level of individual and team achievement is possible when selfless people share a common purpose unconditionally giving 100 percent of themselves to one another by doing *absolutely* everything possible at the limit of their capacity to support the group dynamic to succeed.

The outcome of that magic was the team winning the world's most grueling sporting event an incomprehensible record seven times, the equivalent to winning seven consecutive Superbowls, and Lance, deservedly so, being heralded as one of the greatest all-time athletes in the history of sport. In addition to the immense gratification of seeing the accolades given to the team for their superhuman achievements, it was extremely validating, personally, to be acknowledged for my contribution to those victories by having been given the name "Dr. Magic" by the team and staff and to be acknowledged by Lance in his book *Every Second Counts*, as being "Part doctor, Part guru, Part medicine man" . . . "who we believed could fix any and all of our problems" and "while he fixed us physically, he also fixed us mentally" and "if you judged the most important man on the Postal team by the foot traffic in and out of his door, then it was Jeff. Without him, we knew we'd never make it to Paris." The icing on the cake to this chapter in my life was going back to the Tour a final time after taking a year off from the Tour when Lance retired and, again, helping the team win the Tour for what would be my eighth consecutive Tour victory by putting Alberto Contador on top of the podium in Paris as the new Tour champion.

Unlike the Tour, not everyone has the opportunity to surround themselves with a multitude of coaches and mentors, helping them pave the way toward their goals. That's why I wrote this book. Through *Turn It Up!*, I will teach you how and why creating and sustaining a successful life isn't about one or two super-attributes, intense struggle, or grave sacrifice, but more, about strengthening, in reasonable proportion, all of the elements—that when taken as a whole—enable proper planning and execution of the tasks necessary to achieve goals with consistent vitality, confidence, and enthusiasm. In addition, I also advocate that perfectionism, will, and talent are essential parts of, but aren't, the foundations of success. The key to success is developing and executing a well-constructed plan that is consistent with your skill set, time availability, and resources—something everybody can learn to do.

Turn It Up! is a realistic road map for those who want to turn up the volume on their lives and get in the success fast lane. It is designed to systematically teach the easy-to-learn, step-by-step skills that I know work because I have witnessed it firsthand in my own life and repeatedly with the successes of my clients.

Success is a natural state of living, but there are principles that even the super-successful must follow to consistently reach their goals. *Turn It Up!* is where the foundation of these principles are explained and offered for the taking with examples and anecdotes of the proper mindset, planning, and action steps necessary to precisely formulate and execute your own successful plans to make your dreams and ambitions come true.

The success stories I chronicle throughout this book illustrate a vital element that I believe is overlooked in other books: physical health and fitness and creating a healthy work and home environment. You cannot fully create and maintain a success lifestyle without these four elements, and I will teach you these fundamentals throughout *Turn It Up*

Finally, at the book's conclusion, I offer you proven steps to remain perpetually successful, because, as with anything, recognizing maintenance as one of the biggest challenges is the key to the process.

Success is a skill anybody can learn, but it requires the correct organization and implementation of particular strategies, something everybody can do by following the success plan laid out in *Turn It Up!* Now it's time for you to Turn It Up! and pave your road to continued, prolific success!

1

Why Success Matters

Real success is finding
your lifework in the work that you love.

—David McCullough

Perhaps no other factor is as poignant and ubiquitous to the human experience as the drive to succeed. The impulse to be successful is an indelible, deeply etched primal instinct that profoundly influences each and every one of our thoughts and actions. Everyone defines success in his or her own personal way. Regardless of variations, each definition conveys that success happens the instant a beneficial outcome occurs. When a childhood gymnast performs their first cartwheel perfectly, an astronomer discovers a new comet, a musician has their first hit, or a librarian correctly places a book back on the bookshelf, they have all met the criteria for success and have become a success by doing so.

"Can I be successful?" is a question everyone asks at some point. "Yes, of course you can" is the resounding answer. Success, however, is not reserved just for high-powered Type A personalities or driven individuals. As mentioned in the introduction to this book, we're all born winners. Our inheritance at birth endows us with the innate capacity and drive to succeed; it's just that most of us never learned or have simply forgotten it, or we don't trust our ability to achieve our goals. Yet success is an easily learned skill that anyone can master. Successful people aren't embarrassed or guilty about their success; they recognize and embrace it as the most fundamental force driving their life experience.

Becoming a consistent success is extremely straightforward in concept: *It requires only the timely completion of specific tasks within a well-structured plan that achieves a predetermined outcome.* One or two random successes don't make someone a success. Success is a skill that, when practiced diligently, becomes second nature and consistently produces the desired outcomes, creating a productive, vital, and passionate life.

In broad brushstroke terms, success has a competitive side to it. Every moment of your life pits your desire, knowledge, and ingenuity against your potential, history, and destiny. If your talents, great ideas, and skills are consistent with your plans and actions, achieving your goals becomes commonplace. Conversely, scattered and ill-founded plans, coupled with insufficient skills or resources, predictably lead to sub-par goal achievement and a less fulfilled life.

Success matters to everyone desiring a highly vital, exciting, and rewarding life. Have you ever known anybody whose life ambition was to be a loser or unsuccessful? Can you imagine someone saying to his wife "Hey, honey, I'm going to go to bed early tonight so I'll have plenty of energy to go out and fail tomorrow." This, of course, may seem like an absurd example, yet it reflects the subconscious "failure mentality" countless people reenact day after day in their lives. Many people, if not most, have more confidence in their capacity to fail than to succeed.

Success may be your most vital life resource because it can break the hidden chains that hold you back from becoming the best you can be. Success does this for you by building a strong mind and passionate spirit, creating meaningful relationships, achieving balance in life, securing a better future, manifesting dreams, defining who you are and what you stand for, and enabling you to build and capitalize on your talents.

Success Builds a Winner's Mentality

To prosper and endure in today's hyperkinetic, fast-paced, hectic world requires a special "winner's mentality" that quickly and efficiently converts ideas into success. Each success you have further builds your winning mentality by improving your ability to focus, increasing your belief in the value of your aspirations, increasing your confidence in your decision making, expanding your cognitive capacity, increasing your life passion, and strengthening your purpose.

Your successes will only occur as fast and accurately as you can create and execute successful plans in rapid-fire succession. Success demands and forces you to develop a focused mind and attention span that can continually assist you in determining and acquiring the skills and knowledge necessary to formulate and execute plans consistent with your ambitions. Your ability to focus and concentrate set the upper limit for how far you can develop your capacity for success because that determines what actions you can conceive and are capable of implementing. The legacy you leave will be the product of your thought-focused actions. Proper focus will produce lofty thoughts, big results, and significant legacies. Scattered focus will not.

Repeated success strengthens your ability to make prudent decisions related to achieving the objectives you set for yourself. You will be able to listen selectively to what others tell you, but you will not be persuaded inappropriately. A large reservoir of hidden talent and latent success probably lie buried beneath the layers of expectation and opinion that others have piled on you throughout your life. Others will continue to heap more and more onto that pile until such time as you formulate and pursue your own goals and respectfully inform them that their input is needed only when solicited. No one has the authority to hold you hostage with intrusive thoughts, suggestions, or expectations. Your life is yours to manage in the way you determine will express your greatest talents and build the legacy you desire. Success teaches you to enact those actions that consistently produce your goals, not the goals of others.

Each success you have opens your mind a little further to additional successes you're capable of achieving. And the more you succeed, the more options you will envision and the more you will succeed. Every experience you have, and every fact you learn, reorganizes your knowledge base and prompts fresh and novel ideas related to achieving more success.

Indecision kills opportunity faster than anything. Previous success demonstrates that achievement occurs only as fast and accurately as an opportunity is seized and acted upon. The old adage "He who hesitates is lost" is more poignant today than ever because of the increased number of people vying for the same opportunities. However, the word *hesitation* doesn't exist in the vocabulary of the successful because their successes have given them the confidence to embrace and capitalize on opportunity at the instant it presents itself.

> "The word *hesitation* doesn't exist in the vocabulary of the successful."

Success builds a better brain, a strong spirit, and a champion's outlook by inspiring you to be in constant pursuit of your next success. Success is the ultimate "feel good" prescription because it keeps your mind and body running at peak levels powered by enthusiasm, ambition, motivation, and optimism. The best minds and souls on the planet belong to individuals who have experienced the elation of success, which inspired them to further strive for a lifetime of constructive and positive achievement. I've never met a person with great mental acuity and passion who isn't actively in pursuit of a beneficial goal. Finding solutions to problems so you can achieve a beneficial goal is the exercise your brain needs to create optimal neural pathways to keep your goal setting and achieving at peak levels.

Success improves the speed and accuracy of your decision making. The more success you have, the better your pattern recognition and intuitive skills become. These will increase the rate and authenticity of your successes and fortify your confidence in turning to these vital resources in your choice making. These skills enable you to see problems before they occur because they enhance your capacity to see the impact each factor in your plan will have on every other factor. Few things are worse than seeing someone spend a significant amount of time and resources pursuing a goal, only to have it fall apart due to preventable circumstances that were evident, yet not identified, during the plan's creation, inception, or execution.

Trusting Yourself

Goals achieved shift your mentality from hope to anticipated success. Matters once deemed impossible may now seem doable and within reach. Within weeks after Roger Bannister became the first to run the mile in under four minutes—*a feat thought impossible*—every top runner beat the four-minute mark. Prior to Bannister's achievement, the thought of breaking the "impossible" four-minute barrier was unthinkable, not because it was but because the prevailing mental sentiment said it was, even though it wasn't. When the facts say, and you believe, something is possible regardless of how impossible it seems or what others say, then with a high degree of certainty it is attainable. When you believe in yourself and appropriately match your skills with opportunity, what's possible morphs from possibility to inevitability. Seize it.

No one ever has, nor will you ever, accomplish everything you set out to do. Your inability to reach every goal you pursue is actually healthy, however, because it teaches you to remain trustful in yourself and gracious in defeat, and thereby a more determined individual and a better example for others. When others see you bounce back from a goal not achieved, they realize that not achieving a goal is something everyone must and can confront and overcome. They then realize that defeat isn't personal—it only illustrates that something failed to occur despite the best efforts put forth to make it happen. This is no big deal as it happens millions of times daily and illustrates that committed people are continually reaching for success. This realization inspires others to initiate actions toward goals they might not otherwise set, which helps them develop more trust in themselves and reinforces their hope for more positive outcomes and a better future.

Impeccable timing and patience are fundamental to consistent success. Success teaches you that trusting your instincts and initiating the correct action at the right moment are what make you master of your own time and slave to no one. When you respect your timing, reacting impulsively and unwillingly jumping through others' hoops just doesn't happen. Your confidence in yourself and respect for the opportunities that arise always permit you to take the time necessary to do everything in its own time, while never being blinded by too much self-interest or fear that if you don't react to an opportunity immediately you'll lose it forever.

> "Impeccable timing and patience are fundamental to consistent success."

Busy, productive, task-completion-oriented people who believe in their abilities get more done in any given amount of time than those less certain of their abilities. Experienced doctors having five minutes to complete a ten-minute procedure will do it, correctly and completely, in five minutes. Less experienced doctors, with less confidence in their abilities, with thirty minutes to complete the same ten-minute task, will take thirty minutes to do it. Belief makes you a proficient time manager, enabling you to complete tasks more efficiently in a shorter time and thus making more time available for you to allocate to other endeavors.

Optimism Is Everything

Few actions generate personal empowerment faster than creating a positive outcome out of an idea, and success does that. Success takes an invisible idea and makes it tangible in the physical world. That's the alchemy of human ingenuity. Everyone who's achieved a goal knows the sense of self-pride that manifesting something positive brings. Every goal attained breaks a few more of the invisible chains that hold you back from becoming the best you can be, making your future goals easier to achieve. Each of your successes reconfirms to you that your achievements are the result of your efforts, and each validates your capacity to be the author of your own destiny.

Your successes make you more optimistic than those who don't conceive of, initiate, strive for, or reach for goals. Optimistic people firmly believe they will achieve their aspirations and that their best achievements and times are ahead of them. As your optimism grows, so do your vitality, energy, and enthusiasm, inspiring an even greater sense of purpose and hope that sets the stage for future prosperity.

Success matters because it teaches you to look to yourself, rather than others, for your happiness and validation. As a winner you always know you'll get things done and take care of yourself regardless of circumstances. Your self-generated independence enables you to support others unconditionally without reciprocal expectation.

The hope of having a successful today and a better tomorrow is the driving force that motivates winners to get up every morning. Your anticipation and belief in a more prosperous and fulfilling future keep your mind sharp and your fires of enthusiasm burning bright.

Success happens when preparation meets opportunity. Your ability to capture an opportunity is directly proportional to your optimism, skill level, and preparedness. Optimism allows you to seize an opportunity the moment it shows up, and your skill level and preparedness allow you to transform it into a concrete success. The more optimistic and prepared you are, the more opportunities you will seize and the more successes you will have.

Winning Builds Empowered Relationships

Rarely will your successes go unnoticed. Each success can illustrate to others that they also can become accomplished winners. Empowerment through example is an important gift you can give others. We've all seen the power of notoriety at major sporting events where the kids wear replica jerseys with their favorite star's name and number on the back, hoping someday to "be" them or at least be like them. Always take life's high road—you never know who's watching.

Successful people are often unfairly labeled as being too self-absorbed, too good for others, and indulgent by those who have never experienced much success, when in fact real life winners extend unconditional support to others and never let such sentiments stand in the way of that support. Outreach creates tremendous goodwill. When you extended yourself willingly to others, it will reinforce your conviction in your principles and further strengthen your belief in yourself.

Prosperous individuals always see success as being plentiful enough for everyone to have as much as they want. Sharing abundance is a given for the successful, whose life mission is to respect others—as well as the blessings of their own gifts—enough to encourage others to partake of their own share of universal abundance.

> "Always take life's high road—you never know who is watching."

More than anything, people want validation. Winners always take the time to say thank-you and to acknowledge those who have contributed positively to their lives. Lance Armstrong was once asked about the contribution his team made to his success in the Tour de France, and his response was that he was only the zipper on the yellow jersey (the jersey worn by the active leader of the Tour), while the team was the jersey.

Every word you speak and action you undertake impacts others, whether intentionally or unintentionally. We've all experienced someone telling us how important something we said or did was for them and how it changed their life in a profound way. The right word or action said or done at the right time can make the difference between a good or bad life to some. Winners know the power of words and actions, and they choose both carefully. They know success is bigger than they are, and they uphold that privilege of influence respectfully.

Everyone Wins with Group Synergy

Group synergy is a mainstay of successful lives. No one can do alone

everything necessary to become and remain successful. We all need the assistance of others to do for us
what we can't do for ourselves. Relationships exist
on many levels, each contributing to the grand prize
of shared accomplishment. Win–wins build tremendous affinity among people, inspiring us to seek out
others with whom to collaborate.

> "Winners know the power of words and actions, and they choose both carefully."

Successful people thoughtfully consider the impact
their thoughts, words, and actions have on people, places, and things, and they
only enact those that are beneficial. Such consideration breeds extraordinary
trust and respect among people. As trust increases, people open up more and
more to each other, greater group synergy occurs, and the group dynamic flour-
ishes further. Each member prospers from doing what he or she is best at and
from the group's success in achieving its mutual goals. Trust builds trust and
mutual success.

Sports teams are excellent examples of this, with the most successful
teams composed of players who work well with each other, all unified by
the pursuit of a common goal that brings out the best in everybody. Equally
important to the benefits you receive from others is what they get from you
and from the relationship, including learning how to succeed and build
their own successful futures.

The easiest way to turn a potential success into an achieved one is to
establish optimal communication among those with whom you're working
to accomplish your goals. Once the communication lines are established,
the coordinated efforts of the group to function as a unified whole expand
exponentially, which leads to explosive growth. Becoming a great communicator produces consistent group success by unifying people toward common goals, posting them to positions that match their expertise, providing
clear descriptions of what to do, and giving them responsibility to make
their own decisions regarding how to reach their goals for your plan's successful completion and the benefits they receive from their participation.

Planning for Success Builds a Better You

Perhaps the most important benefit you receive from reaching your goals is what your successes do for you as a person, but to achieve your goals you must first identify precisely what your goals are. Then you must plan and execute the steps of your plan to bring their benefits into the physical world. To accomplish this concept-to-completion cycle, you must develop superior cognitive, technical, physical, and creative skills. Beyond enabling you to achieve your goals, these skills make you a more self-determining and self-sustaining individual who makes a positive contribution to humanity.

Success teaches you to make appropriate, not reckless or overly conservative, decisions. Without some risk, nothing happens in life, making it impossible for you to live any better than you do today. Taking appropriate risk is necessary to surmount those factors that hold you back from fully developing your talents and living your dreams. Living life too much in the safe zone keeps you subordinate to other people, places, and things, which halts the development of your talents and makes living a meaningful and prosperous life more difficult.

At the end of the day, no one but you can do what is necessary to make your success happen. All the great golfers and tennis players must swing their own golf clubs and rackets; no one can do that for them. Success teaches you that the responsibility for success is yours alone.

One of my most valuable life lessons came from my mentor when I was eighteen years old. I was feeling sorry for myself when my mentor asked if I'd like a helping hand to help me through this rough spot. I said, "Yes." Then he looked me straight in the eye and told me in no uncertain terms that if I wanted a helping hand, I had one at the end of each arm. He promptly turned around and left the room. As startled as I was, I knew he was absolutely right. He knew that for me to become self-determining I had to find my own answers.

Successful lives confirm the fact that, regardless of circumstance, there's always enough energy to accomplish everything you need to get done, especially when it's on behalf of others. At the Tours de France I did with the United States Postal and Discovery Channel Professional Cycling Teams, I'd get five hours of sleep each night for three weeks straight while working incessantly mending bodies and minds, but I never felt physically or mentally torched beyond repair at any time. A ten-minute nap here and there helped for sure, but what got the entire team to the finish in Paris intact and in the winner's circle was the team's commitment to one another to be there through thick and thin, doing whatever it took to uphold our obligation to one another and get the job done. There wasn't a single self-serving moment during any of those brutally difficult three-week events.

Identifying and adapting to the best way to achieve a goal is a trait every winner has acquired. No plan ever goes from inception to completion exactly the way you think it will, because no sooner do you get started on something than circumstances change, forcing you to adapt your plan to accommodate the new situation to keep your plan moving toward its best outcome. Often the best results occur when a plan slams dead up against an impenetrable barrier, forcing you to find an alternative way to the goal that inevitably turns out to be better than you could have imagined. Such encounters teach you that there's always a "better way" to a better goal, you only have to find it and act on it.

Skills are the cornerstone that productive, enriched lives are built on, and winners correctly recognize them as their greatest asset. Each skill acquired advances you closer to complete personal independence. A sufficiently diversified skill set gives you the confidence to do just about anything, yet you know that if you can't do something, it's only a matter of acquiring the skills necessary to do it.

If your resource pool, composed of materials, people, and finances, is not sufficient to transform an opportunity into a success, the opportunity will die en route to completion. Worse yet, if resources have already been allocated to a project and it deteriorates midstream, the project not only blows up but the resource pool also evaporates, making future attempts at success impossible. Successful people build their resource pool before they need it when they have the time to do it—*and never delay it*—because they know that once they get busy the time will never be available to create it. When building a resource reserve, it's always prudent to put a little extra into the stockpile for the proverbial rainy day when an unanticipated crisis demands unanticipated additional resources.

Becoming successful teaches you to become a proactive embracer of life instead of a helpless reactor to it. Winners realize that each action they complete catapults them forward toward a goal and has the potential to open three or four more doors to other opportunities. The more actions they initiate, the more success will fill their lives.

> "Becoming successful teaches you to become a proactive embracer of life instead of a helpless reactor to it."

Winning reinforces your planning abilities. All the selecting, sequencing, and completing in minimal time the tasks needed to achieve your aspirations will enhance your abilities. There's only so much time to achieve a goal, and the best step you can take to conserve energy and time is to have a complete and well-organized plan.

Every Second Counts

Ideally, each of your life's moments is motivated by hope and enthusiasm for a better now and an expansive future. Life's seminal moments occur when opportunities meet a mind and skill set capable of converting them into beneficial outcomes. Fabulous legacies are built when great adaptation skills, health, mental clarity, and opportunities converge to create a dynamic platform that makes a highly productive lifestyle possible.

Sixty-three million years ago, a monstrous asteroid plunged into the ocean, creating a massive climate change that led to the extinction of the dinosaurs. Had dinosaurs successfully adapted to the new climate, they

would have survived. Successful people remain successful by adapting moment by moment to changing
life conditions. Mental and physical agility make
effortless transitions possible from old to new and
innovative ways of accomplishing tasks in new climates so you can maintain your competitive advantage. Viewing change as an ally is essential to
capitalizing on opportunity. The only certainty in life

> "Look for change
> and embrace it since
> it's where the
> greatest opportunity
> exists."

is change, which makes constant adaptation an essential survival skill for
you to master. Look for change and embrace it since it's where opportunity
exists.

It's impossible to work 365 days a year at peak intensity without becoming ill or burnt out, and all too frequently great plans terminate because of
those very consequences. The old school "No Pain, No Gain" (and no
future) success mantra has been replaced with a contemporary "Smarter Is
Better" manifesto that states success is achieved by having better health,
thinking smarter, promoting better day-to-day recovery, balancing life
activities, and focusing on long-term success. The best time to make health
changes is before you become ill. Once you're sick it takes more money,
time, and effort to get well than it does to remain healthy in the first place.
Health is your greatest asset. Do everything possible to preserve it.

With each new accomplishment, success snowballs and attracts a flood
of new opportunities to you. Every film star has experienced an avalanche
of new script offers after a successful movie, much like the influx of new
people who come into your life, and the new opportunities that emerge, as
you become successful. Taking advantage of each moment's opportunity
makes the best opportunities surface most often. The more successes you
have, the bigger your sphere of influence becomes and the greater the
impact each of your actions and words has on yourself and others. Your
sphere of influence gives you the platform to inspire others to manifest
their talents as winners, and allows you to build an infrastructure of like-
minded people to support your aspirations. Having a circle of like-minded

peers with whom to exchange information, bounce ideas around, and consult is an invaluable asset to building and maintaining a successful lifestyle. Camaraderie and relationship are vital elements in building great lives. Making use of them as much as possible helps make every second count.

Success Made Simple

Just the mention of the word success can intimidate people. The very thought of being successful can be extremely unsettling, illusive, and foreign to many. At the end of the day, however, success can be distilled into several key concepts that when appropriately integrated can make regular success possible with little investment of effort, time, and resources.

No single characteristic distinguishes you more than your actions. What you do reflects what's important to you and what you stand for. Knowing yourself and investing your energy and confidence in your unique talents gives your life conviction and purpose and gives you the best opportunity to express your greatest attributes most often. Your life's passion, commitment, talents, personal evolution, commercial value, and legacy reflect your core beliefs and life principles as expressed through your most important calling card: your actions. Your life is measured only by what you do and have achieved.

You must always confirm that the successes and goals you desire match what you really want your life to be. To fully understand the impact your dreams and loftiest aspirations can have on your life, it's imperative that you observe and talk with those who are living your dreams before you invest the emotional, physical, and resource capital to achieve them yourself. This is the only way you will know with complete certainty that your dreams match what is possible, that your expectations are realistic, and that your goals are worth pursing. A doctor confided to me that he

> "You must always confirm that the successes and goals you desire match what you really want your life to be."

would never have gone to medical school to become a physician had he known how difficult the hours and demands of medicine were. He could have avoided this difficult challenge by doing a life simulation dry run in medical practice before enrolling in medical school. He could have asked several physicians about the realities of practice, both good and bad, and could have followed them around their practices while they examined and treated their patients. This would have provided the reality check necessary for him to see with precise clarity what medical practice really is on a day-to-day, face-to-face basis. We've all heard, or uttered, the classic line, "It seemed like a good idea at the time, but if I'd only known then what I know now I wouldn't have done it." So goes life. When you do your investigative homework to determine what your dreams really represent in terms of commitment and benefit, you won't disappoint yourself. Many who have blindly chosen fairy-tale dreams have ended up with nightmare endings by neglecting their homework .

> "You will know that you have expressed your life purpose when you have completed an action and feel as energetic as you did before you started it, have brought prosperity to yourself and others, have left the world a better place, have little memory of the episode, and are looking forward to your next project."

Your life purpose is the reason you get up each morning. It's the "why" behind every choice and action you make. Achieving your life purpose is an action, not a state of being. Anyone can say or look like they're a rock star, but it doesn't mean they are. The only thing you have control over in your life is what you do. When your actions express your greatest innate talents and special abilities, you are manifesting your life purpose. You will know that you have expressed your life purpose when you have completed an action and feel as energetic as you did before you started it, have brought prosperity to yourself and others, have left the world a better place, have little memory of the episode, and are looking forward to your next project.

Your hidden talents surface only when you're forced to find a better way to achieve an outcome. Striving for excellence at the edge of your capacity and reaching for unfamiliar goals necessarily bring your best, often unknown, talents forward. The more you expose yourself to new opportunities for success and reach a little farther for them, the more your talents reveal themselves, and the more you will prosper. Always stretch yourself when given the chance. It's the fastest way to build your success capacity.

Your path to your success is highly personalized. Only you can make the decisions required to create and reach your goals. People have information that can help you make your decisions, but nobody has your answers or can make your decisions for you. You will find your own answers in your own time by investigating and doing what is important to you. Your life experience, coupled with the courage to pursue your own path, creates your success. The greatest gift you can give others is to encourage them to follow the path of their own inquiry, investigating everything that has meaning to them despite the opinions of others.

Bartering with Your Talents and Skills

Your unique talents and skills, like dollars and cents, are a currency that can be exchanged for goods and services. The more skills and talents you have, the greater the range of tasks you can exchange with others. The bigger your successes are, the greater your exchange power will be with others and the more life options you will have. For example, Jim Carrey was a relatively unknown actor until extraordinary box office receipts from *Ace Ventura* sent his value soaring to the point where he now commands millions of dollars a film. His versatility as an actor also enables him to star in a variety of film genres without being typecast as a comedian, which has increased his value even further. Each success you create and skill you acquire drives up your personal stock, which enables you to have and do more with less exchange.

Acquiring What You Need

You must acquire all the tangible items that are necessary to achieve your goals. Never hold back on purchasing what's needed to create your success. Prudently buying items that advance your life opens the door to greater success and creates financial returns far in excess of the money you spend. How many times have you delayed buying something you truly needed to complete a project and then said to yourself, "If I knew it was going to be this good, I would have done it a long time ago." We've all said that a million times. Your best investment is in yourself because how well you accomplish things and what you achieve are what determine your future.

Being the Best You Can Be

There are some six billion people on Planet Earth, and only one is you. There's nobody on this planet like you; there never has been, never ever will be. You have unique gifts that, when expressed, optimize your life's potential and contribution to others. Being the best you can be only occurs when your talents are developed sufficiently to manifest success consistent with your talents. Each of your successes creates more chances for you to express and grow your talents further and to inspire others to do the same.

Your talents are only as good as they are refined. The challenge of executing your aspirations brings out the best in you in the same way that rehearsing great scripts brings out the best in the most successful actors. Your mind and body need regular stimulation at or near the edge of their functional capacity to challenge them to develop their ability to perform so you can achieve more sophisticated and rewarding goals. Physically and mentally focusing on success is the best means of developing your mind and body to generate their full capacity.

> "The best way to get back on track during an off day is to remove yourself from it completely, resisting all temptations to salvage it."

How Do You Feel When You Experience Success?

Success is one of the most gratifying and important feelings anyone can ever experience. It's the great validator. It is a statement confirming your capacity to create and execute tasks, make correct decisions, commit to action, be self-motivated, take appropriate risk, and believe in your ability to create a better life for yourself.

Success produces a wide range of feelings, from overwhelming elation to subdued gratitude. Many factors determine the scope of response: degree of success, effort made to achieve it, when it happened, how it impacted self and others, and so on. Take a few moments to consider how success makes you feel by asking yourself a few questions.

- Which emotions have you had when you've experienced small, moderate, and substantial successes?

- What impact do the emotions you experience with success have on your motivation to develop your skills and aspire to a better life?

- What would it feel like if you never had success in your life?

- Which emotion do you experience most frequently with success?

- Name a few successes that have evoked significant emotion in you. What emotions were felt, and what thoughts did you have experiencing them?

- Name the emotions, in order of importance, that you most frequently experience when you've created a success. Which emotion means the most to you? Which is most powerful for you?

- How do your successes influence how you think about yourself, others, and your future?

- Do you ever have any inappropriate reactions to your successes? What are they, and what can you do to change them?

- Of all the feelings you have when you succeed, which do you think is the most important?

Somewhere between too much and too little responsibility and material acquisition resides a sweet spot that provides the time both to continue creating success and to enjoy its rewards. Having too many material encumbrances and too many obligations requires excessive maintenance and monetary outlay and often smothers otherwise successful lifestyles. Success helps you find and maintain the delicate balance between having too much and too little of everything. If you continue to succeed without succumbing to sleepless nights, poor meals, lack of exercise and fun, or relationship strain, you'll be living in the "sweet spot." To prosper and excel even further, you only need to keep doing what you're already doing. If you've been chronically overextended physically or you've compromised important relationships while striving to be successful, your life is seriously out of balance and must be stabilized. Otherwise, burnout, illness, and heartbreak are certain.

Everyone has bad days. Winners know that struggling with life on down days inevitably compounds their challenges and leads to incredible frustration and decisions they may deeply regret. The best way to get back on track during an off day is to remove yourself from it completely, resisting all temptations to salvage it. Enacting desperate measures in an attempt to salvage a bad day or willfully beat it into submission only compounds the difficulties it presents.

As strange as it may seem, losing makes you a better winner. Nobody in their right mind should *want* to lose, but all winners have discovered that losing is an essential part of developing and refining the skills needed to become a consistently top performer. Without exception, all great champions have experienced more losses than wins, but they have also realized that losing is the fundamental means by which they can see how good their winning strategies and skills really are. Losing shows you what aspects of your skill set need to be bolstered in order to improve your performance to a level consistent with your talent. Without knowing which areas need bolstering, it's impossible to create an ultimately winning lifestyle.

TURN IT UP! TIPS

1. Success is a skill anyone can master. The secret to achieving your goals is to match your skill set with a well-organized plan and execute the plan's steps in a timely manner.

2. You're born to pursue success. Take pride in your successes as they validate your capacity as an individual and pay respect to the privilege of life and those who have given you the mentoring, encouragement, and opportunity to develop and express your talents. Make mastering your ability to focus your top priority. Focus empowers you to reach your goals in the shortest time with least effort. Eliminate as many unwanted distractions as possible to make the time and energy available for you to build the life you want and are capable of living.

3. Creating and implementing plans is the exercise your brain needs to keep your goal setting and achievement skills at peak levels. Spend time regularly exercising your brain by conceiving of and developing ideas and plans, playing mentally challenging games, reading books, and engaging in stimulating conversation.

4. Never be pressured into doing something if your instincts tell you the timing isn't right. Always take whatever time is necessary to act when you are ready. Every action has its perfect timing and your respect for that consideration will afford you much opportunity and prosperity.

5. Always take life's high road—you never know who is watching. The word you utter that may have no significance to you may be the one that inspires another to change their life for the better.

6. Take the time to encourage others to pursue their goals. Sharing abundance and prosperity shows respect to them—as well to the blessings of your own good fortune.

7. Before initiating any action always consider its impact on people, places, and things. And, only enact those that are beneficial. This universal goodwill law will create good fortune for all.

TURN IT UP! TIPS (CONT'D)

8. Always take prudent and necessary risks as they are the only way to fully develop your talents and life. Doing so will teach you to overcome the mental blocks that hold you back from living your dreams.

9. Whenever possible learn a new skill to build your success repertoire. Each skill you acquire makes you more capable of achieving loftier goals in less time with less effort and will bring you closer to personal independence.

10. Prior to pursing a major goal, spend time observing, shadowing, and talking with those who are living that dream so you know exactly the commitment and resources necessary for that lifestyle. Forecasting in this way will serve as a reality check to insure your decisions are being made with full discernment.

11. Always stretch yourself and reach a little farther when an opportunity at the edge of your comfort zone presents itself. This action is the fastest way to build your confidence.

2

Embracing Risk

Only those who will risk going too far
can possibly find out how far one can go.

—T. S. Eliot

here's something inherent in all of us that makes us yearn for the best
yet fear the worst. Life in its most rudimentary sense is nothing more
than an endless sequence of moment-by-moment opportunities, all
carrying some degree of risk. Regardless of the choices before you, you'll
confront some level of fear with all of them, at least until you learn to
embrace risk as a partner in opportunity. Risk can be your friend, not your
enemy, once you learn how to use it in your favor.

Risk, like fear, is one of life's secret little four-
letter words. Without risk, moving forward and keeping the sizzle in your life aren't possible. "Nothing
ventured, nothing gained" is the creed of the successful, but life, even for the most successful, is a
two-steps-forward-one-step-back process. Not all
actions turn out to be winning ones, and if they do
that's often no more than an indication that your
goals were set too low, life is being lived too much in the safe zone, and
your best opportunities weren't embraced because you feared they were
beyond reach, which made failure likely.

> "Risk can be your
> friend, not your
> enemy, once you
> learn how to use it
> in your favor."

23

Taking risk teaches you that the only way to future prosperity is to capitalize on the upside potential of today's opportunities by embracing and overcoming risk. When most people think of risk, they tend to fear the worst and worry about what they might lose and how they could get hurt. To winners, however, risk translates to an open opportunity to have a more passionate, purposeful, productive, and prosperous life. The biggest risks carry the biggest gains, and perhaps the biggest risk of all is to do nothing.

Without risk there is no impetus or necessity to excel. Life without risk only heads in one direction: down a long gray tunnel of mediocrity where talents, enthusiasm, and hope lay dormant, encased in the paralyzing trepidation of risk. It's risk that satisfies the mind's lust for creativity, meaning, and excitement. The mind deplores sameness and repetition. Seeking innovative solutions to complex problems is what drives the human spirit. We all know people who watch television for hours on end, and most of them are shrouded in a thick cloud of pessimism, bored out of their gourds from lack of mental stimulation and initiative. Risk is the catalyst that inspires souls to sing and keeps life vital with constant stimulation and challenge. Without risk there can be no reward, and without reward there is no validation for the time, effort, and commitment you've put into your life.

Every top performer begins every action with the expectation of succeeding. If you look at the performance statistics of all great performers, however, most experience more losses than their reputations would suggest. It took Thomas Edison two thousand tries to get the first electric light bulb to work, but when asked for his thoughts on requiring so many tries to get it right, he said he never considered any failure a failure, only another step closer to getting it to work. Failure is a mentor and friend showing you what you need to do to achieve your aspirations efficiently and completely.

Risk taking enhances or diminishes your chances of success. Choosing the right level of risk to take, separating the astute from the reckless, is a learned skill that divides consistent winners from those who randomly stumble into an occasional success. When discussing risk taking, we mean those risks that are beneficial to you, humanity, and the environment, that have an advantage heavily weighted in your favor to succeed.

One characteristic that distinguished Lance Armstrong from his competition during his professional cycling career was his instinctive ability to implement unorthodox winning strategies when prudent and necessary. In Lance's final Tour de France, all his teammates had a bad day on the first mountainous stage. The press emphatically prophesized that Lance's teammates weren't strong enough to provide him with the support he needed to win an unprecedented seventh Tour. What they failed to consider was that riders usually have only one bad day in the Tour and often have their best racing day the next day. That being so, everyone on the team believed the possibility was there to have a terrific result the following day despite the press's prophecy of doom.

For that next day's race, another brutal uphill route, it was decided the team would feign the weakness others presumed by riding very conservatively, hoping to bait the other contenders into prematurely using up their energy by trying too hard too early in the race to beat Lance by a wide enough margin that it would be impossible for him to bounce back and win the Tour. The team's competitors took the bait, as hoped, and fatigued prematurely. This allowed the team, which had conserved maximum energy throughout the day, to take control of that day's race and position Lance to break away with three other riders to finish well ahead of his competition. Ultimately, that race led to Lance's seventh consecutive Tour de France victory.

Never Embrace Risk if the Facts Say Otherwise

There's a monumental difference between appropriate and careless risk taking. Before attempting any task, winners always do a benefit-to-risk analysis, and if they determine the risk is too high, they pass on it. It's always better to be safe than sorry. Whenever you're not sure that it's wise to embrace a risk, do not act until the facts clearly indicate the benefit-to-risk ratio is high enough to warrant moving forward.

If your skills, time, confidence, and other resources match or exceed the identifiable challenges of a risk, the risk has a high probability of converting to success and should be taken. If the challenges outweigh your resources, pass on the risk and move on.

> "If the challenges outweigh your resources, pass on the risk and move on."

Never feel that passing on a risk, if the facts dictate you should, means you're turning your back on opportunity or aren't courageous enough to embrace risk. Wisdom defines your courage and success, not stupidity from egotistically risking precious resources while attempting something with a high chance of failure.

Learning to Risk

An essential fact that you must learn and trust as early as possible in your evolution as a winner is that if you don't succeed at something it doesn't mean you're a failure. As peculiar as it may seem, many people have a deep-seated, unconscious belief that if they haven't achieved much prior success, or don't achieve their goals every time they try, they're incapable of being successful. Of course, nothing could be farther from the truth as we're all born winners and hardwired to succeed. We only need to learn the skills.

For specific clients, I will create a situation that teaches them, despite occasional failure, that they are capable of success at any time. I purposely have them attempt tasks at which they have absolutely no chance of succeeding. This forces them to confront failure head on, to realize that they're not going to shrivel and die if they fail, and to see that success is not defined by a single failure but by succeeding more often than not.

One client, an extremely talented underachiever, despite his meticulous preparation, incredible fitness, talent, and dedication, was unable to express his full potential and prosper because he lacked decisiveness and was unable to assert himself in critical situations. To make him confront and overcome these success-limiting liabilities, I had him attempt a task just slightly beyond his reach that, though we never discussed it, he and I both knew he could never achieve. At the instant he failed at the task, he exuded strength of character and confidence that I had not previously seen in him. He experienced for the first time that failing to achieve a goal is only an isolated, one-time event having absolutely nothing to do with his capacity to be a consistent winner. He also understood that he possessed the ability to overcome the self-fulfilling failure prophecy mind-set he had fallen victim to by not taking appropriate risks. From that transforming moment he went on to become a record-setting legend in his field.

Those Who Hesitate Are Lost

Capitalizing on opportunity demands swift and decisive action. Unfortunately, the paralyzing hesitation most people feel when it actually comes to embracing risk most often allows great opportunity to slip through their fingers. To seize the gift of opportunity without hesitation requires a calm, confident, and steady mind. These characteristics are the product of trusting your ability to convert opportunity into success, as shown by past opportunities achieved in a similar fashion, the rehearsal of correct actions in advance, and having confidence in your capacity to adapt. All of these assets are learned behaviors and can be employed by anybody given enough time to acquire them. Every successful person knows that when the homework's done correctly the test is easy.

> "Timing is most often the difference between a successful or failed risk."

Timing is most often the difference between a successful or failed risk. Appropriate timing turns opportunities, even high-risk opportunities, into extraordinary, often very easily acquired, successes. Timing is much more a product of pattern recognition, spontaneity, and intuition than intellectual decision making. If too much time is spent analyzing a risk intellectually, considering too many choices and conflicting opinions, the brain often succumbs to fatigue-delayed decision making. By the time a decision is finally made under those conditions, the time to capture an opportunity has expired and is lost forever.

The best risks are often taken by coupling a noncognitive, pattern-recognition-based, instinctive response with the relevant knowledge stored in memory. A very skilled graphic artist client was asked by a major account executive why he chose the color green for the award-winning album cover he designed for the account. His answer was "Because it felt right." When your skills are established and instinct silently tells you that an opportunity can be converted into a success, you should strongly consider embracing the opportunity, as it has got the signs of a sure winner.

Remain Focused on the Task at Hand

Among your most important success attributes is your ability to focus and maintain your attention. You can only devote your attention successfully to one thing at a time. Scattered attention and an inability to stay present with a task make plan completion virtually impossible, and one small lapse in attention has permanently ruined many people's lives. Your attention can be deflected in many ways, the most common being from overthinking, fear, and other people.

To capitalize fully on opportunity and minimize its risk, you must learn to commit your attention only to completing tasks that advance your life's ambitions and are of service to others. Every opportunity embraced places you at risk of not completing it, a risk significantly compounded when your attention is divided among too many points of focus. Exceptionally talented people who can do many things well often succumb to the curse of divided focus by doing too many things "half well," leaving their lives "half finished" instead of completing a few things fully, moving forward, and building on their successes. This endless perpetuation of incomplete action keeps their lives in chronic turmoil, excessively burdening them with an endless conveyor belt of unfinished tasks, suffocating their talents, and preventing them from constructively moving forward in life. If your attention begins to wander, consciously draw your focus back to completing the most immediate and important task at hand. Don't risk trying to catch up by attempting to complete unfinished tasks. Stop the chain reaction immediately, and finish the task you're currently doing. Then move forward with new tasks. Task completion requires constant vigilance, a process that gets easier but never becomes automatic. It's a daily battle with which everyone struggles.

By its very nature, the act of embracing risk, or any unknown, creates fear. Paradoxically, this may actually help you succeed. Fear of failure can be a great motivator to finish tasks, often more than the desire to succeed can be. When you feel the fear associated with risk creeping into your plans, remain focused with all your resolve on completing your task and staying fully invested in securing the benefits you will achieve from its completion.

> "Fear of failure can be a great motivator to finish tasks, often more than the desire to succeed can be."

If you allow yourself to be distracted by someone else's actions or personality, you're vulnerable to making mental errors that can take you away from achieving your ambitions. Bruce Penhall, two-time World Speedway Motorcycle Champion, won a championship race with a textbook example of why you need to keep your focus on doing and completing only what produces your successes rather than what's occurring in the lives of others. On the starting line for the final race of the event, Bruce purposely looked down at his main rival's engine and shook his head as if to say "Something's definitely wrong with that engine." Bruce's opponent quickly looked down at his motorcycle's engine to see if he could identify the problem Bruce "saw." Of course, nothing was wrong with the engine, but he was so flustered from Bruce's purposeful distraction ploy that when the flag dropped, he got a bad start and Bruce sailed to capture the victory.

To maximize your success and minimize your risk when implementing actions, there's no substitute for proper preparation. Proper preparation impregnates your mind and body with as much "real life" capacity to deliver as possible so you can step up and perform when it's demanded of you in the here and now. It's not enough to have the right facts swimming around in your mind. Those facts must be connected to actual circumstances and experiences by rehearsing them in conditions that simulate those happening in real life in real time. Nobody can "think" their way through a performance if the skills haven't been adequately rehearsed and embedded into their mind-body response pattern in advance of live task execution.

An example of this is how the United States Postal Service and Discovery Channel Professional Cycling Teams would prepare for the Tour de France. They would hold training camps to pre-ride the racecourse—rain, wind, or shine—to ensure they knew exactly what challenges they would face during the Tour. Then they would adapt their training accordingly to maximize their preparation for the race by minimizing the risk of encountering surprises. Unfortunately for their competitors, most didn't do the same, giving the team an advantage to dominate seven consecutive Tours.

Similarly, most top rock and performance groups simulate live-audience conditions when they rehearse. In addition, they often rehearse at the same times of their scheduled live performances, often as late as ten in the evening. Most review video tapes of their rehearsals to further refine their shows before the actual performance. For final preparation, a live dress rehearsal is conducted with an invited preview audience to simulate the opening night. All of these preparations insure all the elements for a spectacular debut show are in place.

Expect to Succeed

All great performers expect to succeed each time they take the stage. They all exude an air of certainty about their future successes, almost as if they'd already happened. They all fully expect to produce a winning performance each time they step onto their "center stage."

To prepare a champion Motocross rider for a championship showdown at the last race of the series, I employed an unorthodox, yet highly effective, strategy. My client had the fitness and equipment to win the championship, but needed a confident mind-set that he "owned" the track. The championship would be decided between himself and two other riders racing in a pack of twenty. Whichever rider finished in front of the other two would become the champion. To help my client develop the sense of track "ownership," I arranged with the management at the famous Rose Bowl in Pasadena, California, where the championship race would take place, for my client and me to go there one afternoon a week for several weeks in advance of the event to workout. The entire purpose of my client's training in the Rose Bowl was to instill in his mind and body that this was "his" stadium and "his" championship. At the end of the final lap of the title-deciding race, it was my client who came across the finish line first of the three and won the championship.

When to Embrace Risk

Deciding whether or not to embrace risk can be done by intellect or intuition or a combination of the two. Each method has merit, and everyone has a personal preference. What matters is your preference matching your decision-making style.

Every waking moment of every day your body and mind are bombarded with millions of bits of information that must be collated and acted on to ultimately determine your responses to life. A portion of the input goes to your brain and conscious mind, with the majority going to your unconscious mind and cells. Both compartments interact during every moment of your life to produce your reactions to your life's circumstances, but the brain and conscious mind pathway is considered by some to be slower than your intuitive unconscious in collating and responding to incoming stimuli. We've all experienced instinctive decisions that produce great outcomes quickly and, by contrast, intellectual ones that seem to take forever, conflict us with uncertainty, and often produce subpar results. If given a choice, experience suggests that trusting your instincts may be the better choice, since they may be based on more information and may be closer to reality than your intellectual conscious mind's perceived reality.

All top performers base their decisions upon what they stand to gain, not what they might lose. In my late twenties I sought the advice of my neighbor whose opinion I valued because of his extraordinary business acumen. In discussing the two books I intended to self-publish, I told him all the elements were there for them to be a success. However, my main concern was the tremendous expense it would take to publish them. At the end of our discussion, my neighbor offered to finance my books, though I never asked him to consider it, but he asked me to answer one question first: "What would happen to my life if the books were a success?" His request stopped me dead in my tracks. At that instant it was clear to me there are two basic types of people: those who make decisions based on what they stand to gain, and those who make decisions based on what they might lose. I published the books myself, and they were successful beyond my expectations.

> "All top performers base their decisions upon what they stand to gain, not what they might lose."

Practicing the Present

We've all experienced the massive adrenaline shock felt the instant we make, or think we've made, a huge mistake. It only takes one momentary lapse in concentration to ruin weeks, months, or years of effort that might otherwise have ended in tremendous success. Distractions prompted by telephones, PDAs, radios, CDs, daydreaming, and other people are avoidable causes of catastrophic choice making. Controlling your distractions requires you to constantly practice bringing your attention back to your task at hand and setting boundaries with yourself and others. These skills never become automatic. You must continually apply them to gain mastery over your time and circumstance.

Every successful person has mastered the art of being singularly engaged with their immediate tasks at hand. This focus enables them to be succinct in discussion, extremely lucid in thought, and very present in conversation—exactly the state of mind required to perform at their best under pressure when distraction is at a premium. Time counts for the successful because they know they never have enough time to achieve all their goals, so they eliminate distractions that take them away from completing their life ambitions.

Every top performer experiences uncertainty before performing. A little nervousness, apprehension, and sweaty palms—they all have it—it's just that they control it and make it work for them. Being a touch edgy before performing is a healthy sign, indicating a present readiness to perform. It's a normal physiologic response that mobilizes physical and mental assets to produce a top effort. Being too relaxed when initiating a task indicates a lack of the mental intensity and focus required to make the best goal-achieving decisions and actions. Conversely, overconfidence dulls the mind, slows reflexes, and weakens the body, magnifying the risks inherent in any task. If you feel slightly anxious prior to an action, it's simply a signal that your reflexes and physical readiness are there to make it happen. Combining this with proper preparation, trust in your abilities, and having the correct skill set makes your action's outcome a virtual slam dunk.

As each year comes to an end and you reflect on your successes, you will find that your most successful days were scant. Most days will be uneventful, but half a dozen will be extremely volatile, producing either spectacularly great or tragically bad outcomes. Those atypical days can't be predicted and are of unknown origin. They just show up randomly—and will continue to do so—throughout your life. The trick is to have adequate time and acute presence of mind to know when those days are happening so you can capitalize on them and purposefully create consistent favorable outcomes.

> "If you feel slightly anxious prior to an action, it's simply a signal that your reflexes and physical readiness are there to make it happen."

On routine, uneventful days it's imperative that you finish all present tasks on time to give yourself the time flexibility to appropriately address your spectacular days properly when they occur unexpectedly. Never assume that the time to complete tasks will be available later. If your life is already too congested from delaying task completion, when great days do arrive you won't be able to take advantage of them, which will magnify their potential downside and add to your life's already overburdened gridlock.

If you complete your tasks early and have time left over only then do you have the option of commencing a new project, acquiring a new skill, or, even, resting. Only begin a new project if you have the time, energy, and resources to complete it comfortably within your schedule. Never risk starting a new project if the time isn't truly there to manage it correctly. If you do, you risk further overburdening your already full life. This becomes particularly detrimental if something goes wrong with your project, because time to resolve it won't be available.

On those occasional days when you feel mentally dull and out of step with life, it is extremely unwise to embrace risk or, perhaps, even work on a plan. If you do, there's an overwhelming chance you will create a very unforgettable down day for yourself that can drag your entire year down. Your ego might entice and seduce you into rolling up your sleeves, tempting you to "make things happen" willfully, but history is clear that such attempts most often only magnify downside risk and consequences. On mentally down days, always back away from risk and do nothing. Only resume activity when your mental faculties are back up to speed.

When spectacularly great days do appear, step aside and let them occur naturally without your help. If you try to make them even better or prolong such days, most often they will unravel quickly. Great days are gifts that are best appreciated. When they occur, bless them and ride the wave as long as possible. Enjoy them because they won't last forever.

On days when everything caves in, never push too hard to resurrect or salvage anything because that will usually make matters worse. And never look for magic answers, as there aren't any. Manage the process delicately with the intention of stabilizing it. Once stabilized, initiate proven success strategies that lead to the best resolution possible. When you've gotten the maximum benefit the day offers, back away from the circumstance, let go, and move on before the next landslide occurs.

When to Bypass Risk

Risky situations provide the greatest chance to catapult you into greater success faster than anything, but they also have the biggest potential to trip you up. You must absolutely, unequivocally avoid risk when things are going too well, when desperation sets in, when you are in ill health, or when you have become too willful about attaining success.

When life is almost too good, you risk believing you have become a permanent, self-perpetuating winner and are exempt from following the prudent rules governing benefit to risk—the same rules you applied previously to achieve your successes. Belief in this exemption is perhaps the fastest way to derail a successful life. When life is going well, step back, give thanks, continue to follow the principles that have created your success, and enjoy the ride because every successful life will have its bumps in the road.

A client worked very hard for more than a decade to win his first athletic championship, after which he proclaimed he "deserved time off" and would resume his preparation for the coming season when he was "ready." During his off-season he spent considerable time traveling internationally, took more time off than normal, and gained more weight than is customary during the off-season. As his preseason was fully in stride and moving toward the new season's first competition, it was evident he was well behind in his preparation due to his neglect. Unfortunately, he never caught up, failed to defend his title, and never regained the passion that originally made him a winner.

Desperation has prompted many people to take risks that have ended in catastrophe. A man loses his job, panics, and heads to Las Vegas to win money to get his life back in order. Inevitably, he ends up losing everything because his desperation drove him into bad decision making. Never impulsively embrace anything. It always backfires.

Similarly, risk should be avoided if your health may prevent you from transforming opportunity into success. Without good health you're incapable of completing the actions necessary to produce beneficial outcomes, so always do everything possible to promote and maintain your health.

Sometimes, despite heroic efforts to create success, a risk implodes from willfulness. Risk and willfulness add up to a very destructive combination that most often ends in failure. Appropriate willfulness is absolutely necessary for times of crisis and survival, but it's not an acceptable long-term motivation for success. Willful people who pride themselves on using their strong will and mental toughness to convert risks to successes often do achieve their goals but, regrettably, leave behind a trail of broken promises and ruined lives, while usually forfeiting their health in the process. Never take a risk when the will to conquer is the motivating force, since the result will usually be disastrous for you and others.

> "Never take a risk when the will to conquer is the motivating force."

Risk Is the Fastest Way to Success

All winners look for risk because they know it's the fastest way to advance their lives. One well-embraced risk at the right time can put you into the record books, doing for your life what ten or twenty minimal-risk, minimal-return actions could never do. Travis Pastrana, a fearlessly gifted freestyle motocross rider, put himself into the record books by doing the one and only double back-flip jump in freestyle motocross history. Travis's feat contains many extremely important examples of the power that embracing risk offers.

First, the jump met the criteria for being a high-risk, high-return investment. It did this to such an extent that when people learned Travis was going to attempt it, some thought he shouldn't even consider doing it because the chances of sustaining a serious injury were high and even inevitable.

INTUITIVE RISK AND RECKLESS RISK

Taking appropriate risk is an essential skill you must master to become a consistent success. Most successful people would agree that the biggest risk of all is not taking a risk when presented with an opportunity that has success written all over it. Often your best impulses to embrace opportunity come from your spontaneous intuition.

Intuitive risk may appear to be reckless because it often happens very quickly and under atypical circumstances, but it actually carries a very low degree of risk. The magic of your intuition is that it simultaneously considers all the risk factors of an opportunity in a split second then refers back to you either a "yes, do it" or "no, don't do it" impression within the same moment. Reckless risk, most frequently fueled by exuberant emotion and blind passion, is extremely risky and has a very high failure rate.

Several mental and physical responses to opportunity will identify whether you're engaging the opportunity through intuition or recklessness. If it's by constructive intuition, then proceed with confidence as the probability of success is high. If not, back away until the reckless indicators abate so you can determine rationally whether a risk is worth taking. When you know the difference between intuitive and reckless risk, it will pay great dividends for you, sparing you immense grief and generating spectacular prosperity.

INTUITIVE RISK AND RECKLESS RISK (CONT'D)

Mental and Physical Responses to Risk Factors	Intuitive Risk Response	Reckless Risk Response
Body tension	Calmness	Nervousness
Response time	Time slows down	Time speeds up
Mental activity	Mind slows	Mind races
Appropriateness of timing	Well synchronized	Erratic, out of step
Reactions to opportunity	Appropriate	Exaggerated, over the top
Breathing	Slows down	Speeds up
Perspiration	None	Forehead, underarms
Mouth	Moist	Dry
Frustration	Decreases	Increases

A poignant example of intuitive versus reckless risk is seen in two motocross motorcycle racing peers. Nathan Ramsey broke one wrist and dislocated another in a serious accident during practice. Surgery was done immediately on both wrists to insure maximum recovery. During the early stages of recovery, Nathan intuitively felt that based on the circumstances he was facing the best thing to do was retire from professional competition due to his injuries. Several weeks later, though, he reconsidered his retirement and decided to embark on a systematic re-entry program into the sport to see if his injuries were, in fact, career limiting. After several months of graduated physical training and riding on his motorcycle he concluded that he was capable of racing at his former level and made plans to resume his professional racing career. To his pleasant surprise when he returned to competition he actually rode better than prior to his injuries.

In contrast, a peer of his who had a malingering knee injury that most likely warranted surgery continued to compete despite his faulty knee. And, as the result of a minor and typically benign accident his injured knee was further injured requiring he take the remainder of the year off. To further compound the situation, he attempted to race yet again before his knee was completely healed and was forced to withdraw from a race because his knee couldn't tolerate the stress during a practice run.

Second, before attempting the jump, Travis did his homework by practicing the trick so many times into a foam-filled practice pit that it had become second nature.

Third, when warming up for the jump, Travis made a practice run at the ramp to ensure that his motorcycle was working properly and that the ramp was set up perfectly in its correct position. He made one small correction to the jump location, got on his motorcycle, turned around, and went back to his starting spot. Then he sped toward and up the ramp, launching himself several stories into the air, and successfully executed the precedent-shattering double back-flip jump.

The execution of the jump happened the way every successful accomplishment is achieved. Travis made the correction to the jump ramp location by intuitive feel based on his countless hours of painstaking preparation, manually shifted its position, then got on his motorcycle and took off without giving himself time to overanalyze the process. He trusted his preparation because he'd successfully practiced the jump in his foam pit countless times. Perhaps the crowning achievement of his accomplishment is that afterward he publicly stated he would never attempt it again because of its extreme risk.

Too Much of Anything Creates Huge Downside Risk

Overtraining isn't just an athletic phenomenon. Successful people know they can't fully capitalize on opportunity if they're tired and listless. We've all experienced what it's like to commence an action only to realize we don't have the energy or motivation to see it through to the end. Too much activity and not enough recovery render success unattainable. Embracing risk successfully demands a body that is well rested and a mind working at peak capacity, otherwise producing consistent success becomes impossible.

TURN IT UP! TIPS

1. Perhaps the biggest risk of all in life is to do nothing. Spending life too much in the safe zone never challenges your best abilities to surface and express themselves. Never hesitate to take a risk if your intuition and the facts tell you it can be achieved.

2. Always begin every action with the expectation of succeeding. The more this is practiced, the more success will occur.

3. Avoid risk if circumstances or your intuition suggests it is unwise to undertake. Backing away from risk is a sign of intelligence and respect in such instances and never a mark of indecision or cowardice.

4. Failing at something doesn't mean you're a failure. Lack of periodic failure is, often, more a sign of lack of initiative and confidence in the ability to succeed than insufficient competence. Make your decisions on what you stand to gain, not what you might lose.

5. Often, the best successes occur when risks are taken based on intuition and pattern recognition rather than intellect alone. When opportunity presents itself trust your instincts, as they are often closer to reality than your perceived reality, and embrace risk.

6. Having time or opportunity in the future is never guaranteed. Always complete a task or embrace an opportunity when the time is available. By doing so you will continue the forward momentum of your plan.

7. Only begin a new project if you have the time, energy, and resources to complete it comfortably within your schedule. Too many plans too close together dilute your resource pool and greatly increase the risk of compromising them. On those days when you feel mentally out of step with life it is extremely unwise to embrace risk or even work on a plan. It's better to back away and regroup and come back the following day.

TURN IT UP! TIPS (CONT'D)

8. When you're having one of those magic days when everything seems to happen effortlessly and beyond your expectations, step aside and let it occur naturally without your help. If you try to make it better or prolong it, you risk interrupting its inertia and having it slip out from under you.

9. On those days when nothings seems to be going right, never willfully try to salvage a lost cause, as that most often compounds existing problems. It's best to immediately change activities to put distance between you and the problems.

10. In the following instances, avoid taking risks: when life seems to be going a "little too well," when desperation sets in, when health is compromised, or when you have become too willful about attaining success. These moments increase the risk of failure significantly.

3

Learning to Control Fear

Fear is the mind killer.
Fear is the little death that brings total obliteration.

—Frank Herbert

Before you can go any farther in learning to achieve your goals, you need to get a grip on the single most destructive thing holding you back: *fear*. Whether you're afraid of failure, others' opinions, embarrassment, change, or physical harm, when you let fear dictate your choices and run your life, you'll never be able to have the vision, construct the plan, complete the steps, or take the risks necessary to make your dreams a reality. Even when you do you manage to take important risks despite your trepidation, if you don't master fear every step of the way to your goal, that destructive emotion will inevitably wiggle its way into the process, and it may force you to abandon your dream before you achieve it.

Although anyone can suppress fear with sheer will every once in a while, winners know that conquering fear only on occasion won't be enough to allow them to achieve consistent success. If you don't manage fear consistently, it will trip you up when you're most vulnerable. This emotion is uncanny in its ability to detect when your mental resistance is down and you're most susceptible to its damaging intrusion.

A helpful way of understanding the relationship between you and fear is to view the struggle as if fear were a human opponent vying for control over your decision-making process. Either you master it and make your own decisions, or it makes them for you, leaving you at the mercy of its counterproductive imperative. When you realize fear is a game, understand the rules of the game, and understand your opponent, gaining mastery over fear becomes possible.

Don't think, though, that you need to be 100 percent fear free to be a successful person. The idea that great leaders and "natural-born" winners are innately fearless is one of the most harmful and inaccurate fallacies of all. Fear is a fact of life and part of our hardwired humanity. In fact, it's the most primitive, and essential, self-preservation mechanism we have.

> "If you don't manage fear consistently, it will trip you up when you're most vulnerable."

The human species evolved with the help of fear—and the physical fight-or-flight reaction that accompanies it—in order to mobilize physical resources so humans could recognize and fend off physical threats (like predatory wild animals) or flee for self-preservation. You know you're having a fight-or-flight response when you're confronted with a situation and your breathing increases, palms get sweaty, blood pressure rises, or muscles tense. That's your survival instinct in action.

These days the threats we encounter generally aren't to our immediate physical survival but to our psychological well-being and emotional self-esteem. When your primitive, physical, fight-or-flight self-preservation response butts up against a modern social or professional confrontation (think of an unsolicited suggestion from a bullying coworker or an intimidating meeting with a group of people), it produces reactions that are totally counterproductive to your goals.

When you transfer the fear response to what challenges you psychologically and emotionally, it deflects you from achieving your goals in four ways:

1. **Action paralysis.** Remember when, as a kid, you were startled by a terrifying surprise while watching a horror movie, and your body and mind felt paralyzed and you couldn't move or think? Well, the same thing can

happen when you're blindsided by an unexpected event as you reach for your goal: you respond with total mental, then physical, paralysis, so that moving forward becomes impossible. For example, someone you're counting on quits without notice at a critical juncture in your project, leaving you high and dry, and you feel like your mind and body have turned to stone. Or you discover you've jeopardized an important opportunity by failing to check your e-mail or voice mail, and you're struck by a nauseating shock wave of fear that reverberates throughout your entire mind and body. Or you lose your note-filled PDA prior to an important meeting and your brain feels as if it's been thrown into a high-speed blender.

It's not just external events, however, that cause action paralysis. You can cause it in yourself, through fear of making a bad choice, botching a task, letting yourself down, or being rejected by others.

2. **Overreaction.** Fear can cause you to react with hair-trigger impulsiveness to the smallest, most insignificant things, often making you say and do what can cause irreparable damage to your goals and relationships. I witnessed a classic example of this when I was coaching a well-known sports figure. One day I videotaped him during his training so he could objectively evaluate his technique. At the time, a very precocious younger competitor was staying with him so they could train together in preparation for a major competition. Later that day, the athlete I had videotaped walked into his house and found the younger athlete watching the video of him training. He mentally snapped and became furious. He assumed we were conspiring against him and that I had taped him specifically so the younger athlete could study his technique to advance his own career. This, of course, was totally false. The intent in shooting the video was solely to help him improve his performance.

Unfortunately, no amount of discussion could quell his anger. Tragically, the athlete's career went into a tailspin. His anger consumed his mind to such an extent that he was unable to maintain focus on his training and repeat his past successes. This scenario is all too common. When fear distorts life perceptions, it causes overreaction to obstacles—or in the case of the athlete I just described, the perception of obstacles where none exist—and barriers are created that prevent plans from moving forward toward successful completion.

3. **Feeling overwhelmed.** "I'm so overwhelmed" is a modern-day mantra. Most people feel they never have enough time to do everything necessary to "stay on top of things." The effect of feeling overwhelmed is similar to action paralysis in that both create a catatonic state that kills your initiative to complete tasks. Anytime you feel like you can't see your way out from under the sheer volume of what you need to do can paralyze you. Your mind seizes up, eyes glaze over, shoulders stiffen, and you feel as if your body's frozen in place.

This feeling of being overwhelmed, however, is often something other than what it appears to be. Sure, you're busy, with lots of demands on your time, but when something's *truly* important to you (your biweekly golf game? your weekly shopping excursions?) you probably have to admit that you always find a way to make time for it. On the other hand, when feeling overwhelmed by life keeps you from going after the things you say you want, one of two things is happening: Either you don't *really* desire what you say you do (like finding time to exercise, or reading a special book) or you do want those things, sincerely, but fear is preventing you from embracing them with the feeling of being overwhelmed.

Feeling too overwhelmed to move toward your goals is one of fear's sneakiest guises—and one of the oldest excuses in the book. You see, as long as you're overwhelmed you don't have to take risks or feel inadequate. So, taking on more commitments than you have time for and then letting them freeze you in an overwhelmed state becomes a method of eluding challenges that would lead you to achieve your dream of success. Often we blame our overwhelmed feelings on others, telling ourselves they've placed too many demands on and overburdened us. Ultimately, however, you're responsible for your own actions, and if you're truly doing so much for others that it keeps you from going after your own dreams, you need to recognize that the blame for that entrapment ultimately rests with you. You created it, and only you can change it. And, that change can happen quickly. All you need to do is say no to others and set boundaries with them.

4. **Anger.** Although fear and anger may seem to be polar opposites—since we tend to picture scared people cowering from confrontation and angry people aggressively going after something—anger is actually just another form of fear. When we're insecure about our abilities, uncertain about the future, or otherwise scared of a situation, we'll often react angrily in a misguided attempt to defend ourselves from whatever we're scared of, disguising the very fact that we're scared. Anger may be fear's most destructive variant. It clouds judgment and destroys the ability to maintain concentration—and often the difference between a poor performance and a great one hinges on the ability to make good judgments at a critical time.

> "Feeling too overwhelmed to move toward your goals is one of fear's sneakiest guises—and one of the oldest excuses in the book."

For example, a client of mine was about to race in a national championship supercross race, and right before his motorcycle was to be placed on the starting line its engine stopped running. He waited calmly on the starting line while his mechanic fixed the problem, within the two-minute time allotment allowed for repairing such problems. When the starting flag dropped, he was the first rider to the first turn, never looked back, and won the race. A few races later one of my client's competitors encountered a similar mechanical problem, but unlike my client he threw a major tantrum on the starting line while his crew frantically fixed his motorcycle. When the race was finished, he'd placed quite low in the results, throwing out the window his very achievable preseason goal of finishing top three in the series. I'd be willing to bet good money that his anger distracted him and led to his poor performance. Not only does anger fatally throw off your focus; it also totally erodes your self-confidence.

For example, think of how you feel after you've lashed out irately at somebody over a minor offense or a perceived trespass. A mix of guilt, for making the person feel bad, and embarrassment, for losing control so visibly, washes over you. Few things dissolve your self-worth more than that, and it's nearly impossible to succeed with your confidence wounded.

And have you ever noticed how exhausted you feel after an outburst of anger? Anger consumes tremendous amounts of energy that could otherwise be channeled toward achieving your goals. When you let anger seize control of your emotions, you rob yourself of the focus, confidence, and energy necessary to move forward. In the end, anger produces no winners, only losers.

> "When you let anger seize control of your emotions, you rob yourself of the focus, confidence, and energy necessary to move forward."

Winners don't have any natural immunity to fear and its liabilities, but what sets them apart is how they manage their fear so that it never gets the upper hand. By actively controlling their worries and anxieties—neither surrendering to them nor getting locked in battle with them—they can transcend them and can maximize every opportunity to achieve success without fear getting in the way. The following five strategies can help you overcome fear:

1. **Remember that everyone is scared.** When you see fear as a sign of weakness in yourself, it can exert a viselike grip on you, thereby leading you to conclude that you're incapable or unworthy of success. This deceptive emotional process goes something like this: You decide that you want to achieve something, but going after it involves some risk—you'll have to put yourself on the line in pursuit of it, and there's no guarantee you'll succeed. So your fear mechanism kicks in, taunting you with thoughts of all the things that possibly could go wrong, what you might lose, and the humiliation you might feel if you fail. These negative thoughts and feelings, however, aren't what actually sabotage your chances of success. The truly disastrous thought process is what happens next: Because of your fearful feelings, your self-esteem plummets because

you don't really believe you can do what it takes to succeed. You conclude that if you're fearful, you must be inadequate, and if you're inadequate, you're certainly not capable of pulling off your plan. You interpret the fact that you're scared as a confirmation that your fear of failure is justified.

This is, however, a logical fallacy, and recognizing it as such is the first step in releasing fear's hold over you and moving forward to claim success. You need to understand that fear in itself is *not* a sign of weakness. It's not a sign that you're incapable of achievement. In truth, the fact that you feel fear has absolutely no bearing on your chances of success. The big secret is that everyone feels fear, but we all think we're the exception, the minority, and that others actually feel as confident as they look.

So, take a minute to understand and accept this fact: *Everybody* feels fear. Even people who've won Olympic gold medals, Academy Awards, and mind-boggling financial contracts feel it. The day before each of the eight Tour de France's for which I worked with the United States Postal and Discovery Professional Cycling Teams, most team members were withdrawn and kept to themselves, each in his own private world confronting the uncertainty and apprehension of how they would hold up under the severe physical and mental challenges facing them over the next three extremely demanding weeks. They knew full well that they could deprive the team of victory if they faltered. They didn't, and the team won all eight Tours.

> "Winners don't have any natural immunity to fear and its liabilities, but what sets them apart is how they manage their fear so that it never gets the upper hand."

Olympic athletes have knots in their stomachs before the games begin, superstar businessmen get sweaty palms before walking into make-or-break meetings, and great actors' throats tighten before uttering their first words on stage. What separates these winners from those who never even get to the starting line, or freeze when it's time to perform, is that they know how to manage fear. They know that controlling it systematically is an essential step on the road to success that's every bit as important as that dramatic final step across the finish line.

Now that you see that fear is absolutely, 100 percent normal, that everyone has it, and that it's part of every success, you can learn to manage it so that it doesn't sabotage your winning potential.

2. **Learn to recognize "The Voice."** You can't manage fear without confronting "The Voice." The Voice is something we all encounter at one time or another: that obnoxious little chatterbox inside our heads that tries to talk us out of everything good. Every time we start to do something of value, The Voice pipes in saying something like "Are you sure that's a good idea? What if you screw it up? Remember last time when you took a risk and it didn't work? Why do you think you're so special that you'll be able to succeed at this when others have failed?" If you're not proactive in putting a muzzle on The Voice, it will trip you up on the road to achieving your goals.

As with the other aspects of fear, nobody is immune from the taunts of his or her own heckling inner Voice, or its destructive power. After a Tour de France stage, one of the riders told me that when he was on that day's race's starting line The Voice told him he was going to "crack" (cycling parlance's term for physically blowing up) on that day's tough uphill race. Prophetically, he had tremendous physical difficulty that day on the final race climb and has called it the worst day of his professional career. Fortunately, he was able to recover for the next day and support the team to another Tour victory. Similarly, a major league baseball pitcher client once confided to me that one day The Voice told him he was going to throw a pivotal pitch into the dirt in front of the catcher, and, sure enough, when that make-or-break pitch came, he did just that.

Both of those stories illustrate one of the reasons The Voice is so powerful: What we *think* about doing is almost always what we end up doing, even when it brings about the outcome we fear most. I learned this lesson in a painful and humbling way once when I was riding my mountain bike on a trail along the edge of a steep cliff. Instead of keeping my eyes on the path where I wanted to go, I looked over the edge and thought about how bad it would be if I went off the trail and over the cliff. Sure enough, next thing I knew I rode off the cliff, and I have scars as a permanent reminder of my misdirected intention. So, when you allow The Voice to taunt you with worst-case scenarios and draw you into its snare of fear and self-doubt, it's more than likely that those nightmare outcomes will be realized.

Nobody knows for sure the exact origin of The Voice, but it most likely has its roots in your past. Every put-down, criticism, or negative comment you've heard from childhood forward sets up a pattern of response in you, even if your conscious mind doesn't remember them. Every criticism you've ever heard is tucked away somewhere in your memory, and the negative residue of those comments rears its head in the form of The Voice.

People spend years and decades in therapy trying to understand the nature and origin of their blocks to success, feelings of inadequacy, and taunts of negative self-talk. In my experience, a critical step in breaking The Voice's stranglehold is to be very clear about one thing: The Voice's whole purpose is to make your life one long bad day, to make you confused, self-doubting, and scared to take action. It's almost as if it's a separate person who is only happy when you're miserable. Once you understand, however, that The Voice's game is to keep you in check, preventing you from enjoying happiness and prosperity, you can mount a successful counteroffensive.

To do away with The Voice's power over you, you first need to accept that, like fear, it has the tendency to be with you to some extent throughout your life. Again, this isn't exclusive to you. Everybody I know has it. Remember, The Voice is one of humanity's "little secrets" that rarely gets talked about, yet we all have it. You won't be able to silence it entirely, but as you get better at recognizing its pattern of operation you'll be able to identify it earlier as it tries to weasel its way into your consciousness, and you'll eventually learn to disarm it the moment it pops up in your life.

The Voice isn't always easy to recognize because it can take many forms. Sometimes you perceive it as self-criticism; sometimes it masquerades as your "rational" mind, simply questioning your goals. Often it takes the form of a person from your past or present who criticized you (or, possibly, who you perceived to be critical of you, regardless of whether or not that was true). The Voice is a master of ill timing, and it most often worms its way into your thought process when you're vulnerable and your mental defenses are down from being overly tired or hungry, or when your nerves are frayed, or when you're feeling a little lonely or down.

If you listen to its seductive babble, The Voice will send you into a mental tailspin, leading you to doubt that you'll ever be able to achieve your goals and most likely preventing you from even trying. Another ploy The Voice uses to lure you into its trap is to harass you to your breaking point, so that you egotistically roll up your sleeves and jump into the boxing ring with it, wanting to "show it who's boss" and "shut it up once and for all." Doing that, however, only gives The Voice even more power over you and throws you further off balance, leaving you unable to focus and execute your success strategies and causing you to make poor decisions at critical moments.

"The only effective way to push the mute button on The Voice is this: don't engage it; don't start a dialogue with it; don't get into a wrestling match with it; and don't get drawn into its web of confusion."

The only effective way to push the mute button on The Voice is this: don't engage it; don't start a dialogue with it; don't get into a wrestling match with it; and don't get drawn into its web of confusion. Just observe it and continue completing the tasks that carry you closer toward your goals. Recognize that its whole game is to keep you mentally off balance by making you doubt yourself, realize how it tries to draw you into its snare, and observe its seductive taunts trying to persuade you into dialoguing with it. Just watch its meaningless chatter in the same way you might passively observe an obnoxious late-night infomercial host for a few minutes before

WHEN DOES YOUR VOICE POP UP?

Since everyone's particular set of vulnerabilities is unique, The Voice has special entry points it chooses to gain access into your consciousness. Identifying the situations in which The Voice is most likely to sneak in and start scrambling your mind is the key to choking off its portal of entry. Ask yourself these questions to assist you in identifying when your Voice is most likely to surface. Once you understand your Voice's mode of operation, you can work to overcome its taunting and to achieve your goals by learning to trust your talents and your past history as a success.

- Can you think of a time when you were certain that you wanted to do something but were suddenly plagued by thoughts that created confusion and caused you to doubt your plan? What were the circumstances? What were the thoughts?

- Are there certain people who knock you off balance mentally? Do you feel uncomfortable or uneasy around them, regardless of what they say or how they act? Who are those people? What goes through your mind during and after your interactions with them? How do you feel around them? Do you feel tired, doubt yourself, and question your capacity to succeed around them?

- Think of events in your life when you have done especially well and when you have done poorly. What were the differences between the situations that led to those different outcomes? What thoughts were going through your mind beforehand that led to either a better or worse than expected outcome?

- Can you think of a time (or times) that an opportunity you'd been wanting came along, and for some reason you didn't take it? Why didn't you take it?

changing the channel. You can watch it without wasting emotional energy or buying into what it has to say. Rather than jumping into the ring and battling it by contradicting its taunts ("I can do it!"), just observe it, as you would watch someone ranting and raving on a street corner, and go on about your business. ("There's that Voice trying to scare me again," or "There's that infomercial buffoon again, trying to get me to buy something I don't need.") By remaining aware of The Voice but refusing to engage it, you rob it of its power over you. If you react to it you give it energy to perpetuate itself, but if you starve it of attention it will wither. Dispassionate observation is the only true antidote to The Voice.

3. **Don't give anyone or anything more credit than is due.** Whatever it is that stands between you and your goals, whether it's a task, a person going after the same goal, or some barrier that stands in your way, do not give in to the temptation to exaggerate its strengths. We're all inclined to see our challenges as greater than they are and to discount our own assets by comparison. Being so focused on others' abilities that we don't give proper attention to our own hurts us both by increasing our fear—and with it the likelihood that we won't even try to succeed—and by reducing our chances of gaining the competitive edge. I learned this when, during my first international cycling competition, I was competing against Olympic and world champions and knew from their practice times that my training times were similar. I figured I had as much chance to win as they did, but in the preliminary races I didn't perform up to my capacity because I was so intimidated by my competitors' past achievements that I didn't concentrate on applying all my abilities toward winning. The moment I stopped paying attention to my competitors it became a competition against myself, and by simply focusing on making my best times ever, not on beating theirs, I made my first international podium finish.

So, first of all, if you're vying for the same goal as others in a competitive situation, remember that they are only human, that they put on their shoes one at a time just like you do, and that you have as much right to succeed as they do. It's a public-speaking cliché that picturing the audience in their underwear will make them seem less intimidating, but the principle behind it—finding a way to remember that others have their vulnerabilities, too—is a great truth to remember when you're going for a win.

One of my friends had breakfast with a legendary multi-time world motocross champion who many consider to be the greatest ever in his field, and later told me incredulously, "He puts sugar on his cereal!" Because of a minute breakfast preference that seemed incredibly ordinary and human, my friend was never able to see the person as a motocross "god" again. So try to find a few small but shining examples of ways your competition is human and fallible, just like everybody else. If you look long and hard enough, even the seemingly invincible reveal their cracks.

> "Success is a ladder and nobody has a fixed place on it."

Now even if there's strong evidence that someone you're up against might have an advantage—your colleague has won "salesperson of the year" twice already—remember that success is a ladder and nobody has a fixed place on it. No matter how far ahead competitors might seem, you're at most just a few rungs behind them. And who knows: in the time since your abilities were last measured against each other, you might have moved up a few steps and they might have moved down, putting you on a level playing field.

The most important way to keep yourself from being intimidated, whether by the competition or by the enormity of a task or obstacle you're confronting, is to complete the first step of your goal's plan on time. This accomplishment is its own minivictory, and it's crucial to achieving your goals because once you have accomplished it, you realize wins are only a matter of applying the correct skill set to the plan and completing the steps one by one to reach your goal. It's as simple as that. Then you can focus on your own progress and capacity for achievement, rather than obsessing over any perceived advantages held by the competition or the challenges in front of you.

4. Expose the bogeyman. As with anything we fear, what terrifies us, prevents us from going after what we want, and thwarts our efforts when we do is always much smaller and less powerful than we make it out to be. We tend to forget this because we spend so much energy trying not to deal with our fears that we lose all perspective on what they really look like and what the true consequences would be if they came true. When you avoid confronting what you fear, you give it strength, so that in your mind it grows into a Godzilla-size monster, when in fact it more likely resembles a pesky insect—grotesque and unsettling when you see it crawling across the floor or buzzing around your head, but nothing a flyswatter couldn't take care of in a few seconds.

It's ridiculous, really, how much strength we give our fears when we avoid confronting them, because the second we do examine them for what they are—when we open the closed door and take a long hard look at the bogeyman—whatever it is quickly loses its paralyzing grip over us. Think of how the Great Oz lost his power in Dorothy's eyes once Toto pulled back the curtain to reveal him for the imposter he really was.

Now is the time to take an unflinching look at what petrifies you. Think of your dreams and goals, what you want more than anything. Now think of the reasons why you haven't achieved them and what you need to do to accomplish them. What feelings come up? Does your body recoil—through a little pit in your stomach, a flutter of anxiety in your chest—when you think about what you want and what needs to happen for you to achieve it? Why? What is really so scary about going after your desires? You probably feel some type of fear of failure ("If I screw up people will laugh at me behind my back," or "I might lose all my money pursuing this, and then what will I do?") but—and this is harder to recognize—there also could be some degree of fear of success percolating inside you. Success means change, and even if it's change that you consider positive, changing your status quo can be frightening nonetheless. The "Fearing Failure, Fearing Success" chart to follow lists some of the most common fears of both failure and success. Do any of them ring true for you?

FEARING FAILURE, FEARING SUCCESS

It's understandable that we fear failure, but why fear success? Fear is a natural instinct we're born with and an ever-present reality everyone must deal with throughout life. Fear is our best friend in critical situations of physical danger or when vital decisions must be made, but it can hurt us when it impairs our decision making and compromises our ability to manifest our highest attributes and aspirations. People have different fears for different reasons. The key to overcoming fear is first to identify why failure and success produce fear. Then learn appropriate responses to fear-producing situations so that you neither overreact nor underreact to them. Abnormal fear is often the product of learned behavior and, perhaps to some degree, genetics. Take a moment to examine the most common reasons people fear failure and success, and see which apply to you.

Reasons People Are Afraid of Failure	Reasons People Are Afraid of Success
• It's associated with being a bad person.	• If the bar is raised, they must then perform indefinitely at that level.
• It's associated with incompetence.	• Fear of the unknown.
• It's associated with certain rejection.	• They might not have the capacity to learn the necessary skills.
• It's associated with embarrassment and looking foolish to others.	• If successful, their life will change and they'll have to leave people behind.
• It might induce mental conflict and psychological pain.	• Jealous people will have bad feelings toward them for being successful.
• It might result in criticism from others.	• They might have to make decisions outside their scope or understanding, which would cause them to fail.
• Material acquisitions will be lost and never gotten back.	• They will be unable to keep up with the more knowledgeable and sophisticated people they have to be around.

FEARING FAILURE, FEARING SUCCESS (CONT'D)

Reasons People Are Afraid of Failure	Reasons People Are Afraid of Success
• It might result in a predicament that is difficult to get out of. • It might decrease self-esteem. • If the goal is not achieved, others might label them a failure. • It might take more resources than available to rectify a goal not achieved. • Success might never be experienced.	• They might be put in situations where they're expected to be competent but aren't. • Others might realize that they're not capable of achieving success consistently. • They might not feel comfortable with people in the socioeconomic strata associated with their success. • They might feel guilty if they have more success than others. • They might become overwhelmed by the demands and opportunities their success brings.

5. **When you're trembling, proceed anyway.** Although, like all of us, winners feel fear, what distinguishes them from those who never get to the top is that they cope with the fear and embrace opportunity, regardless. Winners know that feeling insecure or afraid is not a reason to turn back. On the contrary, taking action in the face of fear often results in the greatest successes. They also believe more than anything that the greatest possible failure, the only thing truly worth fearing, is what you lose when you don't take a chance on an opportunity you may never get again.

"Winners know that feeling insecure or afraid is not a reason to turn back."

Of course, you would be justified to say "Easier said than done." After all, if it were easy to ignore your fears and take action, then nearly everybody would be chasing and manifesting their dreams, when in fact most people let unjustified fear rule their decision-making process. No, it's not always easy, but like many things that aren't easy, it's necessary.

CONTROLLING THE FEAR IMPULSE

Everyone's experienced temporary moments of fear before, during, or after an action or circumstance. Someone calls on the phone and presents a tantalizing opportunity that you're not sure you're equipped to accept; you receive an e-mail informing you of a significant unexpected dilemma; or perhaps you're on the verge of a personal breakthrough and the tension is mounting and the time has come to make your move. This type of situational fear differs from generalized anxiety—being in a constant low-grade state of fear—that permeates one's every thought and action.

The most prevalent signs and symptoms of the situational fear impulse include any combination of a racing mind, cold hands, and stiff body. Though the mechanism for such responses may be unknown, what's important is that you capitalize on the situation regardless of your fear reactions to it, by having a strategy in place to control them.

I know of a very talented and committed individual who, on at least half a dozen occasions, would predictably collapse under the weight of anticipation because he couldn't transcend his racing mind. You could see the breakdown coming like clockwork. As the critical moment approached, he would start second-guessing and changing his entire success routine and then mentally crumble when it came time to execute.

When you find the fear impulse gaining the upper hand on your mind, there are several simple measures that can be used to control it. The common link these mechanisms share is they anchor your mind in the present and allow you to make rational decisions under pressure. When you feel you may freeze under pressure, here are some strategies to unwind your mind:

1. **Separation breathing.** An effective technique to reduce the racing mind associated with the fear impulse is an exercise I call separation breathing. It's essentially breathing from the diaphragm as done in athletics, martial arts, and meditation practices that slows the mind for better

CONTROLLING THE FEAR IMPULSE (cont'd)

performances. The exercise can be done sitting or standing. To begin, draw your attention to a point a few inches below your navel. Then, without lifting your rib cage, gently inhale through your nostrils, so your abdomen moves forward from your spine as your lungs inflate. At the conclusion of your inhalation slowly exhale through your open mouth—as your ribcage and abdomen naturally recoil back toward your spine—and then begin your inhalation cycle again for thirty to sixty more seconds. You can discontinue the diaphragmatic breathing when your mind starts to slow down and you think more objectively.

2. **Outline and rehearse your response.** When the mind starts to race it's vital to step back and mentally, and perhaps, also, in writing, outline in exact detail what you want your alternate response to be. The objectivity this provides gives you a choice as to how *you* truly want to react to circumstance, instead of just *blindly* responding in a way that is more reactionary than deliberate. Once you've decided on a nonimpulsive, rational response, rehearse it enough times to build your confidence in delivering it. This process should never be rushed. Take as much time as needed to make sure your response is exactly as you intend it and respond in *your* time and not that of others.

3. **Do something physical.** Physical activity takes the mind away from itself and is often the best means of putting objective distance between you and your reactions. When the body is moving and the mind is idle, clarity and solutions often come easily and quickly. Go for a walk or a bicycle ride; shop, garden, or go to the gym, and spend enough time and intensity doing the activity so your mind is redirected on the "doing" of the activity and not on the subject of your fear impulse. When the mental feathers settle you can then return to the topic at hand with a calmer mind and greater objectivity.

4. **Change activities.** Another effective way to take the edge off the fear impulse is to change activities. By engaging in a completely different activity your mind has space between itself and what it is reacting to. Once you settle down you can then return to the previous topic with composure and reason.

CONTROLLING THE FEAR IMPULSE (cont'd)

Fear is an emotion that can be managed. Realizing that situational fear is always temporary can help you take back the power over the situation. Using the simple (and sometimes most obvious) coping mechanisms, such as the ones described above, can help you step out of your own way and unblock your natural pathway to success.

To show you how to "press on regardless," I first want to dispel a big myth about fear and performance: people think it's necessary to be super "calm" to perform well, but that's absolutely not the case. Sure, it would be nice to feel totally at ease, but there will be times when you can feel your body react in fear just as you're about to make a move that's crucial to achieving your goal. No matter what, you shouldn't give in to that fear and wait to regain your "calm" before taking action. Your pulse might race, your palms might get sweaty, your throat might dry up, and your physical fight-or-flight response might kick in, but *do not* view your physical symptoms as a sign of surrender. When you take necessary action despite your body's fear response—when you feel the fear and do it anyway—you empower yourself and take an important step toward developing a new, full-time, "This is what I stand to gain" temperament as opposed to the old fear-controlled "This is what I stand to lose" operating system that keeps most people stuck in mediocrity. Try it. It's easy. Once you've done it, you can do it over and over, lessening fear's grip on you.

Action, you see, creates reorganization. When you suffer an injury to an ankle or shoulder, the worst thing you can do is rest too much. If you try to heal the injury with total inactivity, the result is increased scar formation, poor muscle function, limited range of motion, and a prolonged recovery. If, however, you begin moving the injury early in the rehabilitation process, you reorganize the injured tissue faster, leading to accelerated, more complete healing. That's pretty much the way it works when you act through your fear. The fact that you're *doing*, and not freezing with fear or waiting to relax, shows you what you're capable of, gives you confidence, and quickly dispels the fear response.

When we're terrified, we tend to think something awful is going to happen if we act, but that's virtually never the case. You're not going to self-destruct or fade into oblivion. On the contrary, taking action dramatically enhances your capacity to succeed. How many times have you balked at doing something, yet once you've done it and experienced its benefit, you've asked yourself why you didn't do it before. That simple act of moving forward reorganizes your mind and body, enabling the process of being a consistent winner to occur more easily.

TURN IT UP! TIPS

1. Remember, everyone experiences fear. It is our species' most important survival mechanism. Experiencing it signals that your physiology is working as intended. You need only apply it to your advantage.

2. Looking at what's behind your fear to identify its cause is the first step to overcoming it. Never blame your fear on anyone else, as it is your personal reaction to circumstance.

3. Understand that fear is not a weakness. If you assume your fear represents a character flaw, you will ultimately conclude that you are undeserving of success.

4. Whenever you feel fear you must think about what you should be doing, not what you shouldn't be doing. What you think about is what you will do.

5. When that little voice inside you starts to make you doubt yourself, don't dialogue with it, resent it, or try to struggle with it. Redirect your attention to what *you* want to happen and do it.

TURN IT UP! TIPS (CONT'D)

6. Make the first step of your plan the easiest to accomplish. Having steps that are doable will build your confidence as you accomplish them.

7. Face your fears as directly and as soon as possible so you can see them for what they are and move on. Your mind will make your fears bigger than they really are if you do not directly face them.

8. Under no circumstances should you ever assume that you must regain your composure before moving forward. Sometimes the best way to overcome fear is feel it, be aware of it, and proceed with your plans anyway.

9. Be more committed to reaching your goal than to caving into fear. It takes less energy to reach your goal than to contend with self-doubt and irrational emotions.

10. Never think that you need to be completely fearless to be a successful person. All successful people feel fear.

4

Being Principled,
Not Perfect

Pleasure in the job puts perfection in the work.

—Aristotle

B eing perfect is an aspiration many have, but one that no one ever has or ever will achieve. Ironically, you are more apt to have an imperfect life by compulsively striving to be perfect than by accepting the fact that simply being human makes you imperfect.

Striving too hard to be perfect will most often lead to chronic frustration with yourself and others and with life in general, which takes a heavy toll on your health, self-worth, and relationships. Top performers have learned to become more perfect by reconciling their imperfections with themselves while investing their confidence, trust, resources, time, and effort into their mental and physical strengths and aptitudes, not their weaknesses. This way they are able to live a more perfect life despite their flaws. How do they do this? These top performers have shifted their attention to embracing their not-so-perfect selves and focusing on an even better alternative to perfection: embracing their principled selves. By reconciling their weaknesses and accepting their limitations, they have created guidelines for themselves—a

> "You set the perfection bar. That's what being principled is all about."

set of principles—to personally strive for. You, too, can come to terms with your imperfections and stop letting them hold you back by adopting a life strategy—your own set of principles—that minimizes your imperfections and maximizes your strengths, in accordance with your own rules and definition of perfection. In essence, you set the perfection bar. That's what being principled is all about.

Defining Principles

Every successful individual has a highly personalized set of principles that govern their life choices and actions. Principles are "rules" that determine what decisions and actions are made and how they are carried out. Appropriately defined and applied, principles bring out the highest potential in the person. The trick is to find exactly what those principles are. For some, determining those principles comes easily. For others, it's more difficult. Generally, for most, their principles evolve and require refinement throughout life.

Those individuals with well-defined principles, meaning they align with their talents and knowledge-base, consistently outperform those who do not have this infrastructure. The benefits to having well-founded principles are plentiful. Perhaps the most important is that they provide a baseline reference for evaluating and responding to every life moment and how you are reacting to it. Without that reference, life can become extremely inconsistent and chaotic and very disruptive to productivity. It's analogous to being in a china shop blindfolded trying to find your way to the exit. There's absolutely no telling where you are and when you're going to bump into a table causing plates, cups, and bowls to crash to the floor shattering into a million pieces. Your principles also attract like-minded people to you who can enrich your life, while also alerting you to the people with whom you share very little compatibility. Your principles serve as your life pillars during adverse personal circumstances, providing the decision-making structure that reduces mental confusion and helps you remain committed to the task at hand and ultimate goals.

Putting Principles to Work

Once established, the efficacy of your principles will be put to the test on a daily basis and will identify to you how successfully your principles match your expectations and practicality with others'. This valuable feedback provides you vital information on how refinements can be made to your principles so you can gain their maximum benefits. The following considerations will help you begin to develop your own set of principles.

1. **Know what you stand for.** Perhaps the most important quality to have is to know what you stand for, what you will or will not do, and what your actions represent. This defined line empowers you to make swift, decisive, and beneficial decisions that keep your life directed toward a prosperous future. Your actions will also inspire others to search for, define, and create their own individual life platforms, empowering them to be the best they can be and to leave their best personal stamp on humanity.

People who lack set criteria on which to base their actions seldom have the personal infrastructure, authority, and commitment needed to create extraordinary lives. With a solid grasp of what you represent, you can build an infrastructure that is focused on setting appropriate goals, decreasing hesitation and fear, and being capable of reaching your objectives. Without principles, every time you are confronted with a decision, you must reconstruct the principles that govern your decision making. This lack of preparation squanders valuable time, reduces spontaneity, creates considerable mental confusion, and erodes confidence, all of which produce poor decisions, uninspiring performances, and unfulfilled dreams.

2. **Know your strengths and weaknesses.** One trait all successful people share is that they know what their personal strengths and weaknesses are and build their lives only on their strengths. They never dilute their time and

energy by trying to be perfect at something when they have no aptitude for it. You only have so much energy in life, and if you expend energy trying to be perfect at too many things, you're going to be a very frustrated and tired individual who is, at best, half good at some things and great at nothing, with your best talents buried under a blanket of mediocrity. All successful people do what they are best at, which is exactly what you should devote yourself to doing. To become as perfect as your imperfections allow, you must develop a highly refined, yet workable methodology to keep your goals lofty and attainable and your plans moving efficiently. For you to be the best you can be, your life must be built on your unique talents, not on the talents you have in common with others.

> "One trait all successful people share is that they know what their personal strengths and weaknesses are and build their lives only on their strengths."

3. **Flow with life's twists and turns.** Life, for each of us, will never be a straight line from here to there. Instead it is a meandering whirlwind with unanticipated twists and turns. This circuitous path, however, provides you with your greatest opportunities and possibilities that you could never have deliberately conjured up. Essential to becoming the best you can be is that you must trust your life path, embracing its twists and turns as opportunities, not as unwanted detours.

4. **Turn adversity into benefit.** No life or plan ever runs perfectly from start to finish without hiccups along the way. A major component of a successful life is being able to adapt as you go, while turning adversity into benefit. Those who can think on their feet and embrace challenge as an opportunity to exercise their improvisational skills and trust their instincts, consistently come out on top when confronted with circumstances under which many would buckle. This agility also helps establish and reinforce the size and scope of what circumstances most allow you to function at your best most often.

5. **Establish boundaries.** Defining your principles and adhering to them requires that you concisely identify how much life responsibility you can

reasonably and realistically handle and how much you are *willing* and *want* to obligate yourself to. These parameters set the boundaries for how far you will take your principles. For example, if one of your principles is to get a consistent good night's sleep, one of your boundaries might be to not accept phone calls after eight o'clock. Without establishing and vigilantly adhering to your boundaries, despite the principle, the inevitable slide into being overburdened by incomplete tasks and over-obligation can easily occur. This imbalance can quickly compound when the chokehold of over-commitment prompts the impulse to unload the burden of over-obligation as quickly as possible. Too often this leads to employing impulsive, untested measures, which, unfortunately, lead to greater counterproductive chaos.

6. **Modify as needed.** Skilled achievers appropriately modify their boundaries and principles. Most peoples' boundaries undergo subtle refinement throughout their lives and without sweeping change. However, significant alteration in boundaries can occur, especially for those who have experienced extreme personal hardship or tragedy. One of the most beautiful human beings I ever met was Alex Baum, who mentored me when I was training for the Olympics. Alex was a World War II concentration camp survivor who'd been exposed to unimaginable cruelty, yet he didn't have an ounce of resentment in his body—only strength, wisdom, and appreciation. His commitment to supporting others in every imaginable way exemplified the highest definition of caring and compassion. If there was ever a saint and role model representing the highest principles of the human experience it was Alex. He knew no boundaries when it came to his human outreach and putting his principles into action.

What matters, as Alex Baum demonstrated, is that you remain open to and solicit from others as many life-governing principles for consideration as possible, adopting those that resonate with your core beliefs, regardless of others' opinions. Being completely authentic regarding what works for you is the only way you will ever live a fully committed, individualized life, making your best contribution to others and experiencing ultimate personal empowerment.

Define Your Principles

Every life event you have follows a trajectory determined by the forces acting on you in exactly the same way as the force of gravity influences the planets orbiting the sun. The more defined and refined your personal set of principles is, the more purposeful and focused your life becomes and the more easily your successes are achieved. Decisions are made more easily when backed by well-defined personal guidelines that enable you to see your options with increased clarity and perspective. With a strong set of principles guiding your aspirations, your goals are achieved with more certainty than if your choices are made without those strong parameters. With well-defined principles, it's very easy to see where opportunities do and do not fit into your life, which ensures that your efforts will produce their greatest dividends. A valuable exercise to do, periodically, is to reassess and refine your life-governing principles by asking yourself the following questions:

- Which of your principles have helped you achieve your goals, and which have taken you farther away from them?
- Which principles don't you have that you wish you had? Also, what would it take to acquire those principles you would like to have?
- What are some of the consequences you've experienced as a result of your principles? Which ones did you profit from, and which worked against you?
- Where did your principles come from? Which of your friends, family, or mentors have influenced you in positive ways?
- How have you influenced the principles of others?
- How do your principles at this stage of your life compare with those you had in the past?
- What are your most prized principles that have served you well?
- What principles do you see in others that have brought them success or failure?

Deemphasizing Perfection Creates Better Performance

The concept of being principled but not perfect is something every top performer has reconciled. Ask any of them and most will tell you flat out that the more perfect they try to be when performing, the worse their performances are. It seems completely contradictory that people perform better if perfection is deemphasized, but most of us have experienced just that. The moment we stop caring so much about something, it happens. Being less perfect will help you in many ways.

> "Being less perfect will help you in many ways."

SIMPLE ACTIONS CREATE SIGNIFICANT SUCCESS

Your imperfections will make you a better communicator. You're not a mind reader, nor do you speak a universal language everyone understands, so you must develop the language skills to communicate precisely with others to reach your objectives efficiently. Succinctly expressing to others what you need from them to support your plan aids its timely completion. The most successful actions are those initiated with the least complex strategies and fewest words spoken.

Those who step up and perform well when it counts never try to be too perfect when performing; they just trust their abilities and execute the process without thought. Others who try too hard to be too perfect and control their performance by thinking their way through it inevitably perform too rigidly and end up out of sync. That's what happens to figure skaters who easily perform the most difficult tricks in practice but fall during competition. Their timing is off and they lose their spontaneity so that their actions don't flow and they end up falling on the ice. A simple rule here could be "Don't think about it—do it." One of the distinguishing characteristics of all great musical groups is their ability to create and synchronize the flow of their music with their audience.

An important strategy to adopt—one that will allow you to remain principled and not succumb to the perils of trying to be perfect—is to emphasize life's big picture and deemphasize the smaller (even if significant) details. When the big picture is well visualized and set within the context of your principles, it becomes easier to identify and exclude nonessential details that clog your mind and strangle your path to success. Whenever you're feeling too much pressure to complete too many things to keep your plans alive, always take a step back and look at the big picture. The pressure you feel is almost always from drowning in insignificant details, while completely overlooking the larger reality.

The 90 Percent Rule

We have previously discussed the negative impact that trying to be too perfect has on creating success, but finding the sweet spot where the best life experiences and successes happen can also be elusive. We should, therefore, understand that the sweet spot resides somewhere slightly below perfection but significantly above average. The sweet spot is analogous to getting all As in school. That may seem like an inaccessible goal, but to do it you really only need to answer questions correctly 90 percent of the time because 90 percent is still an A. Statistically speaking, missing 10 percent is missing a lot, yet to be perfect in an imperfect world you only need to get life correct 90 percent of the time.

This doesn't mean not putting 100 percent effort into your pursuits. It means making a 100 percent commitment to doing it and putting 100 percent effort toward achieving the 90 percent of what's necessary to live an abundantly successful life. Personally, I follow the 90 percent rule in everything I do. I'm very well aware that it's not possible to know everything about the mind and body and be a specialist in every area. So, with a 100 percent commitment, I direct 100 percent of my effort to learning and applying with 100 percent competence the 90 percent I need to know to address 95 to 98 percent of the needs of my clients. And, for those clients with circumstances outside my expertise I refer them to the appropriate professional within my professional network. The same holds true for my clients. I only expect them to do what's reasonable and necessary to meet their goals; no less, no more. I know that's the only way they will be capable of maintaining the long-term enthusiasm and commitment to doing the work to live life in the sweet spot.

The perfect program for anybody is the one that's doable and gets done. Rarely is the textbook program sustainable over the long term. For example, a client was involved in a very serious professional car racing accident that resulted in many broken bones and extensive surgery. Once home from the hospital his goal was to speed his recovery as quickly as possible by going to the best physical therapy clinic in his region, despite the several hours a day commute to and from the clinic. After a few weeks of this extremely time-intensive regime, his enthusiasm met the practicality of his therapy's exhaustive requirements, and he realized the only reasonable solution to meet his therapy needs and economize his time and energy was to forego the long commute to therapy in favor of a guided home therapy program. This decision ultimately proved correct because his home therapy led to his recovery in the shortest time possible.

In summary, even history's most successful people have failed *at least* 10 percent of the time—even Albert Einstein considered himself a failure because he couldn't find the unifying link between gravity and magnetism. So, don't sweat the 10 percent you don't know or do perfectly as success occurs from correctly doing the 90 percent of what's relevant and not the insignificant 10 percent. Enjoy the 90 percent you do know by living in the sweet spot following the 90 percent rule.

Remaining in the Sweet Spot

Living in the sweet spot is a delicate balancing act between too much and too little of everything. Either side of the correct amount of anything unbalances life, making you less effective in everything you do. Being kicked out of the sweet spot's orbit can occur for several reasons.

One ubiquitous life tenet that everyone is force-fed early in our imperfect world is that the harder you work and push yourself, the better your life will be. The theory may make rational sense, but, unfortunately, it is wrong. Too much of any sustained effort for too long always compromises long-term peak productivity, because it inevitably exceeds the mind and body's functional capacity. This eventually leads to mental and physical breakdown, which creates illness, injury, and burnout and makes the consistent attainment of your life's ambitions impossible. Countless people have been injured while subscribing to the "No Pain, No Gain" theory of exercise. Likewise, many have made unintentional mental errors that have seriously damaged their lives due to mental fatigue brought on by too much mental activity for too long. More rest and less work are always better because it improves short-term performance and long-term productivity. Many people find this counterintuitive and hard to accept, but anyone who's overworked too long, too often knows the shoddy quality, poor productivity, and poor decisions brought on by too much, too often.

> "More rest and less work are always better."

This burnout scenario is commonly seen with people who believe they're behind in their work and then work extra hard to catch up with their responsibilities. Unfortunately, they most often overextend their minds and bodies by pushing too hard and then become ill, physically injured, or mentally burned out putting them even farther behind. The only reasonable way to make sustainable life advances without overexposure is to do a little less than maximum each day—following the 90 percent rule—and then string together consistent days to make predictable, regular progress toward achieving goals. When Lance Armstrong was training to race the Tour de France he strictly controlled how often he trained and raced to insure that he never overtrained and was always fresh to race in top performance. He could have put in 110 percent on one day, only to have enough energy to train at 60 percent the next. What's the point of that, when you can consistently perform at your top every day?

Undoubtedly, perfection is an admirable aspiration for everyone, but rarely, if ever, has anyone with perfectionist tendencies been a great success. Most people driven by perfectionism are so compulsively overfocused about getting every single detail in their life—and the lives of others—so perfect that they fail to create and complete their own life ambitions, regrettably rendering them perennial underachievers. To remain in the sweet spot always do a little less to achieve a lot more.

Building Your Dream Team

Since no one is perfect, none of us is perfectly qualified to do everything necessary to finish all the tasks required to complete our plans and become consistent successes. A lesson all successful entrepreneurs learn is how to delegate to those more skilled to do for them what they can't do for themselves. This is not always an easy thing for entrepreneurially minded people to do because they tend to micromanage everything and everyone and, regrettably, impede reaching their goals in the process.

All successful businesses are appropriately staffed with the best people for the job, positioned at the posts that best align with their skills. Team sports are a good example, not necessarily for actual delegation but for the way tasks are assigned by ability to make the team work better as a whole. We see how players of certain ability are better suited for specific tasks within the team structure. In football, for instance, big guys are linemen, fast guys are running backs or receivers, and so forth.

Since everyone is "the best" at something, always delegate those things in which you excel to yourself and leave the rest to those who can perform the remaining tasks of your plan better. You should never feel let down or guilty about not having the skills to do everything, because nobody ever does. It's actually good that you don't, because if you were good at everything, you'd end up doing everything yourself and taking so much time to complete your plans you'd barely make a dent in the number of successful plans you're capable of achieving in life. While it may take a bit of time, effort, and resources to get the correct people involved in your plans, that's the cost of success, and each success you achieve leads to greater successes in the future. That's what partnerships are all about.

Delegation also gives you more time to acquire and fully develop those skills you're good at and must have to achieve your greatest successes in life. You can never have enough of the right skills. The more skills you have, the more creative and diverse successes you can produce in your life.

To delegate successfully, you must ensure that those you're delegating to are not only qualified by job description but also aligned with your plan's goals and purposes. If they aren't in agreement with your project's goals and purposes, they won't be fully committed to your plan. This can be highly disruptive to the integrity of your plan's group synergy. Few things are worse than having those assisting you also working against you and each other because of philosophical differences. If the fit's not right, it never will be. This is where having your defined set of principles is most helpful. Basing your assessment of your team on the principles that define you and your strategy for success will enable you to quickly discover who is not appropriate for your team, which wastes less time and enables you to surround yourself with others who can help you reach your goal effectively.

Ten Steps to Qualifying Your Dream Team

Many are the examples of dream teams that, on paper, should have become dominant in their fields, yet didn't come remotely close to living up to their potential. This is seen quite often in sports where dream teams composed of superior players get beaten by average teams composed of "less talented" individuals. They fail because there is no team cohesion, with too many stars playing only for themselves instead of playing unselfishly for the team to serve a unified purpose.

Teamwork is everything. And, everything possible should be done to assemble a team that works together harmoniously toward the same goal. That's how the unthinkable becomes thinkable and achieved.

Consequently, you must carefully qualify all potential team members before selecting them for your dream team. Several key items should be considered to ensure their skill compatibility with and allegiance to your plan. If they are lacking in any area, they shouldn't be considered qualified for your team because one area drags down all the other areas and everyone associated with them.

1. All team members must align with the goal and purpose of your plan, as well as your set principles. If they don't, their full commitment to you and your plan is impossible, regardless of their talents and promises to support you to their fullest.

2. They must have the education and experience to complete the tasks your plan requires of them. If they do, your plan will sail to completion most easily. If not, it will be fraught with delays, frustration, and resource consumption.

3. All candidates must be self-motivated to finish their tasks completely and on time. Otherwise, micromanaging them consumes valuable resources and their incompetent or passive–aggressive delays can stall or even prevent your plan from reaching completion.

4. Everyone must be committed to doing only what their job description requires and never meddling in others' tasks. Members must never be inclined to assist or take over other people's jobs if not defined in their job description. This not only dilutes energy and slows plan completion, but others may resent the intrusions, which will hurt group harmony.

5. Your team members must only do their tasks as stated and never put

their own creative spin on them. Doing so wastes valuable time and resources. For example, several years ago I designed a metal table and gave the fabricator a very detailed three-view drawing of the table. When I came to pick up the finished table, however, it was different from my drawing. The fabricator explained that he thought the table looked better his way. He was quite angry about my not accepting the table unless it was exactly as my plan specified. Grudgingly, he modified the table back to its original design—on his time and money. He admitted painfully, "There's always enough time to do it correctly the second time."

6. When selecting team members, be sure their problem-solving skills and decision-making methods are fully compatible with your expectations. If you have any suspicion about someone's ability to perform, it's probably accurate and likely won't improve over time despite his or her efforts. People may be able to change their behavior for a few weeks or months, but given enough time everyone tends to drift back into their habitual ways of doing things. Trust your instincts implicitly on this one.

I was having a conversation with several of the riders prior to the start of one of the Tours de France we did together, and when discussing who the toughest competitors would be, I told them that it was impossible to know at that moment who the greatest rivals would be that year, but one thing was certain: given enough time and pressure, each of them would reveal their true strengths and vulnerabilities. The team faithfully executed their race strategy day to day and, as predicted, each rival revealed his weakness, which the team exploited in order to win seven consecutive Tours de France.

7. Each of your team members must perform flawlessly under the pressure of their responsibility for the plan. In assessing whether a team candidate is right for your plan, always have them execute a task similar in difficulty and pressure to those they will be required to do in your plan. If they stand up to the task, they are suitable for inclusion on your team. If not, let them go.

8. For your plan to run smoothly to completion, everyone must be able

to communicate succinctly with the other team members. Each member must have both proven and appropriate written and verbal communication skills that allow information to be accurately disseminated, ensuring that your plan steps are completed on time.

9. Subtle warning signs about incompatibility are often evident early in any relationship, but they are often obscured by the individual's positive traits. If your initial interview with a prospective team member raises suspicion about their competency, or if you're uneasy about something you can't fully identify, pay heed to the warning because your first impressions are usually right. Never bring someone onto your team until you're fully convinced they are qualified.

10. Every team member must show up on time. Being on time shows respect for all and a commitment to your plan, while allowing it to move forward with the fewest delays.

Challenge Is Your Best Teacher

Your imperfections are actually good for you. They create challenges in your life that motivate you to find creative solutions, which makes you a more capable problem solver and gives you more confidence in yourself as a success creator.

Not being perfect makes you more tolerant of the imperfections of others. You learn to use their strengths to support your plan's completion, while reducing the plan's exposure to their liabilities. Few things are better in life than to collaborate with others and succeed at a project that benefits everyone by using everyone's greatest strengths.

Assembling a team capable of creating and completing a perfect plan from imperfect people requires you to form an organizational hierarchy that shuttles information between people through well-organized pathways to minimize the risk of anything going wrong through miscommunication. A final authority who will make the ultimate decisions that steer the direction of the team must be situated at the top of the communication pyramid—and in the context of this discussion, that is you. When the perfect hierarchy is in place, with all plan members correctly posted and communication lines in place, the plan can be executed most effectively.

It's inevitable whenever people work closely together on any plan that challenges and confrontations will occur between those inside and outside the plan. That's part of doing business in an imperfect world. To advance your plan to completion, then, you and your team need to learn to be equally good listeners as you are communicators. That way the common ground with others can be found most quickly so everyone works in harmony to advance your plan toward completion. Listening is often more productive than talking, not only because it shows respect for others but also because it lets their needs and attitudes be known. People who feel respected are much better contributors than those who don't.

> "Listening is often more productive than talking."

Making Peace with Your Imperfections

Matching your best skills and attributes with the best environment that allows you to make a great living is one of life's greatest achievements. Your foremost task is to clearly define and be comfortable with what you are best at. Everyone has the capacity to excel at something, and that something is where you need to invest your trust, time, effort, and resources.

Never invest too much in trying to be good at what you're not good at inherently. That's where your delegation skills can be put to use. While you should always strive to improve your weaknesses so they can support your strengths, you should avoid spending excess time trying to compensate for an ability you don't have inherently. In any endeavor, the right fit between you and your task is everything.

For example, expecting someone who has great people skills, but no aptitude for manual tasks, to thrive working alone stuffing envelopes is about as ludicrous as believing an abstract artist would prosper tabulating profit and loss statements in an accounting office. Only do what you're best at doing. It's the only way true fulfillment happens. Shaquille O'Neal, one of the greatest basketball players in history, is known as a poor free-throw shooter despite his constant practice to become better at the skill, yet he's brilliant in every other aspect

> "Your foremost task is to clearly define and be comfortable with what you are best at."

of the game. He is crystal clear on where his strengths and liabilities lie and doesn't spend a disproportionate amount of time trying to be good at something for which he has little aptitude at the expense of his strengths.

Finding the best environment that allows you to use your skills to their fullest capacity is also an absolute necessity for you to be a top performer. The best work environments are highly individualized, and what's good for one person may not be the best situation for another. For example, an artist may only be capable of creating his or her best work in a chaotic, messy studio, and, conversely, an accountant may work well only in a spotless, well-organized office, but it will never be vice versa. There are no rules for you here, since only you know what works best for you. Find and stick with the setting that works best for you.

Almost all people are aware of where their aptitudes do and don't lie. The most successful people invest their confidence, time, effort, and resources in what they're best at, and they never feel guilty because they may perform less well than others in certain areas due to a lack of innate ability. Michael Jordan is arguably the greatest basketball player of all time. He did what he did best. After retiring from basketball the first time, he tried to be a professional baseball player and a professional golfer but succeeded at neither. His lack of success had nothing to do with his will, intelligence, or desire; he just didn't possess the innate capacity to make it happen at that level.

The message is crystal clear: you're uniquely qualified to do brilliant things in life, but you're never going to be all things to all people. If you try,

> "The only way to live life successfully and to its fullest is to do what you're best at and delegate to others those things they can do better than you."

you'll likely end up being the proverbial jack-of-all-trades but the master of none. The only way to live life successfully and to its fullest is to do what you're best at and delegate to others those things they can do better than you. The sooner that's done, the faster you'll be on the road to success.

Recognizing Your Uniqueness as Your Greatest Asset

Throughout time, historic achievements have always come from those who see life differently than most and take action to manifest their uniqueness. Da Vinci, Michelangelo, Madame Curie, Mozart, and Helen Keller all had unique visions and attributes that represented the pinnacle of the human spirit. Each trusted and cultivated their unique talents and followed the path of their inquiry, manifesting achievements that landed them in the history books.

None of us are so different from them. We all have distinct aptitudes that uniquely qualify us to do great things, yet we live in a world of comparison where we're always being measured against our sameness with others. Magazine covers, newscasts, television shows, and others constantly remind us of our differences, usually impressing upon us that we are lacking in some sort of way. This is especially true in regard to today's standard of success. Our uniqueness can be seen by some, even ourselves, as a liability, but it's really our greatest strength. I remember as a teen being made fun of by a friend's mother who ridiculed me for wearing tight, form fitting cycling shorts when I would ride my bike many miles to my friend's house. Despite the sting of the comment, cycling was a perfect match for my mental and physical abilities, ultimately culminating in a berth on the United States Olympic Cycling Team. Another example comes from a success theme television show that featured a guest who started the first model

MAKE A LIST OF YOUR UNIQUE ATTRIBUTES

There are some six billion people on this planet—and *only one you.* Nobody else has your specific constitution or attributes. Those who have matched their personalized aptitudes with their life passions and then placed themselves in environments that allow their unique combination to be expressed most often produce the most successful lives.

It's always worthwhile to spend a few minutes reflecting on your unique talents. This can help you reacquaint yourself with your gifts, and remind you how your life should be ordered to get the most out of it. The first half dozen talents will be fairly easy to list, but as you expand your list the remaining ones may become increasingly more difficult to identify as they are often obscured by your more obvious talents. Take your time and deliberately ponder what it is about you that makes you a distinct human being and sets you apart from others. You may even identify qualities that others have criticized in you that might actually be your greatest asset because of their uniqueness. In this exercise you must investigate every aspect of your life to find your greatest assets. Areas to assess include academics, sports, art, hobbies, recreational activities, social situations, home activities, and relationships. Begin your investigation by answering the questions below. They will provide you with useful information and spawn other questions to assist you in compiling a complete list of your uniqueness. Keep doing the exercise and never discount anything that comes up as being insignificant. Continue to reflect on the following questions until you have thoroughly identified your distinguishing characteristics. You'll know the drill is finished when no further insights percolate into your consciousness.

- What skills did you possess that made you different from others as a child?

- What activities did you naturally like doing as a child? What attributes do you have in common with others? How much of your life is built on those similarities?

Make a List of Your Unique Attributes (cont'd)

- What do you find most pleasure in doing?

- What skills do you have that could be adapted to working in other professions?

- What are your greatest academic skills?

- What are your best social skills?

- What are your best interpersonal skills?

- What tasks come easy to you in life?

- What classes in school did you excel in without much study?

- What are your passions?

- What aptitudes do others say you have?

- What special classes or training have you had?

- What are your hobbies?

---

agency for people with unique physical characteristics. The models in his agency ran the gamut in physical characteristics coming in every conceivable shape and size. The greatest part about the modeling agency is that many of the models were experiencing great success in their lives because of their uniqueness not in spite of it. So, spending time developing and applying your uniqueness is the distinguishing characteristic that will create an extraordinary life for you—something your weaknesses will never do.

As your successes mount, you will encounter people who say things to make you doubt that your uniqueness is a strength. The irony is that the detractors often fare much less well in life than those who capitalize on their uniqueness and go on to lead extremely prosperous lives. Detractors are motivated by a variety of things—mostly envy and their perception of their own inadequacy—but what's important is that you understand them (because they're probably never going to understand you) and that you stay committed to a life course you're passionate about that represents your highest calling.

Most people are born with malleable personalities that allow the expectations of others to be deeply embedded in their psyche. The exception is the "black sheep" of a family or group who, usually early in life, shows evidence of different interests or views than others. These people are most often strongly driven to pursue their own life path despite the opinion of others. For example, I know a person who comes from a very influential family in the world of high-stakes politics, and instead of becoming the professional his parents expected him to be he became an award-winning independent filmmaker and a gifted healer. As expected, they don't understand him, but he understands them, which makes it that much easier for him to stay on track cultivating his own life path and not be conflicted with his family tradition.

As discussed previously in this book, you have a unique set of abilities and capacities that nobody who's ever existed, or will exist, on earth has. These gifts come from your genes and are cultivated by your developmental environment, giving you a singularly unique capacity to see and execute life in a very special way and enabling you to live a life fueled by passion, productivity, prosperity, and purpose. In the final analysis, to achieve consistent and spectacular successes you only need to match your assets correctly with your goals and to create the right environment for them to surface.

TURN IT UP! TIPS

1. Be mindful that no one has or ever will lead a perfect life. Life has its peaks and valleys, and as long as you have more peaks than valleys, you will lead a successful life. Living unwaveringly by your principles will get you as close to perfection as humanly possible.

2. To become more perfect realize that everyone has imperfections and invest your confidence, trust, resources, time, and effort into your mental and physical strengths and aptitudes, not your weaknesses.

3. For you to be the best you can be, build your life on your unique talents, not on the talents you have in common with others.

4. Perhaps the most important quality to have is to know what you stand for, what you will or will not do, and what your actions represent. Once identified, stand firm on your convictions and never cross the line.

5. Never dilute your time and energy by trying to be perfect at something you have no aptitude for. Base your life solely on those talents and aspirations that you're passionate about. That's what all great performers do.

6. To become the best you can be, you must trust your life path— embracing its twists and turns as opportunities, not as detours. It's not possible to act on every opportunity that you are presented with, so seize the ones that come easily to you.

7. A major component of a successful life is being able to adapt as you go, while turning adversity into benefit. Regardless of circumstance you can always optimize any experience by remaining mentally fluid and allowing the appropriate actions to interface with the given conditions.

8. Before acting on any opportunity, always concisely identify how much life responsibility you can reasonably and realistically devote to it and how much you are willing and want to obligate yourself to.

TURN IT UP! TIPS (CONT'D)

9. Deemphasize perfection and your life will become easier and more prosperous. It's ironic that the moment you stop caring so much about something, it happens. Most have experienced this. The key is to do it and trust it.

10. A successful formula for life is to commit 100 percent effort to learning and applying with 100 percent competence the 90 percent needed to know to address 95–98 percent of life's experiences successfully.

11. Enlist the help of others and delegate to them the tasks that you know you don't excel in. This division of labor creates win-wins for everybody.

5

See Yourself as a Student

Learn everything you can, anytime you can,
from anyone you can—there will always
come a time when you will be grateful you did.

—Sarah Caldwell

The most prolific people are those who continuously and most success-fully adapt to life's ever-changing circumstances. They do so by mak-ing appropriately timed and sufficiently appropriate life course corrections based on accurate information. Mark Twain once said, "It ain't what you don't know that gets you into trouble. It's what you know for sure that just ain't so." Without correct facts, life becomes, at best, one giant spin of the roulette wheel. Winners calculate but never randomly guess at any-thing. They remain students of their discipline to acquire the knowledge necessary to become and remain at the top of their game. Just to break even in life, let alone hit its pinnacle, requires a steady influx of new information.

The day you stop learning is the day your competitive edge starts plum-meting downhill. Every consistent winner is dedicated to remaining a perennial student. They know full well that their talents, ideas, actions, and aspirations are only as strong as they are refined through knowledge and applied with wisdom toward reaching their goals. Their winning

> "Every consistent winner is dedicated to remaining a perennial student."

formula is simple: the best facts gathered equal the best plans conceived and greatest successes achieved.

Students are in the business of collecting data to reach specific goals. The origin of the information is irrelevant. The only consequence of importance is that their goals are achieved. Formal educations are absolutely necessary for foundational knowledge in specific domains but not in others. Some of life's most successful people have little or no formal education, yet they possess wisdom and prosperity that can be the envy of even the most impeccably educated. What is significant to your success is that you regularly collect relevant data and apply it toward manifesting your highest aspirations. Your life validates your education. How well you live reflects how well you've learned. The better your life is, the better the specificity of your education has been.

> "How well you live reflects how well you've learned."

The Facts of Life

In the final analysis, your life is merely a sequence of moment-by-moment choices producing specific outcomes that constitute your legacy. The facts you learn and apply throughout your life will determine that legacy. Each moment of your life presents you with a set of conditions that can be responded to in multiple ways. Each option produces a specific result regardless of your intention. Successful people understand and respect this irrefutable relationship between intention and outcome. To work with it, as opposed to against it, they learn as much as they can to formulate plans and exercise options that perfectly align their goals with their actions to achieve their ambitions.

THE IMPORTANCE OF MENTORING

Perhaps the best way of pursuing your life as a student is to shorten your learning timeline by finding a mentor skilled in the area of expertise you want to become proficient in. Mentors are people successful in what they do because they have learned to integrate their knowledge into the everyday activities of their disciplines. They have learned by doing and know how to weave new knowledge and skills into the real world in usable ways. Having done this, they are generally very skilled in contextualizing and teaching what they know to others.

Being mentored also can lead to apprenticing with the mentor, which in many instances is by far the best way to learn. If you want to learn from someone who has no mentorship program, consider going to work for or volunteering with that person. This will give you a real-life, hands-on education, providing you with the know-how to integrate your mentor's model into your personal success system. No amount of money could buy that experience.

Examples of mentors facilitating successful careers are abundant, with two of the most relevant coming from the world of professional boxing. Early in his career, Muhammad Ali came under the influence of legendary trainer Angelo Dundee, and their twenty-one-year partnership earned both men Hall of Fame recognition as Ali became, as he would so often remind us, "The Greatest of All Time."

Two decades after Ali and Dundee hooked up, a talented young fighter fresh from reform school named Mike Tyson met Gus D'Amato, who had previously trained former heavyweight champion Floyd Patterson. D'Amato took Tyson under his wing but, sadly, died before Tyson could become the youngest heavyweight champion ever. Tyson replaced D'Amato with former boxer Kevin Rooney, who guided him to stardom in the early years of his pro career, but then Tyson made the mistake of firing Rooney, after which his career began almost immediately to go downhill.

THE IMPORTANCE OF MENTORING (CONT'D)

Becoming a mentor to others will help you become a better student. Mentoring others helps you learn the skills of leadership and how to inspire and guide others to become successful, a skill you need to rally others to support you in your projects. Nobody can create success without the assistance of others, and your ability to lead a charge to complete a goal is essential to your capacity to create consistent successes.

Mentoring also teaches you to understand the full impact of what you say to someone, because even a well intended comment at the wrong time can destroy a person. At an athletic competition I was at with a client, I overheard another competitor's coach reading him the riot act about everything he was doing wrong in his warm-up. I could tell by the athlete's blank "deer in the headlights" frozen stare that the well-intended, but extremely destructive, verbal thrashing he'd just received was so traumatic that his confidence had been crushed and his mind so blocked from the pummeling that it would be impossible for him to perform up to his potential. Predictably, he did horribly, which drove whatever sense of self-worth he may have had left even further down the drain. A true mentor would have provided positive direction rather than destructive criticism.

Currently, we're living right smack in the middle of the inception of the information age. This unique period in human history has given you an almost unlimited choice of life options that affords you opportunities to advance your life in ways never before possible in human history. The innumerable options available can overwhelm you all by themselves, create massive stress, and compromise your ability to choose your options wisely and express your talent fully. You can become terminally preoccupied with worry about which opportunity you should engage. Is this the right time to exercise that option? What might happen if I choose the wrong option? What if these are the last options I'll ever have in life? The list is endless. Stress is epidemic in today's world, and is the common link to every poor decision, plan, and action made. Your best decisions are made when your mind is composed, and your worst are made when your mind is under stress. Only when you control stress in your life will your decisions mirror your talents and manifest your highest aspirations.

None of us knows everything or ever will, and what we do and don't know distinguishes each of us from the other six billion people on Earth. Your individuality is the platform your personal life experience must be built on, and it's also your greatest asset in making your greatest contribution to life. Each new fact you garner during each second of your life changes how you see life, what you place value on, and how you respond to life. The more facts you have, the more clarity your visions have and the more obvious it becomes which opportunities should be pursued and which shouldn't.

> "Your best teacher is the act of doing."

A profound realization all winners have is that it's not necessary to know everything about something before taking action on it. Too many people delay acting on something because they fear they don't know enough. They falsely believe they need more time to prepare, read one more book, or hear one more speaker before they are ready to initiate an action. Your best teacher is the act of doing. The responses to your actions tell you what to do next. Winners never hesitate to commence an action when an opportunity presents itself because they know that they'll learn what they don't know.

Many people mistakenly assume that with enough time, effort, and success they will arrive at a point where they know enough that their knowledge will perpetuate their lives without further study. Fortunately, that point never comes—and never will. The day you stop acquiring knowledge is the day your decline toward irrelevancy begins. It then becomes only a matter of time before others who have remained steadfast in acquiring knowledge and have gained significant momentum pass you by.

The Power of Facts

Facts are an extremely powerful currency of exchange that bolsters your success proficiency dramatically. The more relevant facts you have at your disposal, the bigger your achievements will be and the faster they will happen.

Facts, words, and concepts can be loyal allies or formidable foes, depending on how they're defined. Few things prevent or disrupt success faster than miscommunication from poorly expressed thoughts that leave interpretation up to each individual's reality. When in doubt as to the meaning of a word, always clarify its meaning and context. A trip to the dictionary is always a good idea whenever definitions are in question.

Each new piece of information you learn affects your entire knowledge base, making once-hidden opportunities and solutions to problems readily evident. Information also expands your capacity to achieve your goals with more precision in less time, while helping you to create more sophisticated goals. Everyone has had the "Aha!" experience when that elusive detail you have needed to solve a problem shows up. Make it your practice to learn a few facts daily, as they might be exactly what you need to revolutionize your life.

To enhance the breadth of your knowledge, always spend a portion of your study time exploring subjects not directly relevant to your specific areas of interest. Many of the best innovations occur when facts from distinctly separate disciplines merge into a new paradigm. An excellent example of this interdisciplinary cross-pollination is the invention of shock-absorbing front forks for mountain bicycles. A motorcycle mechanic specializing in motorcycle shock absorbers invented a shock-absorbing system for bicycles, and his innovation not only revolutionized the mountain bike industry but also made him a millionaire.

The only time your facts become relevant is when they're converted to actions that reach your goals and advance your life. When not used, facts are quickly shuttled to your memory for future problem solving. Study only what interests you. You'll always learn more when you do.

Challenge Is Your Best Teacher

Speaking metaphorically, two days in your life will determine, to a large extent, how successful your life will be. The "best day" of your life is when you show up in a new town with one suitcase, no road map, and only a few dollars and have to figure out how to create a viable life. Where you will live, how you will meet people, and how you will find employment, are all matters that have to be addressed quickly and with precision since you have no time for indecision or error. This scenario may seem scary, but it is life's greatest gift. Being backed into a corner like this forces you to dig deep into your problem-solving tool kit and find a way to make life happen. Under these circumstances, you don't have the luxury of feeling sorry for yourself, calling a friend to rescue you, pouting, or throwing a tantrum. The only option is to find a way out quickly. This is real life. The faster you find solutions, the more confidence you will have in yourself to deal with circumstances and the more experiences you'll be able to capitalize on. These experiences make good people great achievers.

Buried within you is the capacity to achieve extraordinary things. Challenge is the mechanism that life has provided for you to unearth your talents and excel. Unless you're challenged to find solutions to your life's dilemmas, you have no incentive to seek, risk, and bring forth your hidden talents because they aren't needed and, consequently, would remain dormant forever. You already have the solution to everything and only need to draw it forth.

Your moments of challenge are essential rites of passage for you to become everything you're capable of becoming. You become a better person when you get through them. Lance Armstrong won his seven Tours de France after, not before, his cancer. Overcoming adversity instills

> "Your moments of challenge are essential rites of passage for you to become everything you're capable of becoming."

confidence in your ability to get through anything at anytime. With a history of success, you know it's possible because you've done it. If done once, it can be done again and again. Few things are insurmountable.

The other most important day in your life is the "worst day" of your life, which is when you believe you've finally arrived at the point when your life becomes self-perpetuating and no longer requires your initiative and inventiveness to maintain itself. At that moment your competitive edge starts to crumble, because you begin leading a defensive—rather than offensive—life by spending increasingly more and more time preserving, protecting, and maintaining your accumulations and status at the expense of embracing new opportunity. No great champions ever believe that their past success guarantees or entitles them to future success. They consider success to be life privileges acquired through knowledge, initiative, great planning, and impeccable plan execution. The great Argentinean racing driver Juan Manuel Fangio would always say, "You should never believe you are the best, but you should always try to be the best."

Once prolific winners have prospered from learning the skill of being successful, the incentive to remain a student often comes from the mental trial of pitting their knowledge and planning skills against a challenging aspiration. Most great achievers will tell you that the success game, once learned, is ultimately won more in the mind than with the body. To win the mental game, all the facts must be known, well organized, up to date, and continuously woven into every plan and action. Otherwise, game-winning life moves will be based on incomplete information and never completely reach their intended goals.

Another motivation that perpetually successful people use to pursue success is to embrace an opportunity only if it offers the challenge of crafting an unconventional means of achieving their goal by exceeding the expectations of others. They love using their minds to seek out new information to create unorthodox goal-achieving strategies that blow people's minds as to how the success was achieved. The method to success becomes more important to them than the success itself.

One of the best and fastest ways to remain a top student and build your success methodology repertoire is to plan and execute a project you'd consider slightly beyond your abilities. Such a plan makes you confront and overcome fear, find new skills, learn new things, and construct methods for task completion that you don't currently possess. If you have some extra time, challenge your problem-solving skills by doing a small task you've never done before. You may surprise yourself with how easily you can do it. Once done, try again with a more difficult plan.

Another creative means of building your success capability is periodically to choose a challenging and novel learning setting. For example, try reading a book on a busy street corner with horns blaring, tires screeching, and music blasting in the background; or attempt to complete a task following an operations manual while in the vicinity of a practicing rock band or construction site with jackhammers and tools banging away and people yelling at each other. These controlled settings will take your learning abilities to a higher level so you can acquire knowledge under any circumstances and at any time, which most people can't do.

Winners Remain Students

The best way for you to keep your competitive advantage is to make and execute better plans than you have in the past. To do so, you must continuously implement new facts and concepts into your current plans. The moment your acquisition of information ceases and your plans fail to evolve and keep pace with current circumstances, your extinction process begins.

"Whenever you have a spare moment, learn something new."

Today's headlines are tomorrow's old news. Life doesn't stand still or wait for anyone. Today's fast-paced world changes so rapidly that information often becomes obsolete the moment it's available. This gives knowledge a very limited shelf life, making the injection of new information into your plans mandatory for you to remain successful. Winners constantly scout for new ways to be first in line to seize opportunity. They know that the more current their information is, the greater the likelihood is that they will get to the front of the opportunity line. Whenever you have a spare moment, learn something new.

Continuously acquiring new information helps you adapt quickly to a rapidly changing world. Quick adaptation strengthens both your existing communication lines and the trust others have in you for maintaining your inflow and outflow of new information with them at peak velocity. As information moves more and more quickly among diverse cultures, political arenas, and faith traditions, it's imperative that you fully understand how the people you interface with see and interpret what you say and do. That way you can create the most efficient communication possible to facilitate the biggest mutual wins for you and others. Ignorance and lack of understanding breed division between people due to fear of the unknown. Better communication creates the most mutual successes and the best harmony among people.

An important benefit to your becoming a more informed and experienced student of your discipline is that you evolve into a more creative, nonlinear problem solver, capable of succeeding at a wider variety of more sophisticated tasks. Successful lives are more than just applying standardized cookie-cutter solutions to problems. One-size-fits-all solutions only produce average, run-of-the-mill, and—quite frankly—boring results. They never produce optimal or spectacular results because every situation is its own distinct entity, with a unique personality that demands a personalized solution. The best solutions are achieved with pattern recognition that takes information in, interprets it, and synthesizes an appropriate response, producing quick resolutions to often complex problems.

As you become a better student, you also become a better mentor to others. You understand others' circumstances better, have better words for communicating with others, and can help others achieve their goals more quickly. More knowledge also allows you to have more cross-generational knowledge and vocabulary to make your mentoring ageless and available to more people. When I asked a gentleman, looking much younger than his mid-seventies age, what the secret to his youthful looks and vitality was, he replied, "Learn to become ageless by spending time around people of all ages, learning what and how they think. And never spend too much time around old, complaining people."

"As you become a better student, you also become a better mentor to others."

A decided advantage you will have by remaining a student is that the more you learn, the less you'll feel you know. Understanding this takes the pressure off you to believe that you need to know everything to perform at your best. This reconciliation of never having to know everything also promotes a more relaxed mind that struggles less for—but always finds—better answers. A relaxed mind aids memory by allowing the brain to more easily retrieve and collate facts into superior decisions that quickly find their way to your consciousness for better plan creation and implementation. Conversely, a tight mind constricts the memory function, choking off the information pipeline and making the answers to even the simplest questions less accessible.

Facts and information are the great clarifiers. Every bit of information you learn makes you better at everything you do because it confirms or denies theories and beliefs, showing you that something you think either is or isn't true. It also shows you the accuracy of your uncertainties. Some clarified facts may be unsettling and may challenge your deepest notions or beliefs. This is beneficial, however, and is encouraged because it forces you to remain a student, doing your homework to discover both the truth of your convictions and whether modification is required so your life can be built on truth rather than assumption. Winners win on correct and accurate information, not on misinformed hearsay or speculation.

Being a student improves your confidence. New information reinforces your trust in your existing knowledge base, instilling greater confidence to use what you know to achieve greater goals. Confidence also inspires you to take appropriate risks, reduces fear associated with new tasks, and enables you to complete plans on time because you trust your knowledge. Winners know that the longer it takes to accomplish a task, the less likely it will get done. Being confident facilitates on-time plan completion.

Remaining a student keeps your learning skills razor sharp and your mind alert. In today's world people are working later in life, which often dictates making several major career changes in a lifetime. Winners are able to adapt easily to new work environments and to effectively redirect their skills and knowledge to any new enterprise because—unlike their "It's difficult to teach old dogs new tricks" counterparts—they've learned that the trick of never losing their learning skills is always to keep learning.

Being a student helps you perform under pressure. Learning to step up and create what you want in critical situations, as well as in less important circumstances, is the difference between mediocre and profound goal outcomes. Championships and gold medals often are won by only a few thousandths of a second. Purposely creating tasks that challenge your knowledge under pressure is highly recommended and commonly practiced by winners. Whether it is in a classroom, on the street, in an elevator, or anywhere else, always look for opportunities where you can learn to express your talents under pressure. These dress rehearsals will prepare you to respond appropriately in real-life settings when the pressure is truly on. Taking charge of your life only occurs when the conviction of your knowledge overrides the pressure. Practice this skill daily in all that you do until it becomes second nature.

Understanding How You Learn

Learning happens in many different ways, with individual preferences based on how our brain works best. We've all experienced that person who understands written instructions perfectly but is absolutely clueless about how to proceed when told verbally what to do. So it is with each of us. Learning preferences are visual, auditory, kinesthetic, or a combination of the three. Most of us prefer a subtle combination of all with a strong bias toward one of the three. Visual learners like to see what needs to be done; diagrams and written instructions are perfect for their learning style. Auditory learners learn by being told how to do something; they hear their way though processes. Kinesthetic learners feel their way to solutions; as long as they can touch it, feel it, or taste it, they can understand it. Once you've found the process that works best for you, always use it. Never stifle your learning by being placed in a mismatched learning setting.

Each of us learns best in a preferred environment. Some prefer highly structured scholastic settings, like those found in formal learning institutions. Others do best in hands-on apprentice-type arrangements where learning takes place by doing under the direction of, or in association with, an instructor or tutor. Others prefer self-teaching, so they read books, talk to people, attend classes, and do tasks related to their area of study. As with your learning style, once you've found your best learning setting, never deviate from it.

Becoming a Faster, More Accurate Learner

Lack of intellectual stimulation creates a stale mind, lazy body, and dull spirit. When you engage often in mental activities, your mind will be kept alert and finely tuned so that when you must jump into mental action, your neurophysiology is already up and running at high efficiency, ready and able to produce your best mental responses. Minds are like bodies in that both need regular challenge and exercise to function at their best. Putting together puzzles, solving crossword puzzles, and playing Scrabble, chess, dominoes, or cards are activities that build a better thinking brain. Do these frequently to maintain a fresh mind.

At the Tours de France I did with the Postal and Discovery Channel Professional Cycling Teams, having fresh reading material daily brought the

REPETITION AIDS COMPREHENSION

The best students learn through frequent repetition. Conventional wisdom says that for information to be lodged in long-term memory it must be repeated ten or eleven times. Repeating something several times a day at short intervals—rather than at intermittent periods of long duration—promotes much faster learning and retention. Try to find a few short moments during your day that can be used to study or learn something without requiring a special time to do it. Small facts that require only a brief reminder to reinforce are much of what you need to learn. Each of these several-second encounters can be one of the eleven times you repeat something to learn it so "it's yours." Stopped at a traffic light, standing in a bank line, or waiting for an appointment are all perfect examples of empty time slots that could be used to reinforce some point of learning. Learn to make your wait times productive in this way.

To facilitate your retention of the facts, make a set of index cards and write no more information on them than necessary to remind you of what you need to review. You only want the entry on the card to spark your recall of what you need to learn so that you consciously become aware of it and review the information intentionally once or twice for a few seconds before carrying on with your activities. These few-second reviews will reinforce the information stored in your brain and make recall on demand easier. If you do this enough times, the information will become part of your permanent memory bank while taking hardly any time from your day. Carry your index cards with you at all times so that you can capitalize on the opportunity to reinforce your memory whenever you've got a few seconds to glance at the cards.

riders intellectual stimulation that got their minds off the physical pain of the event's severe difficulty and built their morale with familiar, comforting subject matter in challenging circumstances. Every day, new magazines and newspapers were used to engage their minds and soothe their souls.

Top students always have the best equipment so they can learn at peak velocity, so always obtain the best equipment possible so you can learn fast. Learning quickly gives you the capacity to adapt and stay abreast of new innovations the moment they become available. The faster you learn the skills and knowledge you need to be at the top of your game, the more opportunities you will have and successfully initiate. Many people are slow to embrace change. Never kid yourself that old ways of doing things that were once successful will come back in vogue and replace today's innovations, because they won't. We live today in a world of high-speed communication in which old ideas have little viability.

> "Minds are like bodies in that both need regular challenge and exercise to function at their best."

An effective way to increase your learning speed is to form a study group with compatible success students. Surrounding yourself with a network of peers and colleagues with whom you can exchange information—while self-mentoring each other to become greater successes—creates a phenomenal synergy in learning. Information flows faster, ideas catalyze, insights occur, and possibilities unfold in ways impossible for you to conjure up in isolation. This can be done in person, by phone, or via e-mail. Most often one-on-one or small group arrangements are best because they limit distractions and allow information specific to the topic to occur with the least impedance. Regular study times are best, as they can be written down on calendars and can become anticipated and welcomed events.

Another advantage of group learning is that it encourages preparation. Contributing to the group dynamic is an important means of learning. Whether you bring a question to the session, have something you want to share with others on a specific topic, or believe you've found something relevant to the group, it all facilitates learning. Your preparation to share with others will help them learn by exposing them to new information. It also helps you learn by serving as a form of homework, making you research and deliberately think about and conceive exactly what and how you want to share.

Study Less to Learn More

People seem to learn more and see greater possibilities when studying a variety of subjects throughout a day and spending less time on each. This may defy conventional wisdom, but true wisdom is based on the facts, and the facts are that diversity of thought and multiple areas of study create the best learning. Renaissance-type people are examples of this. They have the ability to do many things well, yet they don't seem to spend excessive amounts of time studying or working on them, and they don't get tired of doing anything. Renaissance types seem to move effortlessly among diverse subject matter and to have brains that function differently from most. Actually, their brains probably aren't different—it's just that they've learned the secret to getting more out of life by shifting their focus and energy between the thinking and doing the instant their minds start to lose focus in either area.

Your brain is composed of many compartments designed to receive, interpret, send, and store information. Each compartment is finite in size, requires large amounts of energy to run, and is only capable of taking in specific amounts of information per set periods of time before hitting saturation and becoming fatigued. Like every other part of the body, each brain compartment requires regular recharging to continue to function efficiently. The time to shift between compartments is when your attention starts to wander, your brain feels a little fried, and your eyes begin to glaze over. If you delay the shift, you'll transpose information in your memory risking faulty decisions.

Shifting among compartments often occurs several times a day, depending on your productivity level. Most people can only maintain continuous concentration for a few hours. That's why movies and sporting events only last two or three hours. If they're longer than that, people's minds go flat so they become bored and disinterested. Never overstay your visit on a subject. When it's time to move on, move on to something else.

At times, every student feels the need to push harder and longer and to go without some sleep in order to study enough to pass an exam. Life's the same. At times it's absolutely necessary that you push beyond your normal limits to get the job done. During those periods of purposeful push, sound nutrition and micro-naps become indispensable. To avoid the energy swings often seen with intermittent eating during periods of push, it's advisable to eat and drink more frequently and in smaller quantities so that your brain's energy supply will remain at peak levels. Micro-naps, approximately ten minutes long, throughout the day can work wonders. The best time to nap is midafternoon. (Proper nutrition for demanding times is thoroughly covered in Chapter 11.)

> "Never overstay your visit on a subject. When it's time to move on, move on to something else."

Life's Only Guarantee Is Change

My wife is a great example of someone who has always seen herself as a student. During her twenty-two years as a nurse, she continually took courses, read books, and spent time with others and tutors, researching and studying topics that interested her, including a wide range of subjects outside the healthcare field. She passionately studied these subjects until she had gotten from them what was needed to enrich her life and enable her to be of greater service to others. During her twenty-second year of nursing, she decided it was time to retire from that discipline and begin a new career in interior design. She enrolled in school and spent the next six and a half years studying interior design. She inspired countless people, graduating at fifty years of age to fulfill a lifelong dream.

Going to school also taught her classmates, through example, that anything can be done at any age if you plan and do the steps necessary to achieve your goal. She also showed that age is a matter of attitude, not chronology. You can go back to school at any age and graduate. Success is a never-ending process predicated on inspiration and knowledge. With the right vision and tools, success is only a matter of time and effort. My wife is as fresh today as she was at twenty because she has consistently engaged her passion and tapped into her talents so they could surface. That option is open to all of us.

Remaining a Student

As you become more skilled at creating success, it may become increasingly difficult to remain a prolific student and producer of success. Success spawns responsibilities and opportunities that crowd schedules and consume available time. When the time crunch comes, the first things shelved are often the foundational skills that led to the original successes. Unfortunately, purposeful learning ranks high among those discarded skills. To remain a successful student, then, several key strategies exist.

The most important and easiest way to remain a student is to expose yourself regularly to diverse forms of intellectual stimulation. This stimulation can come from taking a seminar, taking a cruise, taking a day off, or engaging in discussions with colleagues. It doesn't matter what you do, as long as you avail yourself of new and exciting intellectual stimulation on a regular basis. Exposure to new ideas, concepts, and facts has been shown to build a better-thinking brain, especially when exposed to a variety of subjects that require all five senses to participate in the learning process. Always study and expose yourself to what you're interested in, what can easily be studied, and what suits your learning style. Every minute you do so, you'll enhance your knowledge base. The last piece of information learned could make the difference between mediocrity and significant success.

Pursuing your own personal interests vastly accelerates both your motivation to learn and your speed of learning. When you learn for you, there's always more incentive to engage the process. Learning simply for learning's sake, or for others when it's not truly from your highest self and desire, is not nearly as productive as learning with a specific intent in mind. When you pursue and attain your greatest aspirations, you'll be of greatest service to both yourself and others. Investigating multiple areas of interest not only builds a better brain but also creates optimal mental focus and confidence. This keeps your mind fresh and alert so it never gets too fixated and dulled by any one subject.

One-on-one or group tutoring is one of the fastest ways to learn a subject. Dialoguing with experts cuts to the learning quickly. A fast and effective way to access experts is through technical support departments at businesses that have people whose only job is to answer questions, and most of them love doing so. Create concise questions, contact them by phone, and ask your questions. The intellectual rewards can be substantial, and you only have to invest time, effort, and the cost of a phone call. The hardest part of learning is finding the information. When you let the experts do that for you, all you have to do is listen and learn.

Winners thoroughly and regularly rest their minds and brains and never go too long without a proper mental recharge. To pursue and retain knowledge, your mind and body must be fresh, alert, and vital. Retention and clarity nosedive with fatigue, so when your mind starts to wander and your eyelids get heavy while engaging in any form of learning, it's time to take a break. Attempts to learn after a certain point in the day cross the line of diminishing returns. The last thing you need is to make a costly mental error with a tired brain. It's always best to discontinue any mental task at the first sign of fatigue. Even better is to minimize the chance of fatigue occurring by taking brief breaks every hour to rest the eyes, mind, and body.

TURN IT UP! TIPS

1. To become a consistent winner remain a perennial student of your discipline. Remain vigilant in acquiring new information that will keep you on the cutting edge of your discipline. This will allow you to seize an opportunity the moment it presents itself that those less informed will be slow to respond to.

2. Becoming a mentor to others will help shortcut their learning to become their own success, help you refine your communication skills, and give back to others as a gesture of your appreciation for your good fortunes.

3. Never make decisions under stress. Stress clouds judgment and often prompts regrettable choices. Always make your decisions fully informed and with strong presence of mind.

4. It's not necessary to know everything about something before taking action on it. The best way to learn something is by doing it. Never hesitate to seize an opportunity if the timing is right because you'll learn what you need to know in the process of doing it.

5. Exercise your brain frequently by investigating different areas of interest. Many of the best innovations you'll have in your life will come from combining knowledge from distinctly separate disciplines.

6. Don't become too comfortable in your success. If you ever become so comfortable that you stop striving, believing you have "arrived," you will begin to lose your competitive edge and lean toward mediocrity.

7. Always obtain the equipment and skills you need to do the things necessary to reach your goals as quickly as possible. The faster you learn the skills and knowledge you need to achieve your ambitions, the more opportunities you will successfully initiate.

8. Rest your mind and brain frequently throughout the day and get consistent high-quality sleep. Never go too long without a proper mental recharge.

6

Uncensored Possibility Thinking

Stop thinking in terms of limitations and
start thinking in terms of possibilities.

—Terry Josephson

The quality and richness of your life experience are dependent on the creativity and expansiveness of thought behind your plans and your ability to reach your outcomes. Prolific winners know that every waking moment contains a thought, and since you're going to be thinking anyway, your thoughts might just as well be the biggest ones possible. Thoughts are the magnetism that draws opportunity to you and sets the compass heading for your life's direction and success. The least that can happen from being an uncensored possibility thinker is that most of your lofty thoughts manifest themselves.

Thought Begets Action

Your thoughts initiate and direct your actions. What you think about is what you focus on, what you focus on is what you do, what you do sets the direction for your life, and where you end up is the legacy you leave behind. Every moment's thought prompts an action that takes you either closer to or farther away from manifesting your talents, achieving your goals, and creating the life you desire to live. Thoughts are future realities not yet manifest, like an apple seed. The destiny of the minute apple seed is to become a giant apple tree bearing succulent, juicy apples, and it needs only time and nurturing to produce its fruit.

> "Big thoughts generate big opportunities. Small thoughts don't."

Becoming an uncensored possibility thinker creates a life of intense value for you. Big thoughts generate big opportunities, bring out the best in you, increase your life passion, build confidence, create a better world, and inspire others. Small thoughts don't.

Uncensored possibility thinking brings out the best in you by creating ideas that attract opportunities of sufficient magnitude that, in turn, force you to reach for goals that stretch and develop your mental, physical, and skill-set capacities to higher levels of proficiency. This raises your ability to succeed to a much higher level, giving you access to greater opportunities previously beyond your abilities.

Big thoughts reignite your life's passion by revitalizing your mind and tossing out new challenges and problems for which you must find solutions. An active mind becomes sharp, creative, and driven to refine its ability to produce quick and creative solutions to conditions.

Embracing big thoughts increases your confidence and hope in a better future. It makes possible what once seemed impossible. Half the battle in producing a better life is seeing that a more passionate, purposeful life is attainable. Once the vision is clear, the skills and plans needed to produce the successes are much easier to acquire.

Every time you think big and manifest those thoughts, you contribute to a better world. Passionate thoughts mobilize people toward a common goal, create mutual respect between people, and inspire us to learn skills to become self-sufficient. All of that intentionally brings beauty and hope to the world and to one another.

Your loftiest thoughts and visions inspire those around you and attract others to you. Sharing your visions with others is critical to your mutual evolution as expansive, uncensored, possibility thinkers. As you grow, your visions grow. The synergy of sharing with others ignites a chain reaction of possibility thinking that expands the collective field of possibility consciousness for everyone, creating ideas that no single person could ever conceive on their own. Everyone has something to contribute, and you never know who holds the critical piece of information needed to take your thoughts to the highest level.

Why Is Thinking Big So Difficult?

Thinking big comes naturally to very few people, and for most it can be extremely difficult. Most of us are limited by a self-imposed mental "glass ceiling" that prevents us from achieving what we're capable of doing. This isn't because we're incapable but because through the veil of our limited thinking we just can't see our capabilities or figure out how to manifest them. The majority of us know deep down to the depths of our soul what we really want our lives to be and what we dream of having, but for many reasons we find it difficult to give ourselves permission to think big enough thoughts to attain those desires, let alone aspire to them. The most common reasons we're unable to think big are false guilt, suppression by others, belief that we're not worthy of success, or feeling that life needs to find its own way and we're to follow—not facilitate.

Many people can't even begin to contemplate thinking big because they are so bound by the straightjacket of false guilt. For some, no sooner do they start thinking big than their internal self-critic (or another person) or The Voice surfaces and starts confronting them with guilt and producing questions—for example, "You're not qualified to do that, so why are you even considering it?" "Remember your friend who tried the same thing and lost everything? Are you sure want to risk that?" "Who do you think you are thinking like that? I suppose once you start becoming successful you'll think you're too good for us and leave us in the dust." Another classic confidence breaker is "I know you're getting very busy with all you're doing with your new friends, so I'm sure you won't have time for us anymore; but I completely understand and don't want you to feel guilty about it."

Be on the lookout for the guilt-producing specialist who manipulates people into believing that lofty goal setting and its subsequent achievements are egotistical and purely self-serving. This is often seen in relationships in which one person, usually overly dependent on and possessive of the other, makes the other feel guilty for having his or her own aspirations. In reality, these people are completely self-serving and fear they will be abandoned if the other succeeds, so they try every trick they know to manipulate the other person into staying.

Certain other people don't believe they're capable or worthy of thinking big, so they don't even try. So many people have told them for so long that they're not capable of achieving anything that they now believe it, thinking it is useless even to try. Pathetically, it's most often the losers in life who have instilled that belief in them. The only source of validation the losers have comes from tearing others down so they can remain authorities in their own minds and can masquerade as somebody other than the small-minded, unproductive cynics they are.

> "We're born to seek and manifest successful thinking and pursue the best life possible."

The belief that "Life will unfold as it should" is another classic reason people refuse to contemplate best-life scenarios, even though deep inside it's what they really want. For some reason, they believe they have no right to have a say in what their life's outcome should be. This, of course, is completely erroneous, as we all have been given brains to think and talents to express. We're born to seek and manifest successful thinking and pursue the best life possible. For some, the guilt associated with the thought of creating success originates from the lack of creating it, not from success itself.

Thinking Big Is a Learned Skill

Thinking big is a learned skill that everyone can master. It takes time to develop, however, as few of us have been taught, let alone encouraged, to identify and cultivate our greatest aspirations. Therefore, we must consciously set aside time daily to practice the skill of uncensored possibility thinking and then apply it throughout the day so we can become proficient at it. Practicing this basic skill as little as five minutes a day is all it takes to learn and start applying it to become and remain a consistently top performer.

The exercise presented in this chapter has been specifically created for you to Turn It Up! and help you learn the skill of giving yourself permission to think the biggest thoughts possible and evolve them to their fullest; it's not about the practicality of manifesting them. Uncensored possibility thinking will enable you to create your own opportunities and to embrace them fully with confidence and passion. An important byproduct of learning to think big is that every time you openly express your uncensored possibility thinking with others, you serve as an example to them as to what their lives can be, which can inspire them to step up and be their own uncensored possibility thinker.

To successfully incorporate the exercise and art of continually thinking expansively into your life, you must do three things. First, you must consciously commit to yourself that learning and applying uncensored possibility thinking are high priorities for you and that you will do what's necessary to accomplish it. Second, you must write it down in your day planner so you've made a covenant with yourself to learn and apply the skill daily. Third, you must learn and apply uncensored possibility thinking in your daily life consistently so it becomes second nature. Practicing and applying uncensored possibility thinking is the only way it gets learned and integrated into your life.

Examine Your "Craziest" Ideas

Crazy ideas drive the world. Without ideas at the fringe of normalcy—*what some might consider over the top*—the world would only advance at a snail's pace. Innovation and progress only happen when crazy ideas are considered and then acted upon. Who ever seriously considered that going to the moon was actually possible? How about the idea of contacting someone on the other side of the planet within seconds using something called the Internet? It probably did sound insane to most when the Internet idea was first shared, but in today's world it's an essential part of life. That's exactly how it will be with those ideas that may seem a bit far-fetched now.

To build a dynamic future for yourself, it's imperative that you examine your "craziest" ideas often. To become an extraordinarily skilled "crazy" thinker, you need to take the following simple steps:

1. Keep a written "crazy idea" journal. Write down your most insane ideas without any mental censorship as to their practicality or execution requirements.

2. Know what the best environment is for you to think your craziest thoughts. My wife does her best thinking when driving in her car with the music blasting loud enough that the windows in her car seem to bulge with every beat. Find the environment that works best for you and stick with it.

3. Refine your ideas as your natural motivation and time permit. Never force the refinement process at the expense of neglecting plans already in motion. Complete your current plan before you initiate your next "crazy" one.

4. Regularly peruse your journal and examine the ideas you've jotted down previously. Each idea you've written will in some way influence your future for the better. Regardless of how ridiculous or outrageous an idea appears to be, write it down.

> ### EXAMINE YOUR "CRAZIEST" IDEAS (CONT'D)
>
> 5. Watch the tendency for The Voice to pop up and dissuade you from thinking or writing down your wildest ideas. Ignore it and think big anyway.

Cultivating the Best Learning Environment

There are two aspects to becoming a successful uncensored possibility thinker: learning and applying the skill. Learning the skill occurs best in the privacy of your personal experience, while the application takes place in the tumultuous maelstrom of your daily life. Ideally, your goal is to be able to think big in any circumstance.

Everybody has a best learning environment and style that determines how quickly and fully their skills are learned. Your best personal learning environment has the location and furnishings most conducive to your personal learning style. Some people are so easily distracted that they can only concentrate in absolute silence. Even the sound of a neighbor's ultra-quiet pool motor can disrupt their focus. By contrast, a musician acquaintance could only think and perform when his life was in absolute chaos. In fact, he told me that when his life was going too smoothly he purposely "blew things up," including relationships, to create the turmoil he needed to get things done. Unfortunately, both examples illustrate people with immense capacity whose life quirks make it impossible for them to gain the benefits from becoming proficient uncensored possibility thinkers.

Most often, the best location to begin learning to become an uncensored possibility thinker offers solitude and silence to minimize distraction. Personal considerations include temperature settings, furniture style, lighting, room color, and the room's proximity to other people, places, and things. If possible, find or create your ideal learning setting before beginning to learn and practice thinking big. This shouldn't be difficult, as the exercise takes at most five minutes. If, however, the perfect environment can't be found or created, find the best place possible and begin learning the skill regardless since you'll eventually have to employ the skill in real life with all its distractions.

As soon as your uncensored possibility thinking capacity becomes more systematic and familiar to you, begin incorporating it into your daily activities. First, begin implementing the skill in appropriately chosen situations that don't overexpose you to distracting circumstances beyond your skill level. It's best to implement slowly and ratchet up your exposure as your skill level improves. Eventually, you'll be able to take any idea under any circumstance and bring it to its pinnacle in minimal time. For example, a friend of mine told me he wrote his number-one rock hit on the first take in a noisy apartment in Dublin, Ireland.

Now you're ready to begin the uncensored possibility thinking exercise. Your goal is twofold. First, to give yourself *permission* to develop an idea without censoring yourself. And, second, to *develop* an idea without censorship. This should take no more than five minutes. To begin, sit in a firm chair with your feet flat on the floor, hands on your knees, and back comfortably straight but not stiff. Be comfortable but not so comfortable that you doze off or begin daydreaming. With eyes open, gaze straight ahead, not focusing on anything in particular, and direct your attention to the space between your ears where your brain is. For the sake of this exercise we're going to call this your "mind space." Now, gently breathe a few normal diaphragmatic breaths (as previously described in the Controlling the Fear Impulse section in Chapter 3), all the while keeping your attention gently directed toward your mind space.

Next, while continuing to breathe gently, deliberately and consciously give yourself permission to think as big as you can by thinking the words to yourself, "I give myself permission to think the biggest thoughts possible without censoring myself." This may be awkward at first because it's unfamiliar to you, but do it anyway to begin etching into your brain circuitry the new pattern of uncensored possibility thinking. This will make it more natural the next time you do the exercise.

To reinforce the covenant you just made with yourself to think big without censorship, repeat the statement, silently thinking to yourself a second time: "I give myself permission to think the biggest thoughts possible without censoring myself." Make sure you're consciously aware of and understand the words you're thinking. If you think too fast or make thinking a rote ritual, the words will be thought but will have no meaning—and thus no impact—on your becoming a more expansive thinker.

Now draw your attention back to your mind space and you will notice that thoughts start appearing. Eventually, one will show up that captures your attention more than the others. Choose that one to become the subject of your five-minute uncensored possibility thinking session and let the others go. Let's say the one you choose is about creating a beautiful garden.

Next, think about how your idea, in this instance the garden, can be further expanded and refined in explicit detail. For example, what type of garden will it be, where should it be placed in the yard, and what will it look like? Those questions might be answered by describing the garden as a ten-foot-square vegetable garden placed in the northeast corner of the backyard so it gets full-day sun. Once that initial refinement has been completed, further refinement of each of the garden's elements can be done, applying the same uncensored possibility thinking principles as with the original idea. For example, when expanding on the vegetable garden concept, it could be further refined into an organic, vine garden consisting of squash, pumpkin, and zucchini.

Keep expanding and refining each element of your idea until your mind hits the point of saturation where its creative powers start to diminish, as evidenced by a loss of mental focus and slight mental fatigue. At that point the session is finished. That doesn't mean the idea is fully developed. It only means the uncensored possibility thinking is done for that session. Many ideas take multiple sessions to develop fully, but fully developing your idea isn't the objective of your sessions. What's important is that you learn how to begin to think expansively without censorship and learn when to stop developing an idea for that session and move on. Learning when to stop developing an idea can be as critical to its success as the idea itself. Many an art masterpiece has been ruined by an artist who worked too long and too intensively while trying to create the masterpiece too quickly.

While going through each refinement process cycle during your session, your mind will inevitably start to wander and distracting thoughts will appear. That's expected and encouraged, since the whole purpose for the exercise is to learn to evolve an idea to its fullest so you become a skilled uncensored possibility thinker and master of your decision-making process in any surroundings. Each uncensored possibility thinking session you do is a dress rehearsal for every living moment of your life. Once you become proficient at this skill and apply it consistently you will gain mastery over what once distracted and pulled you away from reaching your goals in life. When this skill is practiced and applied diligently day to day, the capacity to bring your attention back to the tasks at hand, allowing you to create your successes, will happen faster and with less effort. However, never practice this exercise more than five minutes a day. If you do, you risk making the exercise too familiar to you, which will reduce your sensitivity to it and make it less effective. Also, never wait to feel like starting or doing your uncensored possibility thinking skill-building exercise. People who wait to feel like it often wait forever as their lives pass them by.

Which Big Thoughts Are Right for Us?

Every one of us knows deep inside what we passionately want our lives to be. We're not talking about what we're willing to settle for but what we really, truly desire more than anything else. Let's not kid ourselves on this. We may say to others, or even to ourselves, that we don't know what we want out of life, but in fact we know very well what we want. When we say we don't know what we want, we're really saying that we haven't yet given ourselves permission to admit to ourselves and others what our true desires and passions are. We're also saying that we're not sure we know how to get what we want or what level of compromise we're willing to settle for if we can't get what we want.

The beauty of doing uncensored possibility thinking each day—both as an exercise and in daily activity—is that it clarifies exactly what our mind conceives as possible for us. Many of the ideas evolved through the uncensored possibility thinking exercise may seem outrageously absurd, but that's a good thing and the very purpose of this exercise: learning to think as big as possible without censorship.

Of course, not all ideas you evolve will be implemented. Those that do are those that fit your skill set, time availability, and risk tolerance at a given time. This doesn't mean those aspirations requiring more skills shouldn't be pursued—it just means they should be reserved until you have the timing and skills to achieve them successfully. You will discard some of your ideas because when they're fully evolved they will fall below your threshold for consideration and leave you uninspired. If you feel stimulated and anxious to start pursuing one of your completely evolved ideas and it matches your capacity to achieve it, and the timing is right to do it, that's the one to pursue.

> "Thinking big requires feeling comfortable with big thoughts."

Thinking big requires feeling comfortable with big thoughts. Not everybody does at first. Some people never do. This is analogous to acquiring a taste for fine wine. Some people, when first exposed to fine wine, don't fully embrace its taste, but over time they acquire an appreciation that makes it inconceivable that they could have ever not fully embraced it. If at first you don't feel comfortable thinking big, be patient and keep doing it anyway. At a certain instant, the conversion to familiarity will occur.

As you start to flex your possibility thinking muscles and expand the horizons of your life, you will start to experience more success and may feel slightly out of place, like being somewhere you just don't quite belong, as if you've just taken up residence in your custom-built dream home that you've yearned for your entire life but never thought you would have. Most of the awkwardness you feel with constructive change comes from being placed in a new and unfamiliar environment that your body and mind belong in but to which you haven't yet fully adapted. It's not that the new environment is inappropriate or wrong for you—it's simply that the adaptation hasn't yet taken hold. Many people mistakenly think that their discomfort comes from being in the wrong place, when in reality they're in the correct place and only need to spend a little more time there for their mind and body to recalibrate to the new conditions.

"Dealing with detractors is pivotal to you becoming an uncensored possibility thinker."

The best way to facilitate the quickest transition from a restricted to an uncensored possibility thinking mind-set is to immerse yourself completely in the new, expansive environment by doing uncensored possibility thinking throughout the day. The tenet here is that through the act of doing, the mindset shifts; the skill is learned through application and doing. The more time spent in your new surroundings, the faster the adaptation occurs. Jumping in and out of environments slows the conversion process and often creates confusion—from being caught between two worlds, contrasting perceptions, feelings, and views—which can bring a reversion to the former, less-conducive environment.

Silencing Your Detractors

Dealing with detractors is pivotal to you becoming an uncensored possibility thinker. Some people love it when someone shares an outrageously great idea with them. Others hate it. Why some people love it and others despise it is one of life's greatest mysteries. Despite the reasons, it's absolutely fundamental that you identify your detractors, understand their modus operandi, and effectively keep them at bay so you can move forward, developing your greatest ideas and building your success portfolio.

There are two categories of detractors: others and, perhaps surprisingly, you. Both can be equally detrimental to your success, but the medium of detraction is most often The Voice initially presented in Chapter 3. The Voice may be heard aloud from another's mouth or silently in your own mind. Regardless of its origin, The Voice can be extremely destructive if you react to it. When the perfect "wrong" word is said at the perfect time, it can throw you headlong into a confidence crisis, inappropriate outburst, or emotional withdrawal.

The simplest way to deal with the unkind, derogatory words of others is to remove yourself from their presence immediately—and permanently, if possible. No amount of dialogue will ever get others to understand why what they say is so destructive to your life. Unfortunately, most hurtful statements are made unconsciously as an automatic and learned pattern of response to a specific stimulus. These reactions are so deeply etched in people's habitual way of responding to life that they don't even know what they are saying, let alone understand the impact it has on others.

We all know such people. At the critical moment, they could say something encouraging, but they say the most discouraging thing possible, almost as if it were premeditated. Unfortunately, they may even be members of your own family. As painful as that may be, often the best solution is to limit or eliminate contact with them, because in most cases the interaction required to create an equally supportive relationship is impossible to achieve.

The best way to deal with your own Voice, as mentioned in Chapter 3, is to ignore it by keeping your attention riveted on doing the things relevant to advancing your life. Every time The Voice pops up with one of its demeaning barbs, immediately draw your attention back to your life-advancing actions, neither acknowledging nor dialoguing with it. Keep repeating this pattern each time it "talks" to you, and gradually its power will recede. You will "hear" from it again, as it's a lifetime nuisance, but whenever you do, simply ignore it, don't engage it, and go back to what you were doing. It works every time.

On the other hand, every big thinker and top performer has a trusted posse of people whom they consult about their visions, thoughts, and plans to confirm that they're sound and capable of being achieved, and, therefore, so should you. Your people support system should be small in size and composed of trusted allies who are readily available, are concise with their recommendations, offer constructive information, and provide counsel freely without expectation of return.

Your plans should never be constructed in written form until the visions that inspired them have been fully developed and tossed over to your trusted quality control allies for input. The benefits of having them examine your plans is that they not only make your ideas the best they can be from their input, but they also make you a better thinker, communicator, listener, and performer, all of which help you to become a more prolific success.

More Knowledge Means Bigger and Better Thoughts

Your brain hates sameness. Sameness dulls your mind from a lack of stimulation, making expansive thinking impossible. Exposing yourself to diverse and new facts and experiences regularly creates new ways of thinking, leading you to new thought paradigms. Every piece of new information added to your knowledge base creates a new way of viewing life and seeing possibilities. The faster and more prolific your fact acquisition is, the bigger and better your thinking becomes, which often makes achievable what once seemed out of reach.

Countless examples of this phenomenon abound in history, but three from the world of science illustrate the point. John F. Kennedy's idea of putting a man on the moon seemed absolutely absurd until a team of experts correlated the facts with the reality and calculated that it could be done, found the people to make it happen, and did it. The same occurred with Nicolaus Copernicus who postulated five centuries ago that Earth revolved around the sun. The mere suggestion of this sent a deafening howl of laughter and criticism throughout the known world because everyone "knew" that Ptolemy's view of the sun revolving around Earth was, without question, "true." Worse happened to Galileo, who confirmed Copernicus's finding that Earth did indeed orbit the sun. When his support of Copernicus became public, he was promptly sent to trial, was forced by the threat of torture and death to declare his opposition to Copernicus's view, and spent his remaining days under house arrest.

Because brilliant ideas can disappear from our minds as quickly as they appear, you should always make sure you write them down the moment they occur. Though this topic is covered in depth in Chapter 9, it is referenced briefly here. Everyone has experienced awakening in the middle of the night with a great idea and assured themselves, "I don't need to write this down—I'll remember it in the morning," only to wake up the next day scratching their head trying to remember the idea they "knew" they wouldn't forget. So always have a pad of paper and pencil, voice recorder, or computer with you so you can store these new ideas permanently—they're invaluable for your goal setting. Keep all your written ideas in the same location so they can be retrieved when necessary.

Pause Is Necessary for Peak Possibility Thinking

Your mind is not different from your body when it comes to needing rest. Although the brain constitutes only 2 percent of the body's mass, it consumes 25 percent of the oxygen you breathe and 20 percent of the bloodstream's glucose to generate the energy to think. Without adequate recharging, your brain can't continue its highly sophisticated and uncensored possibility thinking duties or orchestrate the physiology necessary for body growth, tissue repair, and energy production. A very practical example of this is the rest cycle given to major league baseball pitchers who pitch only every fifth day and rest on the four days between starts. Without their "planned" rests, the pitchers' arms would breakdown prematurely and injury would inevitably happen.

One courtesy all great achievers and performers give themselves is adequate time to evolve their ideas into brilliant workable plans. Whenever they encounter a situation for which they have no immediate solution, they either shift to doing something that requires little or no thought, take a nap, or go to sleep. Your best solutions often come from your unconscious mind once you back away from struggling with circumstances and let your subconscious search through your memory to find the solution. To continue struggling with a problem when your mind is fatigued only further blurs the answers to problems and shuts off your expansive thinking. If you don't remove yourself from the struggle, you will inevitably make matters worse.

> "A fifteen- to twenty-minute mental recharge break of doing nothing is the easiest and best way to recharge."

I heard an athlete tell the press after winning a major event that he had an absolutely terrible pre-competition practice that day, during which he felt as if he couldn't do anything right. So, after practice he went to his motor home, took a nap, woke up feeling great, and put it all together to win the main event. A fifteen- to twenty-minute mental recharge break of doing nothing is the easiest and best way to recharge. Make this a daily ritual whenever possible.

Trusting Your Thoughts

The only thing you have in life that can never be taken away from you are your thoughts. Your thoughts are your possessions alone, and you have an obligation to your talents to make each thought as big as possible. Every time you compromise your most lofty and passionate ideas, goals, and visions, you turn your back on your birthright talents and the privilege of dreaming. This can prevent you from living the life you're capable of having. Your first obligation to the relationship with yourself is to respect your gifts and talents enough to cultivate them daily. As your talents grow and touch others, you will leave your own unique contribution to humanity. Trust your thoughts because, when acted upon, they're what bring your talents forth.

TURN IT UP! TIPS

1. Since you're going to be thinking anyway, think the biggest thoughts possible. The size of your thoughts will draw to you opportunities of corresponding magnitude.

2. Give yourself permission to think the most grandiose thoughts imaginable. Don't hold back. Open up your mind and push through the mental barriers limiting the size and scope of your thinking.

3. Spend time becoming a "crazy thinker." Deliberately take a few minutes each day to think the most outrageous, expansive thoughts possible. The more you do this, the more comfortable and second nature big possibility thinking will become. Standing in lines, waiting at stop lights, and driving are ideal times to practice this skill.

4. Only spend time around those who nourish your spirit and enrich your soul. Remove yourself from all negative situations and people. All they do is drain your energy, give you a mental hangover, and commandeer time that could otherwise advance your life.

5. Create a support system of trusted people who are readily available, who can provide concise opinions on matters, offer constructive criticism, and act as sounding boards.

6. Give yourself adequate time to construct your success plans. Whenever you reach an impasse with your plan, either shift to doing something that requires little or no thought, take a nap, or turn in for the night. Solutions always come when you back away from struggling with circumstances and allow your subconscious to provide the answer.

READER/CUSTOMER CARE SURVEY

We care about your opinions! Please take a moment to fill out our online Reader Survey at **http://survey.hcibooks.com.**

As a **"THANK YOU"** you will receive a **VALUABLE INSTANT COUPON** towards future book purchases as well as a **SPECIAL GIFT** available only online! Or, you may mail this card back to us.

(PLEASE PRINT IN ALL CAPS)

First Name _____ MI. _____ Last Name _____

Address _____ City _____

State _____ Zip _____ Email _____

1. Gender
☐ Female   ☐ Male

2. Age
☐ 8 or younger
☐ 9-12   ☐ 13-16
☐ 17-20   ☐ 21-30
☐ 31+

3. Did you receive this book as a gift?
☐ Yes   ☐ No

4. Annual Household Income
☐ under $25,000
☐ $25,000 - $34,999
☐ $35,000 - $49,999
☐ $50,000 - $74,999
☐ over $75,000

5. What are the ages of the children living in your house?
☐ 0 - 14   ☐ 15+

6. Marital Status
☐ Single
☐ Married
☐ Divorced
☐ Widowed

7. How did you find out about the book?
(please choose one)
☐ Recommendation
☐ Store Display
☐ Online
☐ Catalog/Mailing
☐ Interview/Review

8. Where do you usually buy books?
(please choose one)
☐ Bookstore
☐ Online
☐ Book Club/Mail Order
☐ Price Club (Sam's Club, Costco's, etc.)
☐ Retail Store (Target, Wal-Mart, etc.)

9. What subject do you enjoy reading about the most?
(please choose one)
☐ Parenting/Family
☐ Relationships
☐ Recovery/Addictions
☐ Health/Nutrition
☐ Christianity
☐ Spirituality/Inspiration
☐ Business Self-help
☐ Women's Issues
☐ Sports

10. What attracts you most to a book?
(please choose one)
☐ Title
☐ Cover Design
☐ Author
☐ Content

TAPE IN MIDDLE; DO NOT STAPLE

BUSINESS REPLY MAIL
FIRST-CLASS MAIL PERMIT NO 45 DEERFIELD BEACH, FL

POSTAGE WILL BE PAID BY ADDRESSEE

Health Communications, Inc.
3201 SW 15th Street
Deerfield Beach FL 33442-9875

FOLD HERE

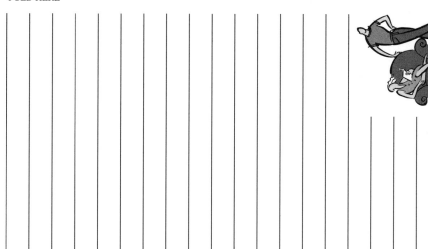

Comments

7

Focus and Finish the Job

*The only place where success comes before work
is in the dictionary.*

—Vidal Sassoon

Baseball legend Yogi Berra said, "The game isn't over until it's over."
We've all heard "It's a done deal" promises a million times only to be
left holding the bag when someone fails to follow through. A job
unfinished is a goal not achieved. The ability to focus and finish the job is
the quintessential hallmark that distinguishes winners from those who fail
to live up to their expectations and achieve their goals. If you can't focus,
you'll be unable to capture each moment's opportunity, and thus you'll
never fully express your full life potential. Focus is a learned skill. Most
people need only to learn and apply it to prosper.

Focus on One Thing at a Time

Culture today in the United States places a large premium on multitasking and shoehorning more activities into already overstuffed schedules,
yet few people's lives have been simplified simply by doing more. In fact,

for most people, life's complexity has increased exponentially because any "extra" time created by multitasking is quickly consumed by more activities force fed into their already top-heavy, bursting-at-the-seams schedules.

Focusing doesn't mean concentrating or multitasking to the point that you become blurry eyed and ineffective. Many mistakenly believe that superfocus and hyperconcentration produce greater results. Unfortunately, this myth usually creates the opposite effect, with those who overfocus too long or too intently falling very short of their goals due to battle-weary, listless, and often very scrambled brains.

"Appropriate focus is born of calmness and presence of mind in the moment; it is not achieved by blindly throwing energy at every opportunity in the hope of a positive outcome."

Nobody has the chameleonlike ability to pay attention successfully to more than one matter at a time. More focus can dramatically increase the risk of mental errors, poor timing, becoming overwhelmed, and burnout. Among the signs of scattered focus are an overwhelming sense of urgency to get things done; fear and preoccupation that nothing is getting or will get done; placing task completion above relationship; agitation with others; the mind going in too many directions simultaneously; a feeling that time is speeding up and you're falling farther behind but that you'll catch up in the future; uncharacteristic mental errors; heightened emotional sensitivity; decreased productivity; nervous eating; and an inability to relax because there's still more to get done. When any of these symptoms are present, you may find your superfocus and multitasking are at peak kinetic levels, but your functional mental focus is in decline and you are underperforming.

A delicate balance exists between appropriate focus and overfocus. Excess focus is extremely detrimental to top performance because it puts too much scattered information into the brain too quickly, slows the mind's reaction time as it tries to collate and make sense of the input, reduces the mind's spontaneity, and often leads to indecision, poor choice making, and bad timing. Overfocus is often the result of excess self-interest, blind ambition, or fear of failure and can lead to shortsighted decisions that often pro-duce disastrous long-term consequences. Appropriate focus is born of calm-ness and presence of mind in the moment; it is not achieved by blindly throwing energy at every opportunity in the hope of a positive outcome.

It's completely predictable who will underperform. Their impulsive and emotionally driven decisions, hyperactivity, or excess introversion or extroversion betray them. Conversely, top performances can be accurately prophesied from those who have mental composure and a strong presence of mind in the here and now, all tempered by an air of subdued confidence. You can vividly see these mannerisms in every great performer. They always have a composed-yet-focused intensity about them, appropriately engaging others but never chattering idly or deflecting their attention away from competing at their highest capability. They have superior concentra-tion skills and, when it comes time to perform, they put their complete trust in their abilities, preparation, and history as a winner.

In contrast to the top performers there are those in every discipline with great potential who continually underperform due to scattered focus. This occurs most often from obsessive fixation on preparation; from preparing too hard or too long; and from overintellectualizing and emotionalizing insignificant details. When they do this, the mind and body are drained by the time it is time to initiate the action and, predictably, they perform well below their potential.

Intention Doesn't Ensure Success

Intention and the law of attraction have for millennia been key princi-ples advocated by devotees of success. The law of attraction maintains that what you think about is what you attract to you. Good thoughts will attract beneficial opportunities, and negative ones will attract undesirable ones. Your intention does the same thing. Intention is, essentially, the goal of your actions. Without intent, you would never initiate anything. However, neither intention nor the law of attraction gets the job done. Each only provides the impulse to initiate the actions to reach your goals. They are not the actions themselves. Your actions do the legwork to complete the tasks necessary to manifest your intentions and capitalize on the opportunities provided by the law of attraction. Intentions and actions are different sides of the same coin, and when appropriately matched they make a potent winning combination. Intentions provide the focus, and actions finish the job.

> "Good thoughts will attract beneficial opportunities, and negative ones will attract undesirable ones."

Focus Is Your Best Friend

Focus is the skill to which all the other components of your success methodology are subservient. Your ability to focus makes reaching your goals achievable. When you have proper focusing skills, producing the successful actions needed to reach your goals becomes commonplace.

Success only occurs when you accept the full responsibility for successfully completing the action steps to achieve your goals on time. Responsibility is a great incentive. People with little responsibility are less likely to achieve their goals because they have little incentive to learn the skills or focus and finish the job. The pressure to achieve your goals on schedule significantly increases your motivation to focus and execute your plans precisely to conserve time so you attain your aspiration efficiently.

Honed focus dramatically enhances your productivity because it directs your attention, energy, and forward momentum toward reaching your goals rather than going sideways or away from their completion because of distraction or uncertainty. Greater focus also helps you complete your plans more quickly, which leaves more energy for additional productive undertakings.

Conversely, poor focus inhibits you from optimizing the potential of your plans by disrupting the communication exchanges necessary to complete them with complete and original authenticity. Inattention disconnects and transposes facts, making it impossible to make accurate, swift decisions to advance your plans. If one small fact is misconstrued or inaccurately transmitted, everything else is perturbed and magnified in proportion to the inaccuracy. When enough distortion occurs in your plan, its outcome may bear little or no resemblance to its original intention. Most attempts to salvage an original plan's intent once it has gone off course and beyond its point of no return only compound its distortion and further amplify the perturbation. Either way, the chaos wastes significant time and energy, further increasing your mental and physical fatigue and frustration and making the achievement of your goals even less likely.

The biggest danger of all from plans gone awry due to poor focus is that you can start to lose confidence in your ability to create and complete plans. If you identify with the person who can't attend to detail from lack of focus as being the real you, embracing future opportunity becomes difficult—especially if you've become gun-shy and reluctant to risk from fear of failure and lack of trust in yourself.

Your Performance Personality

Each of us has a learned disposition that produces success or failure in its own way. These are, like every other behavior, learned and modifiable. When it comes to completing cycles of action, there are four performance personalities: those who start and finish them on time; those who start but can't complete them; those who have difficulty starting them but ultimately get them done; and those who can't get them started or finished. Regardless of the roles genetics and developmental environment play in who has what degree of motivation, in the end they become irrelevant since the only thing that determines your life success is what you accomplish. Despite the influence of your genes and history, completing actions and plans is a learned skill that can be acquired and refined at any point in life. The better and faster you learn that skill, the more you can accomplish and the greater your successes.

Winners are those who start and finish their projects on time. Their performance personalities seemingly have a "finish the job" metronome within them that defines their goals, sets the timeline for their completion, and finishes them on schedule. Such people's lives are extremely straight-forward and run like clockwork. Their dispositions don't require modification for them to remain successful. They simply must keep doing what they're doing without changing anything. Winner personalities are vulnerable to becoming overconfident in their abilities, which disposes them to skipping essential details, breaking protocol, and getting greedy in their aspirations. This may surprise you, but these winners, almost without exception, have all learned their task-completion skills. Very few are born with them. If they can learn and apply them, so can you.

People with the second performance personality, those who can start but not finish tasks, usually have highly creative minds that enjoy, and are more skilled at, dreaming up new ideas and initiating new actions than completing them. They thrive on a steady diet of varied stimulation to remain vital and enthusiastic. Otherwise, they can easily become bored. They never like life to feel like a task or an obligation. Those with this type of performance personality must evaluate their plans at the end of each day to review and refine them, so they get up each morning with a clear outline in their mind as to what steps must be accomplished that day to keep their plan on pace to reach their goal on time. Frequently reviewing and recommitting to finishing their plan's steps each day is the most important thing they can do to ensure they will reach their goals.

The enigmatic performance personality is the one who has difficulty starting a project but at the last minute always gets it done. This is characteristic of very talented people who have learned to rely upon their talent, more than discipline, to pull them through. These people are primarily motivated by a love–hate relationship with time. They need the pressure of time to motivate them to get anything done, but they hate being pushed by it. An example of this is the brilliant, often lazy, student who has the habit of staying up all night studying for tests and miraculously aces them every time. The downside of this performance personality is that these people rarely become perennial successes because they use their talent reactively to get things done rather than proactively to formulate consistently great plans that produce consecutive successes. To succeed consistently, such people must shift their focus away from their talent to planning. Unfortunately, that seldom occurs because this performance-type personality is the one least likely to change. This is not because they lack talent but because they are held hostage by it. Life is just a little too easy for them.

The person who can't plan, start, or finish a task makes reaching a goal categorically impossible since they don't have one. These people often have heavy, bland, gray personalities, devoid of initiative, and are constantly waiting for someone to motivate them to start and complete even their life's simplest tasks, or, preferably, to do it for them. Often they have latent talents to succeed but have become even more skilled as manipulators, having learned to play the helpless "poor me" ploy to get people to feel sorry and do their work for them. Unfortunately, this only disables them further, making them more incompetent and more dependent on others, which can in turn even make them resentful of those on whom they're dependent. Until such people find their own motivation to excel and create a better life for themselves, they will always be dependent on others. To develop their own initiative, they often must descend to the point in life where they're so sick and tired of being unproductive, chained to others for help, and living despondently that they take the appropriate actions to change their lives. People with this personality need to realize that they're the only one who can build and create their success, confront their fears of inadequacy, and find out, by doing, that they can be successful if they learn and apply the success methodology presented in this book. I've known many people who have made this conversion, and the appreciation they have for their newfound self-determination has made them some of the most successful people ever. Change is possible anytime when the will is there.

Building Razor-Sharp Focus

The more acute your focus is the better will be your discernment when it comes to learning and applying your knowledge. There are several simple and effective means of developing your focus to reach your goals on time.

> "Building focus demands that you be in a stimulating and challenging setting."

Building focus demands that you be in a stimulating and challenging setting. Some of the most brilliant students find themselves in classrooms that don't challenge their intellects, so they appear to be defiant, bored, listless, and dull, not because they are, but because they are unchallenged and uninspired. This is exactly the same with you, because lack of challenge can lull you into complacency, downgrade your talents, and make you sloppy, lazy, and inattentive. When possible, take on tasks that put you right up against the edge of your skill level and performance capacity, because the degree of apprehension this type of task creates will challenge and improve your focus and attention skills most quickly and thoroughly. The fear of risk and failure is a great motivator for becoming more proficient. As your proficiency improves, your fear of failure will disappear and your successes will become bigger and occur more quickly. Such tasks will also put some thrill into your life because appropriate apprehension and fear increase excitement.

Playing card games or chess, or any other game that requires thought, strategy, attention, and risk, is a benign, yet very effective, way to learn how to focus and finish the job. It gives you the chance to rehearse your composure and focus skills outside the battlefield of daily life when your choices count. You can experiment with unorthodox game strategies, and if they fail you simply modify your strategy to learn to play better in an impromptu environment, better preparing you for when you have to think and react on your feet in real life.

Another skill you must master is to plan quickly and accurately when little time is available to do so. To build this skill, purposely create situations for yourself in which you must develop small mock plans in time-sensitive situations. These plans shouldn't necessarily be for real-life aspirations. They are practice runs to develop your focus so you can, at a moment's notice, create a solid, workable plan. Some of the best plans have come when someone spontaneously writes a plan on a napkin at a restaurant or on an envelope while waiting in line. Learning to create plans in any circumstance will help you learn to extract the essential details to create a plan that will succeed. Successful plans have more to do with accuracy and coherency of content than with volume. With plans, less is usually more. Creating a plan even while standing in line, stopped at a traffic light, or during commercials, is a great way to help you build the skill.

Losing focus leads to poor decision making that can have disastrous consequences. To remain mentally sharp with precise focus, your mind must be adequately rested. To practice this, whenever you experience the first sign of mental fatigue take a break for a few minutes and do nothing. When you begin your break, be mindful of your tendency to want to keep working to the next logical or convenient stopping point. Also, observe that the longer you wait to take your break, the slower and more disorganized your mind becomes and the more your productivity and decision making deteriorate. What's hardest to learn in taking a break is to give yourself permission to follow the wisdom to do it so you can resume your tasks refreshed, rather than cave in to the fear impulse and keep working, afraid you'll forfeit forward progress by taking the break. Never work on your plan to the point where you are tired and lose focus. Your self-confidence and clarity of thought will dramatically increase when you master this skill.

Everybody has their best personal environment in which to learn, create, and execute their plans. However, you must also learn to do this in conditions that are not ideal. To learn the skill of focusing and directing your attention toward your intended task, calm environments are often best. Too much noise and distraction won't allow you to learn the skill of working around distraction, so you must initially create for yourself a location where you can develop your plans and begin them without interference.

You might even find the absence of distraction foreign to you and the silence unsettling. Fear not, for you will soon recalibrate to this more tranquil setting and further solidify your focusing skills. As you become better able to focus, you'll find you can focus just as well even in more disruptive settings, and you must develop proficiency to do this.

Another way to develop superior focus is to purposely immerse yourself in chaos as a way to challenge yourself to learn to overcome distraction when working. Only do this, however, once your focus skills are sufficiently developed. Find places that have traditionally distracted you and regularly study in them to learn to focus and remain productive when surrounded by chaos. When you periodically practice the skill of focusing in chaotic conditions while studying and planning, you will find that you'll also be able to perform much better around chaos than before.

Once you've learned the skill of staying focused and present with your plans, you need to keep the skill intact and fully operational at all times. This requires constant vigilance to master and maintain but is indispensable to your achieving consistent success. You must vigilantly apply several key strategies to maintain your focus and productivity at peak levels.

At the end of every workday, review your plans for the following day. This will prepare your conscious and unconscious mind for what the next day's plans are so you can take full advantage of advancing your ambitions. If you wait until the following day to review your plans, you'll lose significant time trying to figure out where you are and what you need to do to keep moving your plan toward completion. It's always better to hit the new day running.

Regardless of what you're doing, always do it in the environment most conducive for your productivity style. Avoid attempting to manifest anything in circumstances that aren't compatible with your best way of doing things. Every second lost going nowhere while stuck in surroundings that don't bring out the best in you may be the very second you could have done the one thing that distinguishes your life. Whenever possible, preplan your work setting to get the most out of every productive moment.

To maintain maximum focus, always create plans that have timetables, effort, and resource requirements consistent with your skill level and available time. Never undertake a plan that turns your life upside down because you have to cram it into your schedule or because you're not sure you have the skills for it. If you do, you'll never be able to deliver on it.

Success's Deadliest Sin

Accepting full accountability for task completion aligns perfectly with the no-nonsense, no-excuse-making attitude that is a cornerstone of every successful person. I was consulting with a very talented individual who hadn't yet delivered on the talent he auspiciously debuted at the beginning of his career. He mentioned that the biggest mistake he ever made in life was making his first excuse. After that, he said, it became easier and easier to make excuses, and at the end of his career it amounted to one long excuse with mediocre results and much unfulfilled potential.

> "Whenever possible, preplan your work setting to get the most out of every productive moment."

Excuses not only hurt your ability to acquire the skills to become a more accomplished achiever, but they also erode your confidence in your capacity to deliver on your promises, which compromises your self-respect. Everybody knows that every time an excuse is made, a breach of trust occurs between a person and himself, as well as between himself and others, displacing full disclosure and integrity with a big question mark as to who the person is, what the person stands for, and what the person's capable of achieving.

If excuses become more frequent, it's easier to enter a deadly cycle of nonsuccess, further shredding whatever confidence is left and insidiously imprinting the psyche with the very real message that success isn't deserved because honesty hasn't been upheld. Though certainly true, it's critical that the self-incrimination doesn't go overboard, driving self-esteem so low, and the belief of unworthiness so deep, that the initiative to succeed shuts down and may never turn on again. The truth is, however, that excuse making is the most easily reversible success-sabotaging vice. The moment excuses are no longer made, the chain is broken, the curse is lifted, and life begins to turn around as your belief in yourself returns, restoring—once again—winning ways.

Another downside to excuse making is that every time an excuse is made, it takes away from your ability to stay present in the moment, where your best decisions are made and your best actions accomplished. If decision making isn't fully trusted, deliberation over choices takes too long—while they pass you by. Unfortunately, one of those choices may have been the one to give your life its biggest boost.

Excuse making also compromises your ability to make and maintain relationships, because people can smell an excuse at a distance. An excuse is a calling card that says, "I can't be trusted, I'm not trustworthy with information, I can't complete tasks, and someone else is to blame." Once a person is branded as an excuse maker, regaining trust with others becomes exceedingly difficult. The only policy that keeps your life moving forward in a world of imperfect people is to admit your errors and correct your course. Nobody will ever question that. In fact, some of life's best relationships come from such brutal honesty.

> "There's no future for anyone in making excuses—only losers all around."

Excuses are extremely self-serving, with one purpose and one purpose only: to get the person making them off the hook in their own mind. There's no future for anyone in making excuses—only losers all around. Unfortunately, unwilling people can become entangled in the excuse maker's webs of confusion. Every excuse impacts everyone within range of it, often making people guilty by association. Consequently, you must recognize that your associations play a profound role in your ability to remain credible, and your credibility is, ultimately, all you've got. Avoid excuses and their makers like the plague.

Learning to Say No

Blazing new trails in life becomes possible only when there's a well-lit path in front of you, framed by concretely defined boundaries. Without those two features, life resembles a bottle tossed about by the ocean; bobbing between waves with no say in the direction it's headed. Unfortunately, most people's lives are so cluttered with obligations—many of which they don't really want—that they've completely choked themselves off from life's creative lifeline. All successful people have learned how to set appropriate boundaries with themselves and others.

One of life's sobering realities is that, unfortunately, there's never enough time to do everything we want to do. Since there are only twenty-four hours in each day, you must first prioritize what you want to do and then create the time to do it. The best way to make more time available to do what you're passionate about is to learn to say no. Saying no is difficult for most of us, as our human nature wants to accommodate and please others. However, if you can only say yes, people's requests for your time will consume every second of your life, leaving no time for you to develop your talents and pursue your dreams. The challenge boils down to the fact that you know what your schedules are and others don't, and since nobody's a mind reader it is the prerogative of others to ask for your time, and your job is to say yes or no. It's all very straightforward, and saying no is a skill that all successful people have mastered. When done with respect for life's process and others, saying no can be one of your most empowering actions.

How to say no is a skill in itself. Most people shy away from it because they fear rejection by others. Unfortunately, this often leads to unexpressed resentment toward others that is destructive to your health, relationships, and goal attainment. No matter what you do in life, not everybody's going to be happy with your decisions. What's important is that you do what's best for you to be the best you can be. Saying no should be done quickly, with care and respect for others. Never defer it, because that can hang people up needlessly. When done concisely and with consideration, everyone comes out a winner. Plus, you'll draw to yourself those who respect your stance and appreciate your spirit.

Authenticity is the most important element in setting boundaries. Once you've decided what it is you're going to do, you need to inform those who need to know and state what the ground rules for implementation are so nobody will be caught off guard. This courtesy is only fair and shows respect for all involved. The sooner it's done, the less the chance for complication. Few things are more liberating in life than to be completely transparent about what you're thinking and how you truly feel about something. Far too many people's lives are bottlenecked from not expressing themselves openly, which stifles creative thought and impedes possibility thinking.

Saying no empowers you and makes you stronger because you're taking a public stand on your convictions and honoring the gift of your insights. This freedom of expression is your greatest gift, and the best gift you can give others. Talent and insight only have value when they're expressed and shared. Saying no is more powerful than any half-hearted, insincere yes.

> "Saying no is more powerful than any half-hearted, insincere yes."

Trying to be all things to all people severely limits your abundance. A hallmark of every successful business is that it has clearly defined its products. It knows exactly what it is providing the consumer, and this dictates the entire structure of the company. A fatal mistake entrepreneurs can make is to offer too many products, attempting to capture the largest audience possible, but most often this ends up diluting the company's resources and stunting its growth. Something similar can happen in the business of life. When you dilute yourself by trying to find favor with everybody, you go "success and fulfillment broke" after hemorrhaging your time, energy, and resources to others while satisfying very few. Showing those in your sphere of influence how setting boundaries with others helps you focus and complete your plans on time will inspire them to set their own boundaries with others and help maintain their focus to achieve their aspirations.

OVERCOMING DISTRACTIONS

In today's rush-rush world, distractions are a way of life. From the incessant bombardment of information to automated telephone menus, life has become one big time-gobbling distraction—*unless* you know how to immunize yourself from it. Most distractions are self-inflicted and have simple solutions. The following chart provides solutions to most common distractions. You can conserve enormous amounts of time, energy, and resources by utilizing them.

Distractions	How to Overcome Them
Phone, e-mail, pager, text message, PDAs	Only answer known people; in your electronic address books, put people's names with their numbers so you know who's contacting you.
Fear that you'll miss something	Pursue only your highest priorities; never expend excess energy compulsively looking for your next opportunity: let them come to you.
Junk solicitations, calls, mail	Take yourself off the lists and throw out your junk mail immediately.
Too many choices	Only accept those choices with the biggest returns. Never rush to finish plans just to move on to the next one.
Too much silence	Surround yourself with the correct amount of stimulation that keeps you vital but not overwhelmed.
Horns, traffic, noise, someone else's music	Properly insulate your life space from unwanted noise by using window shades, music, and air purifiers with a gentle background sound that block unwanted noise.

OVERCOMING DISTRACTIONS (CONT'D)

Distractions	How to Overcome Them
Too many unfinished tasks cluttering your mind	Complete the task you're working on before beginning the next one.
Hyperactivity, racing mind	Use no sugar, MSG, or excess caffeine; exercise regularly, stretch before bed.
Taking on too many things	Learn to say no.
Overreaction to people, places, and things	Eat healthy, speak up, have fun, be with people you love, rest well.
Preoccupation with everything that can go wrong in life	Focus on what you stand to gain, not lose, address only those things in life you can constructively influence.
Not minding your own business	Concentrate on achieving your own goals, not those of others.
Trying to do one more thing before going to bed	Drop it and go to bed. The world can live without you until morning.
Incompetent sales or service people consuming your time while they bungle	Always call to confirm appointments and ensure the products and services you need are available before making the trip.

Defining the box you live in makes you the ultimate decision maker in your life. Nobody knows what makes you tick better than you do, and nobody cares about your life as much as you do. Therefore, it's up to you to stage your life for prosperity by developing plans that reflect your personal aspirations, then take the initiative to let others know what you're intending to do and what you expect of them in the process. This is particularly true with intimate relationships at home and in the workplace. Nobody's clairvoyant in knowing what your expectations and plans are unless you tell them. Everyone needs to be adequately informed about your intentions; otherwise reaching goals and creating prosperity grinds to a halt from poor communication with others because they have no idea how to respond to you.

Without boundaries, lives often become excessively top heavy and frequently implode under the extreme gravity of too much obligation, which causes a loss of focus and time necessary to generate and maintain adequate momentum. The best winners regularly weed their garden of unnecessary emotional and physical burdens, which when left untended, only compound further and impact their lives in a negative way.

TURN IT UP! TIPS

1. Realize that to perform at your best you can only successfully focus on one thing at a time. Never multitask to the point you become ineffective. This dilution can create significant confusion and frustration.

2. A major key to performing at your best is to put your entire trust in your abilities, preparation, and history in completing tasks thoroughly and on time. This attitude produces the confidence you need to envision, create, and execute your greatest plans.

3. Never shy away from an opportunity at the edge of your abilities. The challenge to step up and perform at a higher level will motivate you to learn the skills needed to complete the task and focus and finish the job. The confidence and skills you get from this will take you to your next success level.

4. Never identify with the "other" you. There will be times when your focus just isn't there. This temporary "other" you is an imposter who can't perform up to your potential and should never be confused with the "real" you, who has competently achieved goals countless times. If you start to believe the "other" you is you then you risk developing fear of failure and lack of trust in yourself.

5. Always start your projects on time. Starting on time is a learned skill that when practiced diligently completes plans on time allowing more time available for other things.

6. Rest your mind frequently to maintain top focus. When your concentration starts to wander take a break to recharge your mental batteries. This will keep your productivity levels high throughout the day.

TURN IT UP! TIPS (CONT'D)

7. Take a few minutes at the end of every work day to review your plans for the following day. This will prepare you mentally so you can take full advantage of achieving your goals the following day.

8. Regardless of any endeavor, always do it in the most conducive environment for your productivity style. Avoid trying to create or produce anything under circumstances that aren't compatible with your execution style.

9. Only take on those plans that easily fit into your calendar. Undertaking a plan that must be crammed into your schedule risks creating excess clutter in your life, which can easily put you into a mental tailspin from the confusion that it creates.

10. The best way for you to make more time available to do what you're passionate about is to learn to say no. Each time you practice the art of saying no you will feel more confident in your choice making and ability to achieve those things that have the most meaning for *you*.

8

You Must Have
a Winning Plan

*Our goals can only be reached through the vehicle
of a plan, in which we must fervently believe,
and upon which we must vigorously act.
There is no other route to success.*

—Stephen A. Brennan

Plans are the underlying structure and force that make the world turn and create order in the human universe. Without plans it is impossible for you to achieve your life aspirations. When you create and execute a successful plan, reaching your goals becomes a mere formality, requiring only the time and persistence needed to see the plan through to completion. Winning plans save time, energy, and resources, allowing you to reach your goals time and again so you can live the life you choose and be the person you're meant to be.

> "Plans are the underlying structure and force that make the world turn and create order in the human universe."

145

Becoming a Prolific Winner

Winning plans are the glue that holds your life together. They give you just the correct amount of structure to become successful without being inordinately restrictive or permissive. There is a very special zone of living where committed initiative and life's best outcomes coexist. This utopia resides somewhere between not enough and too much life structure. Those who live life "on the fly," making it up as they go, seldom have much success because they lack the planning skills and life framework to construct doable plans that convert their ideas into achieved goals. Conversely, there are those whose lives are governed by so many rules that their spontaneity is suffocated, preventing them from thinking expansively enough or incorporating into their plans better options that may surface during plan implementation that lead to even greater successes. There are also those with superior planning skills, attention spans, and initiative who attain their goals with incredible consistency because they maintain a balance in their lives between structure and freedom.

Certainly, there's no shortage of talent on this planet. Unfortunately, most of it lies dormant, buried beneath people's inability to create and enact plans that draw their best talents to the surface. Most people are acutely aware that they have the ability to do more in life than they're expressing, but they just don't know how to access their talents and transform them into the actions that manifest their full potential.

Countless examples exist of people who may have incredible talent and charisma but are so flighty in thought and action that sustained, predictable, goal-oriented behavior can't be sufficiently generated to gather the forward momentum necessary to reach their goals. This inability makes attaining goals consistent with their talents all but impossible.

At the other end of the spectrum are those whose lives are so structured that they can't completely express their full creativity and genius because of their excessive mental rigidity. They, like those without any structure, know they have the talent to do great things. Yet they are unable to access and mobilize it toward prosperity because the weight and mass of the box they live in is so restrictive and claustrophobic that their skills and talents remain encased in their lack of mental flexibility. Well-conceived plans will give you the objectivity to see how an excessively rigid life structure prevents the full expression of your talents.

This insight empowers you to permit yourself to break out of rigidity's grasp to embrace, cultivate, and use your talents to build a more prosperous life. I have a friend who goes to Europe every year on vacation but will not go unless he knows his exact itinerary for the entire trip, down to the minute, before he leaves. Otherwise, his mind freezes from the uncertainty of his "ambiguous" schedule, making it impossible for him to get the most out of his trip. His obsessive need to have every second of his trip meticulously accounted for makes it very difficult for him with others, so his travel companions are, understandably, few and far between.

Good plans are like crystals balls that allow you to see distant potholes in the road before falling into them. We've all found ourselves in difficult situations with no easy way out. Well-thought-out plans virtually never land you there, but bad plans will, and all too often. Great plans allow you to see the pitfalls in advance, providing time to create contingencies to elude them. An important part of every top planner's daily strategy is to ask what could possibly go wrong with a plan, then to adopt evasive strategies to circumvent any such problems in advance and keep the plan headed in the correct direction. An ounce of prevention in your planning is always worth a pound of cure.

> "Good plans are like crystal balls that allow you to see distant potholes in the road before falling into them."

To transform your plans into completed goals, always have solid contingency plans in place for both best-case and worst-case scenarios before commencing. This is commonly known as "having a Plan B." These contingency plans allow for quick adaptation to maximize any circumstance and often make the difference between success and failure. They may never be needed, but they will help prepare you for any necessity to change course abruptly on the way to a goal. It may be that the only time you will need such contingency plans is when you haven't made them, so remain vigilant about creating them.

The reality is that not every winning plan you make will produce winning results. No matter how meticulously you plan, at times your plans will just not pan out. It's not that it wasn't a good plan or that you didn't deserve to reach your goal. It's just that the plan wasn't destined to succeed. Life often can be like that, without explanation for why something didn't work. This dark cloud, however, has a silver lining: your losses are your best teachers because they show you your weaknesses. Your weaknesses illustrate with exquisite precision what skills and attributes you need to acquire to become more successful. Without these insights you'd mistakenly believe that you're as good as you're going to get in life and that your learning efforts are completely random, without any specificity toward any concrete objective. Defeat also forces you to learn to pick yourself up when you fail, make new plans, and move forward with living. This skill is one of your greatest strengths because life will always be up and down, and life's momentum has more to do with keeping the momentum going in defeat than it does riding the inertia of success. Stalled lives that result from an inability to overcome defeat have prevented untold numbers of people from achieving their greatest life success. Your greatest achievements always come after your defeats.

Often the plans that prove the most profitable and the easiest to execute are the most unconventional. Unconventional plans can appear to be easily implemented and achieved on paper but can be the most difficult to initiate, as can any plan, if the mind isn't fully convinced the plan is viable. There's a monumental difference between being uncertain about a plan's viability because it is unconventional and it truly being unviable. If your confidence in a great plan is waffling because of its uniqueness and untested nature, it may, unfortunately, need to be aborted in favor of the safety of a more conventional, familiar plan. This happens not because the unconventional plan is ill conceived and won't manifest but simply because of the apprehension. This is, of course, completely acceptable if the apprehension created from the unconventional plan produces excessive distraction that disables the plan's correct execution.

If, however, the plan is unconventional and all its steps clearly indicate it has a high probability of success, it should be undertaken without reservation. When unconventional plans are successful, they're often seminal life events that can end up defining your legacy. They also reinforce through example how capable you are of achieving success when supported by a well-constructed plan.

Some plans, by their complex nature, take more time than others to complete. When it's determined that a plan is properly developed and its steps are impeccably sequenced, it becomes easy to remain compliant with plan execution during the inevitable periods of frustration that occur when your plan feels as if it isn't moving toward completion fast enough despite your committed efforts. The commitment to remain vigilant by executing each plan step in its entirety before undertaking the next step—refusing to cave in to frustration during such lag times—makes the difference between average and great plan outcomes.

When Michelangelo painted the Sistine Chapel, he spent a decade looking up at the ceiling as he painstakingly executed each brushstroke. His vision of the finished project and his confidence in his plan kept him motivated to complete the masterwork. It took time, intense concentration, and commitment, yet he remained on track to finish one of the greatest works in art history. He didn't cave in to the myriad of impulses that, like anyone involved in a sophisticated long-term project, he probably had. He stayed true to the mission.

Great Plans Create Self-Trust

Your plans are the reason you get up each morning. They are the purpose for which you were created. Without the motivation plans provide, embracing the new day with passionate enthusiasm becomes difficult. Those without life purpose often live lives resembling not much more than a cold, empty box filled with long, dull, uninspired gray days devoid of passion that leave them longing for connection and meaning. I've never met a happy person who didn't have a well-defined reason for getting up each morning. Achieved plans are the mechanism that enables your life purpose to manifest and your motivation to remain at peak levels.

Everybody wants to be part of a winning team, and the fastest way for you to complete your winning plan is to have a winning team behind you. Having the reputation for being a consistently top performer who creates great plans and secures the best team possible attracts the best people to your plan because they trust you. This gives you the pick of the crop as far as talent goes. Bad plans are like high-powered repelling devices that push people away. People can smell a bad plan a mile away and want nothing to do with it. They know that nothing constructive ever comes from an ill-conceived plan, and the best a bad plan has to offer is frustration, energy drain, and needless consumption of resources.

Once you develop superior planning, you will create a bulletproof self-confidence in your abilities to create and execute plans that will lead to many extraordinary life experiences. This is a pivotal life experience for you because you will learn, deservedly, to trust yourself. Great plans happen because the attention to detail required to make them great was implemented correctly during each step of their creation. When you're confident in your planning abilities, you never rush a plan's creation or execution.

> "Once you develop superior planning, you will create a bulletproof self-confidence in your abilities to create and execute plans that will lead to many extraordinary life experiences."

Experience clearly illustrates that the fastest way to shift a plan's percentages in favor of failure is to compromise its construction and execution through shortcutting. Predictably, too many bad plans too often and with too many failures will severely erode your confidence in your decision-making capacity. Left unchecked, this can degenerate to the point where trusting your decision-making capacity is so severely compromised that your ability to make even the simplest decisions is lost. If that occurs, the risk of completely abandoning choice making altogether becomes possible. Once that occurs, personal growth ceases, placing life in suspended animation until the fires of creation, trust, and confidence burn once again. If you fail at a plan, it was either because the plan was too elaborate for your skill set or you got sloppy in its construction and execution. Only commence constructing and executing a plan when you've got the time, skills and mind-set to do it correctly.

Completing your plans on time and achieving your goals are necessary because they create self-trust, as well as trust between yourself and others. Each time you successfully complete an action, your trust in your ability to create effective plans and execute them properly increases. As you become more proficient at those skills, the more goals you will reach, and the greater your trust in yourself as a creator and executor of productive plans will be, naturally leading to further extraordinary experiences. This also applies to your relationships with others. For each plan you involve others in that ends in success, the more they will trust you and your planning skills. That trust translates into a greater synergism among team members that, in turn, spawns more cohesion and commitment in pursuit of a common goal. This also inspires others to commit to future plans in which you may involve them.

Good plans are important because, when completed, they confirm your capacity to create bigger and better plans in the future. This gives you tremendous hope about creating better outcomes for yourself and others by doing committed acts today that will secure your future tomorrow. Your plans are designed to reach goals, and goals represent freedom, self-determination, and self-sufficiency—the foundation upon which enthusiasm and prosperity are based.

Having the Time of Your Life

Your primal instinct compels you to plan and to be in constant pursuit of goals. Planning keeps your mind fresh, alert, and always looking for better, more innovative, and more efficient ways to achieve your aspirations. Striving for goals is a vital component of the human happiness equation and can often be more satisfying than actually achieving the goal itself. Having a positive focus for a better future keeps your outlook optimistic, which attracts a steady stream of beneficial opportunities to you. Without a plan, moving forward in life is impossible because there's no target. You can't shoot for the bull's-eye if you've got the bow and arrow but not the target.

In the physical world, plans represent a timeline. Since you have only so much time in life to be successful, it behooves you to become the best planner possible as quickly as you can so you can create as many life successes as time allows. Plans are like cars with a new set of tires. Great plans allow you to gain Velcro-like traction on the streets of life, generating forward movement toward achieving your goals quickly with certainty and optimism. Mediocre plans are like spinning your car's wheels on wet pavement, creating little in the way of forward movement toward achieving your goals. If traction is found with a mediocre plan, it is usually only enough to produce an average outcome that usually takes longer than expected to achieve because of the wasted time spent spinning the wheels and going nowhere.

Poor plans are like putting the car in reverse and stomping on the gas pedal. The only things bad plans produce are frustration, confusion, wasted energy, lost time, and high resource consumption, with no return on investment. Worse, they usually end up digging a hole that you can only get out of by using up twice as much of your resources. When a plan is well sequenced and thought out on paper, and the facts indicate it has a high probability of success, consider it a winner. Regardless of your passion for a plan, if the plan has a big, red "This isn't going to work" X on it when it is carefully reviewed, and all the signs point to an unviable plan, shut it down immediately and toss it into the recycle bin because it has no future. It will never succeed no matter how badly you might want.

Good plans help you learn to find, recruit, and post the correct people to assist you in completing your plans efficiently. Without appropriately qualified people posted correctly, goals can seldom, if ever, be reached with ease. The more these people are aligned with their positions and your plan's philosophy, the less training, energy, and communication time are required to keep your plan humming along toward completion. Poor posting has a double-negative impact on your plans. It requires extraordinarily more time to train people to do jobs they aren't qualified for, and additional time and energy just to keep them motivated and trained well enough to execute their jobs, even at a minimal level. Consequently, valuable time and resources are lost that could have been used more productively to keep your momentum steaming you forward toward your goal and success.

When plans begin to stall, as most intermittently do, there's a pronounced risk they will unravel from mental and physical battle fatigue and never reach completion because those executing them are overextended. Too much, too long of anything grinds away at your mental and physical vitality, eventually dulling your capacity to respond to the challenges associated with your plan and severely undermining its successful completion.

All highly motivated people understand the importance of incorporating deliberate time off to recharge their batteries while working on their winning plans. This isn't always easy for high-energy, lofty-thinking winners, and if it's not purposely built into their plans it's unlikely they'll remember or voluntarily take a breather. Most goal-oriented people aren't very good at and, quite frankly, simply have little interest in, planning time off. They tend to believe it means they must give up some time that could be used more appropriately pursuing a project. If time off is neglected often enough, however, illness and poor productivity will inevitably ensue. Purposely scheduling time off is a prime benefit of planning, since most goal-oriented people would seldom do it unless forced. I once heard a nationally syndicated radio talk show host say that as busy as he is, he purposefully sets aside one day every week to do nothing. That's his plan, but even doing nothing on a day off requires a plan.

> "All highly motivated people understand the importance of incorporating deliberate time off to recharge their batteries while working on their winning plans."

It's only possible to have a fulfilling life if you're achieving your dreams and nourishing your spirit through actions that resonate with your soul. Most people need tangible verification that their efforts are advancing their lives. As small as it may seem, one of the strongest validations that you're on your way to completing a task is drawing a line through an item on your plan's to do list. This checkoff ritual represents the successful completion of an individual step within the plan, which brings the goal closer. Considerable personal pride and self-confidence can come from even this seemingly trivial activity. If you can complete a single step, you can complete an entire plan.

Planning is about focus and directing your attention toward what's meaningful. Without focus, energy is always wasted by being randomly scattered in too many directions with the hope, but no guarantee, that productive outcomes will happen. It's a foregone conclusion that goals without well-scripted plans will disintegrate from the steps not being harmonized toward a common goal, making the well-coordinated use of resources impossible. Well-conceived plans, with steps that have been properly sequenced and formulated, anchor your focus and attention in the here and now as action steps are being taken, keeping you on track to finishing your plan steps and making your aspirations attainable.

Achieving More by Doing Less

Reaching your goal can happen quickly or slowly, depending on the accuracy of your plan and how fast each step gets completed. Plans are really no more than a sequence of tasks appropriately strung together to reach a predetermined outcome. The longer it takes to complete a task, finish a project, or reach a goal, the less likely it will happen correctly the first time. Everyone has experienced that. You start something, get distracted, and come back to it later, but every second you're away makes it that much more difficult to get the task going again. Such delays open the door for additional disruptions to sideswipe your plan and delay it further, possibly to the point that it never reaches completion. Critical to finishing steps efficiently and quickly is setting a completion date for each. Timelines and target dates conserve vast amounts of time and energy. Very little punctuates accountability more than completion dates for your tasks.

Incomplete planning is the usual cause of burnout. If at any point in your plan execution the process becomes significantly harder without apparent reason, it's inevitably because either the plan's steps are too large or too difficult and need to be broken down into more achievable steps with smoother transitions between them or essential steps have been inadvertently omitted. In great plans, the spacing between plan steps and step difficulty is always properly proportioned so that the mind and body are never overexposed in terms of time and effort on any step. Doing this allows your plan to advance to completion at peak speed with the least wear and tear on you.

Well-formulated plans must have the correct number of people working on the correct number of appropriately sized and effort-intensive steps to keep the team's morale high. Lopsided work distribution and poor acknowledgement of coworkers can quickly create discontent among team members. Disharmony is one of the fastest ways to sabotage any plan. Given enough time and intimacy with anybody or anything, discontent will inevitably find its way onto the radar. Once there, this discontent can spread, undermining and eventually destroying any plan if not eradicated before reaching the point of no return.

Most discontent comes from giving people responsibilities that are beyond their capacities, or from people who aren't in complete alignment with the objectives and philosophy of your plan. Both sources can contaminate coworkers with their silently hostile, passive-aggressive "Don't just do something, stand there" attitude. Good plans always have appropriate screening protocols to ensure that incompatible people are not selected for the project. If you're not sold on a person's authenticity and capacity to step up and perform, you should trust that intuition and not do business with them. Passive-aggressive types talk a great game but rarely follow through, simply because they don't want to do so. Sometimes they will gum up the plan as a way to express their general discontent with life.

The most direct route from a plan's beginning to its end is a straight line. In a perfect world, each of your plans would directly reach their goals without any detours, but no plan ever gets from conception to completion without some deviation. Well-constructed plans and committed team members gather and maintain momentum much better than uncommitted, fragmented plans and participants. Well-constructed plans provide the impetus to penetrate barriers and reach goals without loss of momentum. Any loss of momentum stalls the process and increases the risk of self-doubt creeping in to stifle the project with the paralysis of indecision. There's always enough time to do anything correctly the second time, and one benefit of a great plan is that its completion always happens on the first pass, leaving additional time for creating other successes. A friend told me his father would always tell him, "If you haven't got time to do it right, then make sure you've got time to do it over." Always construct your plan thoroughly before initiating it to minimize the grief and maximize the joy.

A classic example of this is seen with painting a house. The final coat of paint that creates the house's ultimate visual aesthetic appeal is the byproduct of the preparation that precedes it, including the sanding, patching, and application of a primer coat. When the preparation is done well, the final topcoat is the easiest part of the entire process, just as it is with every great plan and its outcome. In effect, winning plans are a product of a reverse engineering of the process where the goal—the endpoint—of the plan is first established, with the plan and its subtasks and projects then constructed backward from it so there's a smooth, rational, rhythmic transition between the plan's steps.

Building a Better Toolbox

One extremely important benefit of any great plan is that it tells you what skills you will need to complete it successfully. If you don't have those skills, while you're acquiring them you're simultaneously building a better toolbox to create your future successes. Each skill you acquire is another step toward the self-determination that enables you to be the best possible contributor to yourself, others, and humanity.

A good plan provides confidence and clarity in a project, inspiring belief that you can achieve your goals. Many people self-prophesize that they can't succeed because they don't believe they have the necessary history of success to be a winner. Nothing could be farther from the truth. Lack of success for most people is more an issue of never having developed a methodology for setting and reaching goals than any lack of talent or willingness to do it. Once the skill of creating a sound plan for success is learned, reaching goals becomes a lifestyle rather than a hit-or-miss proposition.

One of the most important aspects of living a successful life is to match your goals appropriately with your skill set, available time, and resources. The advantage of accurately constructing your plans before beginning them is that you can identify all the steps required to reach your goal and make sure they're possible within your existing skill set. If your skill set won't provide what you need to complete the steps of your plan, you must either acquire the skills to complete the plan, modify the plan's steps, or change your plan's goal. Never begin a plan until you're absolutely certain you have the skills to see it through to completion.

Another way to expand your skill set is to reduce the complexity of your plan's steps. If you know that your plan is right for you and your skill set indicates you can achieve your goal, yet you stall out on a particular step, that step is probably too complicated and time-consuming. It's a step that needs to be split into smaller, more manageable steps that allow momentum to remain at optimal levels, keeping your plan moving toward completion.

Determining your plan's first step is an art every successful person has learned. Winning plans must always begin at their optimal starting point, which gives them the best possibility that each succeeding step will establish additional momentum. Always devote the time necessary to determine exactly what your plan's first step should be, because that first step sets the tone for the entire plan. It must make a statement to those involved in your plan that it will succeed.

Always make sure your plan's first several steps are easily achieved. This will help your plan gather the initial energy to get rolling, while inspiring others' confidence in it. After successfully completing a handful of successive steps your plan will have a rhythm and be up and running.

> "Always make sure your plan's first several steps are easily achieved."

The better your plans are, the better you can budget and estimate how much time will be needed for you to complete and execute them. All productive people have reconciled that there's not enough time in life to do everything they might like to do, so to get the most out of life they prioritize their plans in order of importance. Then they make the time available to construct their plans correctly, ensuring that they achieve what will bring them the greatest joy and leave the desired legacy. The advantage of accurately forecasting how much time it will take to complete a plan is that you can then budget time for what else you may want to accomplish.

Skillfully constructed plans have very specific goals they are intended to reach. Every step in the plan is designed to take you one step closer to completing your plan with maximum time, energy, and resource conservation. When your plan is sound in its design, you should be able to review it and see with clarity that its steps transition logically and smoothly from one to the next, terminating in the intended goal. If, in your final plan review, the

steps don't look like they'll end up achieving your goal, they can be modified to do so—or the plan can be abandoned. If one step misses the mark,
it can skew your plan off course, making it impossible to reach your original
goal. If such a step is found, remove it from your plan immediately and
replace it with an appropriate step.

You're Only as Successful as Your Last Success

Regardless of your previous accomplishments, you will face the same
daily challenges to create and initiate workable plans to keep your life vital,
attain your aspirations, and remain motivated. Without plans, your life
becomes an uninspired vacuum, void of enthusiasm or the anticipation of
greater things to come. The more time that passes before you initiate and
complete your plans, the less chance they have of occurring and the more
your success skills will atrophy. To fulfill your hopes and dreams, you should
plan to spend time each day creating new plans and revising current ones.
This will keep your planning skills razor sharp and will pave the way for
greater future successes.

History is filled with examples of great plans that have generated great
successes. The first of Lance Armstrong's unprecedented seven consecutive
Tour de France victories is considered by many to be the greatest comeback
in the history of sport. The most distinguishing characteristic about each
of Lance's seven victories was that they were all won in a different way,
based on a specific plan for that specific Tour. The team never tried to win
the same way year after year, as all team members clearly understood that
each year had its own unique circumstances, which dictated how they
needed to prepare and execute. They never attempted to hang onto a plan
that might have been successful in the past but had run its course and
become obsolete. Each off-season, a blueprint for the following year was
created to serve as a guideline to build the best team possible for the
coming season's Tour. In similar fashion, you should always embrace the
best ways to remain at the top of your own game by initiating the most

current and appropriate actions for your specific needs.

Another example of a completely unorthodox but extraordinarily successful plan was implemented by Muhammad Ali, the greatest boxer of all time, for his heavyweight championship fight with George Foreman in Zaire, Africa. At that point in his career, Ali knew Foreman was a vastly more powerful fighter than he was, and he knew that his chances of winning were remote if he tried to match his opponent punch for punch. So instead of moving around the boxing ring to avoid Foreman's punches, as most boxers would do, he deliberately leaned back against the ropes, covering up his head and body with his gloves, to entice Foreman into thinking he was vulnerable. In doing so, he prompted Foreman to consume his energy trying to knock him out. As hoped, Foreman simply punched himself out early in the bout and Ali came back with a vengeance, handily knocking Foreman out to put himself in the history books once again as heavyweight boxing champion of the world.

TURN IT UP! TIPS

1. Maintain a balance between life structure and freedom. People who possess superior planning skills, attention spans, and initiative with incredible consistency also allow themselves room for spontaneity and creativity.

2. To insure your plan reaches completion on schedule always complete each of your plan's steps in its entirety before beginning the next step. This makes the difference between average and great outcomes.

3. To be a top planner, always consider what could possibly go wrong with a plan, and then adopt proactive evasive strategies to circumvent any such problems in advance. This forecasting keeps the plan headed in the correct direction to its timely completion. Remember, an ounce of prevention in your planning is always worth a pound of cure.

TURN IT UP! TIPS (CONT'D)

4. Since you only have so much time in a day and a finite amount sof energy you will only be able to achieve so much in your lifetime. To maximize your life experience and manifest as many of your dreams as possible, prioritize your plans in order of importance. That way those most important aspirations you have will be achieved.

5. Your failures are your greatest life teacher. Life is up and down, and your life momentum and ability to manifest your potential depends more on your keeping your life momentum moving forward in the face of defeat than it does riding the inertia of success. Always remain focused on directing your life momentum forward regardless of circumstances.

6. Never compromise when it comes to the construction and execution of your plans. Shortcutting is the fastest way to make a great plan mediocre.

7. Make sure your skill set matches your plan. Most often, the biggest limiting factor in achieving a goal is not the plan but having the skills to complete the actions steps to reach the plan's goal.

8. Make a formal written plan check-off sheet, so each time you finish a step you can physically check it off. As insignificant as this may seem, it's one of the strongest validations of your success creation program. Every time you check off a completed step it confirms the efficacy of your plan and that your plan will reach its goal.

9

Formulating Your
Winning Plan

*The secret of all victory lies in
the organization of the nonobvious.*

—Oswald Spengler

Formulating your winning plan is easy and very straightforward when
you know your plan is right for you and you have the structure and
skills to create it. It's really no different than if you were to plan a
blowout birthday party for a good friend. It's simply a matter of defining
and putting the steps into a logical sequence to make the party a standout
event. First you decide whom you're going to invite, what the theme of the
party will be, when it will happen, and where it will be held, then fill in
the details.

Like the list you'd make for a party, the starting point for your plan is to
always develop and refine it in written form because you'll accomplish
more in less time with greater results and more resource conservation.

163

Written documents also provide the objectivity for you to see accurately how the steps of your plan move logically from inception to completion while achieving your desired outcome. This lessens the risk that you'll omit necessary steps, include unnecessary steps, or make regretful, impulsive, overemotional decisions, attempting to increase your plan's benefits, when in reality you may be exposing it to significant downside liabilities.

Always make every effort to construct your plan correctly the first time so its execution goes as smoothly as possible from the beginning. Written plans offer that opportunity.

> "Writing out your plan creates an objective life road map."

Written documents also conserve massive amounts of mental energy and time because you know exactly where you are in your plan at all times. This allows you to pace yourself better because you're confident of where your life and plan are headed, unlike people who randomly make life up as they go, treading on the ultrathin ice of letting life "unfold as it should." The mental burden of uncertainty experienced by those who live their lives on the fly can completely disconnect them from ever living carefree, confident, yet appropriately spontaneous lives. Writing out your plan creates an objective life road map that eliminates the "make it up as you go and let's see what happens" factor that predictably produces fear, frustration, inaccuracy, assumption, wasted time, and confusion.

Your written document only needs to be detailed enough so your plan's steps transition smoothly and coherently from one to another on the way to plan completion so you can proceed confidently. Exhaustive, super-detailed, novel-length plans are unnecessary and often serve only to exacerbate already confused lives.

Build the Bond of Commitment

When you write down your winning plan, you also create a greater bond of commitment between you and your plan. What you write, regardless of length, is, in a sense, a contract between you and it, and most people take written agreements much more seriously than verbal ones.

Always have your written plan with you so you can access it at a moment's notice and make spontaneous amendments as they occur to you. Often the most creative and pivotal insights you'll have that influence your plan's success will occur at unanticipated times and vanish as quickly as they appeared. Having your plan at hand also gives you the option of glancing at it when time permits. This is always beneficial, as it gives you a snapshot and overall impression of your plan, exposing weaknesses that need to be improved upon but that might not be so obvious when intently working on the plan's details.

Usually your initial impressions when first looking at your plan indicate where it hits and misses its mark. Remember that it's always best to trust your first impression, make the changes, then leave it alone and come back to review it later. If you look at something too long, too intently, you'll talk yourself out of what you know needs to be done. Given enough refinement time, eventually you'll look at your written plan and know it fully represents your aspirations.

Formulating great plans always takes more time than originally believed, and several generations of refinement are usually necessary to reach final form. This can take minutes, hours, days, or longer to achieve. Always take as much time as you need to make sure everything associated with your plan is written just the way you intend it to happen. That's what the success pros do. Never be in such a hurry that you make an unforced, impulsive mistake. Leave that to the amateurs.

Making a one-page flowchart of your plan can be extremely helpful in creating and executing your winning plan. Whether you have a very elaborate plan or a very simple one, a single-page diagram showing how the steps flow from start to finish will inspire confidence in your plan formulation process, often making it much easier to comply with, especially if you are a visual learner. This also allows you to envision everything on one page so you can readily see the big picture. Without the ability to see the panoramic view of your plan, understanding its subtleties might not happen as easily as necessary for its smooth execution, thereby increasing the risk of poor timing and unforeseen delays that unnecessarily consume time, effort, and resources.

Building your winning plan requires that you incorporate into it your best uncensored possibility thinking ideas. Correctly placing them within your plan for maximum benefit requires that you have a fresh mind, so you must always balance your mental efforts with adequate rest. A rested mind always makes the best decisions. Never mentally or physically push yourself excessively when developing your plan, as that only creates confusion that chips away at your confidence in your judgments about your plan. At the first sign of fatigue, it's time to turn your computer and mind off.

Sharing your thoughts and plans with others is always a great idea. Others' fresh, objective insights can be extremely constructive and make your plans much, much better. Let others help you create your best plans so your dreams manifest quickly and you can move on to your next success. Never be bashful about asking people for their input, because most love to share their knowledge and experience and are honored by your request.

Determining if Your Plan's Right for You

Knowledge, enthusiasm, and passion are the secret ingredients that constitute great plans. These extremely vital and essential attributes only occur when your plan is right for you. Prior to formulating your formal written plan, you must always do a "plan check" analysis to confirm that your plan is a perfect fit for you. You always reach completion more quickly and more efficiently with plans that are fully compatible with you than you do with those that are impulsively embraced and hastily begun without proper evaluation or preparation.

To evaluate whether your plan is right for you requires you to determine with absolute certainty that its vision, intention, viability, impact, and feasibility will create exactly what you intend to accomplish. If even one portion of any of these criteria fails to meet your expectation, it makes reaching your plan's original goal virtually impossible and, perhaps, means the plan is not right for you. Please bear in mind that learning to say no to an incompatible plan is as empowering for you as saying yes to a plan that meets your criteria. You must evaluate and accept the following areas unconditionally to confirm that your plan is right for you.

Vision. Your plan's vision is the original idea to which you aspired. A very good friend of mine, Randy Grubb, had a vision to build a car that Jay Leno would buy for his car collection. Randy's vision wasn't about the practicality of how he would design or build the car. It was purely about his passion to do something he saw was possible. Visions are broad-based, sweeping concepts only detailed enough to allow the evaluation of those elements necessary to confirm that your plan's right for you.

Intention. Your plan's intention is the endpoint your plan is specifically designed to achieve. It is crystal clear, black and white, and never ambiguous. For example, Randy's intention was to build a unique, custom-made, one-of-a-kind car that Leno would buy.

Your plan's intention also gives you the motivation and passion to complete your plans on time. This is important for your evolution as a winner, because to become a consistent goal achiever you must self-generate the vitality, excitement, and anticipation needed to accomplish your goals on time one after another. All great achievers have natural initiative and never require someone else's motivation to get the job done.

Every word you choose to describe your plan's intention must be carefully selected to represent precisely what you want your plan to produce. Your plan's intention entrains your subconscious mind and every cell in your body toward achieving exactly what you've deliberately and consciously defined. We all know that what we ask for most often comes true. So why not intend the biggest and best results as long as you're intending something anyway?

> "All great achievers have natural initiative and never require someone else's motivation to get the job done."

Never settle for anything less than the best.

Viability. "Is my plan viable?" is a question that you must seriously contemplate before investing the time and effort to construct a fully developed, formal, written plan. This is, unfortunately for some, the evaluation point they fail to assess most adequately. To be viable, your plan's outcome must give back to you more than you put into it, and the exchange can be anything as long as you feel you've been given equal to or more than fair value for what you've put into your plan. Intrinsically, every plan's outcome at completion has a free market value in every circumstance that can be used as a currency of exchange in that domain. For example, Randy's car could have tremendous value to Leno and other exotic car collectors but none to someone living in Antarctica. This makes Randy's selling his car in Antarctica unviable, while it is highly viable in the world of Jay Leno and other exotic car collectors.

A good example of a plan intention–viability mismatch comes from an acquaintance I had who designed and built a prototype rifle-shooting bench. The editor of a top marksman magazine told the person his bench was the best sighting bench he'd ever seen. Encouraged by the comments, the person invested significant time and money to secure a booth at a major firearms show to sell his "best ever" sighting bench to fellow marksmen. Unfortunately, he received no orders because he failed to do a viability assessment of the marksmanship community that would have clearly revealed that marksmen did not need or want to buy his bench. Therefore, his currency of exchange was zero because the domain it was placed in wasn't viable.

On the other hand, Randy's car is a spectacular example of perfect plan viability. Prior to spending the time and effort creating the plans for building his car, Randy calculated what cost the car would have to sell for to provide the exchange he needed to create the car. That sum combined with his intimate knowledge of the car collector industry's pricing structure indicated that he would, with almost all certainty, sell his car for the asking price, thus making it an exceedingly viable proposition for him. The first time the car was displayed publicly it drew rave reviews by the press, car collectors, and enthusiasts, with word ultimately reaching Leno, who eventually bought the car for the price Randy determined would be fair and necessary. From this one sale, Randy transformed his life into his dream. He now spends every moment of each day dreaming up, building, and selling one-of-a-kind cars to car collectors.

Impact. You must always consider your plan's impact on everyone and everything. Plans affect you, those involved with your plan, anyone associated with anybody involved in your plan, society, the environment, and, ultimately, all of humanity, in ways you will never even realize. Since, as it's said, there are only six degrees of separation between everyone, and all people share in the health of humanity and the environment, even the smallest, most innocuous event can affect everything and everyone on the planet. To assess the scope of your plan's impact, it's prudent to perform an impact analysis: a simple, structured means of objectively seeing your plan's impact on people, places, and things prior to formulating your written plan. This allows you to identify just how compatible your plan is with your vision, and whether the plan is right for you.

> "You must always consider your plan's impact on everyone and everything."

An impact analysis is easy to do. Simply take out paper and pencil or get on your computer. First, write your plan's intention in the center of the top of a blank page as the title—for example, "Intention: To build a custom, one-of-a-kind car that Jay Leno will buy." Next, divide the page into three equal columns below the title. In the left column, list all the people, places, and things your plan could affect. In the middle column, itemize your plan's positive benefits next to the corresponding item in the left column. In the right column list the negative outcomes of your plan in line with the other two entries. Once completed, the three columns will show you objectively the impact your plan will have on virtually everything. You'll then be able to decide objectively if your plan's impact is consistent with your values and your plan is right for you.

Feasibility. The final step in determining whether your plan's right for you is to assess its feasibility. You've got to know emphatically and with 100 percent certainty that your plan can get done. You can't dream or guess on this. Those who have rolled the dice when the feasibility of their plan is in question have ended up paying a heavy price for their guesstimating. You must be absolutely clear whether or not you have the skills, time, and financial and human resources to execute your plan from start to finish in a timely manner. Few things are worse than having a great plan stop, wilt, and die midway to completion from a lack of resources. To know your plan's feasibility, you must do a feasibility study.

A feasibility study begins by writing "Feasibility Study," the day's date, and your plans intention at the top of a piece of paper or computer screen. Next, on the left side of the page, in order of importance and magnitude from top to bottom, jot down the steps and everything that must get done to complete your plan. To the right of the steps, list the skills, finances, and time you estimate are needed to complete the steps. In the real world it will generally take 25 to 50 percent more resources to get plans completed than you think it will, so go for the maximum on this and add 50 percent to your figures. Once you have placed all the resource requirements next to the steps, you can accurately assess whether the resources are available to manifest your plan's intention.

If the resources aren't there on paper, you must determine what it would take to get them. If you find yourself in the gray zone and uncertain as to whether adequate resources can be acquired, always step back and take all the time necessary to ensure they and be before commencing your formal written plan. Again, always keep in mind that, inevitably, it always takes more time and resources to complete your plans than you think it will. Always make sure you have enough time to get the job done. You never want to come up short once your plan is underway. If all five of your plan's criteria meet your satisfaction in determining if your plan is right for you, it is. If you're not sure, or have determined it isn't, you either need to do what's nec-essary to make all five criteria acceptable or elect not to execute your plan.

It can take minutes, hours, days, or longer to determine if your plan's right for you, but at a specific point in your investigation you will know beyond a doubt whether or not it is. When it is, you may experience, as many people do, an intuitive knowing—most people describe it as being a feeling in their solar plexus (or gut)—that feels as if a door has swung wide open, inviting them to come join the party. If your plan's not right for you, you may find the opposite, with your solar plexus tightening and feeling like a blinking red light has gone off inside you, or as if a wall has been built in front of you, preventing you from proceeding forward to embrace your plan. Never proceed with a plan when you feel like that. Many have done so to their peril. If, however, your internal green light illuminates, immediately proceed with your plan.

Your Winning Plan's Hierarchy

Winning plans always accomplish their goals by following a well-established hierarchy of important elements that establish communication flows that coalesce all your plan's resources, brain power, and energy into doable, well-synchronized steps that, when completed, achieve the plan's goal. This hierarchy is composed of four elements: Goal, Purpose, Outcome, Steps.

Successful plan hierarchies are built from top to bottom in order of importance. Your hierarchy's sole mission is to steer your plan toward successful completion, and for this to happen it's imperative that each of the four elements constituting your plan's hierarchy be in total agreement with your plan's original vision. This agreement is the most fundamental element in formulating your winning plan. When the four elements are aligned, the transitions between your plan's steps occur easily, each step building additional momentum toward attaining your plan's goal in minimal time. Disordered plans, conversely, only produce chaos and frustration, making it impossible for them to create winning outcomes.

Your winning plan's hierarchy of elements, in order of priority, are goal, purpose, outcome, and steps. Each must be worded as concisely as possible, since what each states is, most often, exactly the outcome it produces.

Goal. Your plan's goal is much more than just a culmination of actions; it is a termination point in space and time that affects many people, places, and things. Your plan's goal is the highest-ranking element in its hierarchy, the whole reason your plan exists. It is the single culminating event that concisely states your original vision's outcome that each of your plan's steps is geared toward achieving. Your goal, in effect, is a deliberate, conscious covenant with yourself that creates a bond of trust and commitment between you and you, and you and your plan. It drives your subconscious mind to uphold your commitments to those associated with your plan, pro-vides the mental compass to keep your plan moving toward reaching com-pletion on time, and enables you to find ways to achieve outcomes that were previously outside your reach.

Randy Grubb's goal was to create a car Jay Leno would buy. Once he and his wife committed to the goal, it only required the capital, time, effort, and energy to create and execute his plan to reach his goal.

Purpose. Your plan's purpose states the specific benefits your plan's goal provides. The purpose of Randy's plan was to build a car that, when sold to Jay Leno, would provide him and his wife the capital to allow his greatest talents to flourish by giving him the occupation of his dreams, bringing joy to Leno's life, employing others so they could take care of their families, and inspiring people to strive for, create, and execute their own plans to live highly rewarding lives.

Outcome. Your plan's outcome is extremely straightforward and uncom-plicated. It is where your plan's steps culminate when successfully com-pleted. Randy achieved his plan's outcome when he finished and sold his custom, one-of-a-kind car, exactly as he had envisioned it, to Leno.

Steps. The final element necessary to complete your formalized plan is to determine the steps needed to achieve your plan's outcome. Steps are essentially individualized minigoals constructed to transition seamlessly from one to another in order to achieve your plan's outcome. When all your plan's steps are strung together, your plan should be a single, rational, cohesive chain of steps with logical, well-defined objectives.

The best plans have the fewest number of large steps. Large jumps in difficulty and sophistication between a plan's steps slow its progression and may even exceed skill sets, slowing or preventing step completion or stalling or even terminating the plan. It's much better to make two smaller steps from a single larger step when necessary so your plan's momentum continues unimpeded to completion.

Randy's "Leno car" is a perfect example of step sequencing. Of the thousands of steps required to build the car over eighteen months, the major ones included creating a generalized plan that included designing the car, expanding his garage to house the car's construction, obtaining the equipment required to build the car, purchasing supplies and parts, acquiring help to construct the car, and creating an accounting system to manage capital inflow and outflow. These larger steps were further broken down into smaller tasks, each with its own goal. For example, the large step of doing construction on his garage included the smaller steps of subcontracting with electricians, plumbers, painters, and framers, getting permits, and working with bank financing. These tasks were further broken down into minitasks with their own goals. Ultimately, with enough step divisions, the correct number of steps to achieve his goal was determined and sequenced. At that point, Randy only had to execute his plan, which he did, and Leno now happily owns his car and Randy's living the life of his dreams.

Since effective plan formulation determines your plan's success, always take as much time as necessary to refine your plan's hierarchy fully so its steps are appropriately spaced and sized and consistent with your skill set. Little is more rewarding than to effortlessly achieve a plan's outcome through proper plan formulation. In addition, few things are worse than rushing a plan's construction only to have it fall off track during implementation.

Knowing When to Stretch Yourself

Deciding when and when not to embrace a risk is a dilemma everyone shares. When a doable opportunity isn't capitalized on, it's lost forever, your life fails to improve, and your success baseline isn't raised. Similarly, if you embrace a risk and it fails, you've not only consumed valuable time and resources that can never be retrieved, but also possibly increased the chances you'll never risk success again, only undertaking less than optimal opportunities when you know you can succeed, which creates at best a very bland and noncommitted life.

To grow you must stretch yourself appropriately. At certain times it's critical to undertake a project that forces you to stretch your existing mental and skill limits so you can advance your life and increase your competency. To understand when these times occur, follow these guidelines:

- Always consider embracing an opportunity when you believe you can successfully capitalize on it. Regardless of what the facts say, if you know you can do it, strongly consider doing it, even though you may never have done it before.

- If an opportunity has been dropped into your lap—almost too easily—and you have the time to do it, it instinctively seems the right thing to do, and you question if you have the skills to do it but know you can, you must embrace it without hesitation. These opportunities don't come often and are gifts given to show you that you are capable of greater success. Whenever these signs accompany an opportunity, seize the moment without hesitation.

- As you develop your skills, a time will come when their development is sufficient and their fine-tuning can only be accomplished by using them in real-life situations. When it's time to implement a new skill, do it without restraint. The only way to put the final polish on your new skills is to use them. Once they've

KNOWING WHEN TO STRETCH YOURSELF (CONT'D)

reached a certain point, no amount of thinking or practicing will
refine them to their maximum more than doing them.

• Whenever the signs point to a success and your creative instinct
screams at you to do something but your fear-based self holds you
back from acting, it is without question time to implement. Feel the
fear and do it anyway.

• If you find yourself stagnant and in a period of no growth, it's time to
initiate an action you've never done before. Your slumber isn't from
lack of capacity but from lack of initiative and challenge. The fastest
way to reignite your creativity is to do something beyond your
current level of achievement, because your mind, body, and spirit
have become dormant. Pick something that's easy to do, that you've
never done before, and that you find exhilarating and challenging.
The sooner you do it, the better you'll feel.

Formulating Your Winning Plan from Start to Finish

Now that you've learned the skills to determine if your plan's right for you
and to develop its hierarchy, let's formulate a sample winning plan by combining both of those steps from start to finish. Our hypothetical plan will be
simple but effective to illustrate how to formulate a complete plan with all its
elements. More elaborate plans will require greater detail, but the methodology remains the same, with many plans requiring several generations of refinement to reach their final form. Simple and uncluttered plans are always better
to formulate on your first pass because they show the flow and transitions
between steps better than lengthy, superdetailed, and often confusing initial
plans. Once the overall plan has been visualized, additions and exclusions can
be incorporated into it until it reaches its final incarnation.

The first step to formulating our hypothetical plan is deciding if it's right for us. This step determines if the five areas of plan compatibility meet our criteria for plan acceptance. If all five are compatible with what we want our plan's outcome to be, our plan is right for us and we can move on to its second step: formulating our formal written winning plan. The five areas for review are the plan's vision, intention, viability, impact, and feasibility.

Vision. Our plan's vision is the original idea that inspired its creation. It needs only to be refined enough to confirm that we'll consider the other elements to determine its correctness for us. In this example, let's state our vision as building a two-story, green-design home on a small vacant lot. Let's state that it meets our approval so we can then evaluate the other four factors to determine if the plan is right for us.

Intention. Our plan's intention is the outcome it will produce. This intention is always crystal clear, black and white, and never ambiguous. Let's define our intention in this example as building an affordable, beautiful, contemporary, green-design, 2,000-square-foot, two-story, four-bedroom home constructed of glass, steel, and concrete, with drought-tolerant landscape on a small vacant lot. We'll accept this intention so we move to the next criteria.

Viability. To be viable, our plan's intention and outcome must give back to us more than we put into it. In this example, let's state that our intention is to build and live in our house for five years, then sell it and make a nice profit from the sale and leave the neighborhood a more beautiful place than when we arrived. We'll determine that these meet our criteria so we next look at our plan's impact.

Impact. We must do a plan impact analysis to be certain it will affect us, those involved with our plan, anyone associated with anybody involved in our plan, society, the environment, and humanity in the manner we intended. In our example, our house will be designed using energy-efficient, green-design principles, constructed of ecofriendly materials; it will be fully financed; and the architect and general contractor are known to finish projects on time, so there will be no negative impact to either those associated with the project or the environment. We accept the impact of our plan so, next, move to the final element in deciding if our plan's right for us—feasibility.

Feasibility. For our plan to reflect our vision, we must be absolutely certain the necessary skills, time, and financial and human resources exist to execute it from start to finish unimpeded. In our mock plan, let's say that the proper architect and building contractor have been secured to design and construct our home, the financing for construction is in place, and the construction timeline meets our needs perfectly.

In our hypothetical plan example, all of the criteria have met our standards for accepting our plan as being right for us. In reality, if any didn't meet our standards, we would have the option of upgrading them so they do or foregoing the plan.

Since we've determined that our plan is right for us, we must now formulate our formal, written, winning plan. It is composed of four elements constituting our plan's hierarchy of importance: its goal, purpose, outcome, and steps.

Goal. Our goal is a highly refined, precisely worded statement expressing our original vision's outcome. It is the focal point that each of our plan's steps is geared toward achieving. In our example, our goal is to build an affordable, beautiful, contemporary, green-design, 2,000-square-foot, two-story, four-bedroom home constructed of glass, steel, and concrete, with drought-tolerant landscape on a small vacant lot. Doing so will allow us, and those living there, to develop the best relationships possible, have the optimal space to perform life's tasks the best they can be done, in the least time, with the least effort, while fully recovering from the stresses and strains of daily life, and having fun doing it.

Purpose. Our plan's purpose is to express the specific benefits its goal provides. Let's state this hypothetically as being able to provide shelter and the best living environment possible for everyone living in the house, enabling them to complete the tasks of daily living necessary to become the best people they can be while helping and supporting others to become the best they can be. Further, we want to make the neighborhood a more

KNOWING WHEN A PLAN IS BEYOND YOUR REACH

There are times when a plan you're considering will be beyond your reach and you might not even know it. There are also those plans that you want to undertake but fear they may be too advanced for your skills and resources. Before committing to any plan, always take the time to answer a few questions to determine if it is within or beyond your reach. If any of the questions can't be answered in the affirmative toward successfully completing your plan, give that plan a pass until such time as they can be given a resounding affirmative answer. To know whether a plan is within or beyond your reach, it's most important to take a long, hard, objective look at it when you have clarity of thought and are not blinded by being overly excited about it. Being too excited can blind you to the reality of what it takes to achieve the goal, which sets you up for failure.

- Is the timing right to undertake the plan so that it's not being stuffed into an imaginary time slot that's not really there?
- Are the skills, time, and financial resources available to complete your plan successfully with a little in reserve?
- Should it be required, is there enough flexibility to accommodate additional time to complete the plan? Remember, it always takes more time than you expect to finish a project.
- Has your intuitive "Do not do this" internal red light come on at any time while contemplating your plan? If it has, have you ignored it or tried to pretend it's not there?
- Does your plan cause you anxiety throughout the day or keep you up at night?
- Are your friends encouraging you to do the plan even though you have reservations about it?
- Can you undertake your plan without suspending a plan that's already in motion?

beautiful place and turn a nice profit when the house is sold in five years.

Outcome. Our plan's outcome is the endpoint at which the plan's steps will culminate once they are successfully completed. Our desired outcome in our example will be to build an affordable, beautiful, contemporary, green-design home, with drought-tolerant landscape, on a small vacant lot, so those living there can grow closer together and become the best that they can be while having fun doing it. And, when the house sells in five years, a nice profit will be made.

Steps. Our plan's steps are essentially individualized minigoals constructed to transition seamlessly from one to another, ultimately achieving our plan's outcome. The main steps to be done to reach our goal in our example are to secure the construction loan, contract with the architect and general contractor for the job, formulate appropriate substeps under our plan's main steps, and regularly go to the construction site to ensure that everything's proceeding forward on time.

The hypothetical formal written plan we've just formulated has confirmed that our plan is right for us and that the hierarchy is doable within our timeframe, resource pool, financial abilities, and skill set. To refine the plan further, we could have it reviewed by trusted and capable people who can provide constructive ideas for improvement. Once their useful ideas have been placed within the plan, it will be fully developed and ready for implementation.

> "If you find yourself stagnant and in a period of no growth, it's time to initiate an action you've never done before."

TURN IT UP! TIPS

1. Write your plans down. Written plans produce the best results because they have well-thought-out, logical, and appropriately sequenced steps that inspire a high level of commitment from those involved in the plan. Writing down your plan will also reduce mental stress and simplify plan modification.

2. Make sure your plan's right for you. When your plan's vision, intention, viability, and impact represent your wishes, your plans are right. If they aren't, then they must be modified for compliance or abandoned altogether.

3. Solicit the input of others. Your plan is only as strong as its vision, organization, and execution. Always share your plan with trusted people and enlist their input for constructive criticism. A fresh pair of eyes often sees the missing links that make average plans spectacular. Don't be bashful to ask for input, because most people love to share their knowledge and experience and will be honored by your request.

4. Be very specific in what you want your plan's goal to achieve because it will significantly affect you, others, places, and things.

5. All great achievers have natural initiative and never require someone else's motivation to get the job done. If you have questionable motivation to begin or complete a plan, then either the plan is not right for you, you are tired and need more recovery, or the plan is being executed at the wrong time.

6. Don't proceed with a plan if your gut is telling you it's not right for you. Conversely, if your instincts tell you the plan is a fit, move ahead. Your instincts are often the best criteria for plan selection because they are based on more information and pattern recognition than your intellect.

7. When it's time to implement a new skill, do it without hesitation. The only way to know your skill competency is to employ the skill in a real-life situation—something practice will never do. The process of implementation is its own skill-learning tutorial.

TURN IT UP! TIPS (CONT'D)

8. Your mind deplores sameness. If you find yourself unmotivated, bored, or restless, then it is time to wake up your mind, body, and spirit by undertaking a small project that you find exhilarating and challenging. Pick something crazy and outrageous that excites you. The sooner you do it, the better you'll feel.

9. When devising your plan's outcome always make sure it has the potential to return to you an equal or higher investment. Fairness of exchange is a universal criterion to create win-wins.

10

How to Execute
Your Winning Plan

*Continuous effort—not strength or
intelligence—is the key to unlocking our potential.*

—Liane Cardes

Now that you've finished formulating your winning plan, it's time to get on with the business of successfully executing and completing your plan. Successful plan execution requires that you continually make appropriate adjustments to your plan during its implementation so your plan can be completed on time.

By far, the most challenging feat is to gather and maintain maximum plan momentum so you achieve your goal on schedule. Every plan is bombarded incessantly by external forces that chip away relentlessly at its integrity and continuity—all potentially neutralizing its forward progress toward an on-time completion. The key to successful plan implementation is to have your well-constructed plan supported by sound implementation strategies. This chapter shows you winning methods to execute your plan's action steps efficiently, which enables you to manifest your plan and your visions, hopes, and dreams on time.

Communication Flows

Effective communication makes the difference between mediocrity and greatness when it comes to the execution and outcome of any plan. When correct information can be exchanged quickly and efficiently among the proper people, plans generate peak momentum and roll on to completion on or ahead of schedule. Conversely, poor information exchange produces ineffective decisions and actions that, unfortunately, consume time, energy, and expense, stalling, or—worse—rendering a plan unviable.

> "Effective communication makes the difference between mediocrity and greatness when it comes to the execution and outcome of any plan."

To keep your plan screaming along to completion you'll need to create two documents: one that indicates how information flows among people and another showing plan step completion dates.

To maximize the accuracy and speed of correct information exchange within your plan, always make sure everyone associated with your plan clearly understands who's responsible for what and how information flows between people. This allows people to complete their jobs efficiently without constantly being interrupted by requests and questions that don't fall under their jurisdiction. Always create and distribute a short and concise written policy statement to everyone associated with your plan describing in detail who is responsible for what and where inquiries should be directed. Solid communication lines will not only save a tremendous amount of time and reduce frustration, but also will fortify unity of purpose and solidarity of commitment among those associated with your plan, facilitating its timely arrival at its outcome.

A step-completion timeline illustrating each of your plan's steps, in sequence, with their completion dates will dramatically enhance your and your team's confidence in your plan's initial execution and, once the plan is underway, its pacing and accuracy toward an on-time completion. During intense periods of plan execution, when much is happening simultaneously within your plan, it's quite easy to lose track of where you are, how much you've accomplished, and how far you have yet to go. This can easily lead to mental confusion, frustration, and errors that can quickly compromise a great plan.

Knowing exactly what plan step you're on by glancing at your timeline diagram also gives you the ability to adapt your step-execution pacing quickly. You can speed it up, slow it down, or maintain the same pace. This keeps your plan moving progressively forward toward a predictable completion and gives you the confidence of knowing you haven't overlooked any steps that could cause you to backtrack and lose valuable time. Being uncertain about where you are in your plan implementation consumes tremendous mental energy from worry, which fatigues the physical body and, thereby, reduces your productivity and increases the risk of mental errors. Correct pacing allows plan modifications to occur most easily.

Ready for Liftoff

Just prior to the commencement of any plan, a brief period of apprehension is often experienced by almost everyone involved. Most often this produces either a withdrawal response or exaggerated extroverted behavior. Both can be either good or bad for the plan's kickoff. If the behavior puts minds at ease, producing precise plan execution, it's a good thing. If, however, it paralyzes or skews your mind off course, disrupting the ability to implement your plan, it's a bad thing.

An effective way to put minds at ease and ensure the best mind-set possible for successfully initiating your plan is to have a brief meeting immediately prior to your plan launch with all involved in your plan, even if it's only with yourself. This is where you review what your initial plan execution process will be so everybody is crystal clear on when and where the plan will be executed, what the circumstances are expected to be, what their tasks will consist of, and what the communication lines will be. Once that's done, any questions can be answered. Always provide a written handout that summarizes your plan's launch and all points discussed, because it will serve as a reference to keep people on track at that critical time.

Such a meeting serves to steady minds and emotions, and it will also strengthen the bonds of commitment among those involved in executing your plan. A poignant example of this was seen at Tours de France I did with the United States Postal Service and Discovery Professional Cycling Teams. The day before each Tour de France began, every team member would withdraw to the privacy of their own room to contemplate what the three-week-long Tour might bring them and the team. Customarily, the team director would call a meeting with team and staff the night before the Tour began to brief everyone on strategic and logistic issues and answer any questions pertaining to the event's beginning the next day. The benefit of the meeting, beyond the simple mechanical passing on of information and the restating of each individual's role in the team's race structure, was that it put everyone's mind at ease by answering any questions and providing concrete facts that framed the reality of what that year's Tour would most likely bring. Steady minds always produce better results than apprehensive ones, especially during the exceptionally tense period surrounding any plan's inception.

> "Steady minds always produce better results than apprehensive ones."

You must do everything possible to start your plan on time. The longer it takes to begin your plan, the more energy it will take to get it going and the less likely it will be to get done. There will be days when you don't feel like working on your plan, but you can never wait until you do because you probably never will. Just commit to doing it, step up, and do it. You'll feel incredibly empowered each time you do this. Transcending the inclination to shun working on your plan elevates your self-respect, confidence, and commitment to excellence. Since there's no assurance that time will be available in the future to do what can be done at the moment, the best time to do something is when it's on the calendar and the time has arrived.

Keeping Your Plan on Track

Once you've initiated the first step of your plan, your focus must shift to keeping it on track, enabling it to proceed on schedule toward reaching its goal on time. Keeping your plan on track is a very dynamic process requiring skill, composure, and good judgment. Every plan has its own unique challenges that, if not quickly overcome, unravel it—often to the point of making it unviable. The best defense against these undesirable intrusions is the aggressive and swift implementation of proven proactive strategies that eliminate doubt and provide early intervention to keep your plan proceeding forward.

Show up for duty. Some of your best plan outcomes occur just from showing up day after day and executing your plan. The magic of "doing" generates innovation and many times leads to unanticipated plan modifications that create spectacular outcomes that can dramatically transcend your original intention. Both Silly Putty and Post-it notes are examples of incredibly successful products that were actually byproducts of other plans. We all have days when we don't feel like working on our plan, but that day may just turn out to be the one when the new innovation shows up to become your meal ticket to a life-advancing occurrence. That's an opportunity no one should ever miss.

Never assume anything. Every successful enterprise succeeds because of its clarity and certainty about who's doing what, when, and how. Nothing ever runs on assumption. Assumptions are infamous consumers of time and breeders of disappointment. When in doubt about anything, always get immediate clarification directly from the primary source. Never get information secondhand. Nobody has a crystal ball or is a mind reader, and assumptions that don't represent what something really is always lead to disharmony, loss of trust, and wasted time, all of which can tear a great plan to shreds.

Always expect the unexpected. An axiom all successful people live by is "One should always expect the unexpected," so when it occurs they're ready for it. Life is peculiar in that it seems whenever you're not prepared for something, it will happen. Though all plans come with the promise of a life-enriching payoff, no plan ever comes with a money-back guarantee. Regardless of how good a plan is, or how much you may believe in its outcome, every plan has an inherent wild-card factor to it. Your best plan outcome is determined by how quickly you identify the skewing and how astute your course corrections are. When reviewing your daily plan, it's always wise to identify and be mindful of any undesirable direction any step in your plan may take, so if it begins to drift off course you can quickly make course corrections to maintain optimal momentum. Cover your bases by making contingencies for what will most likely happen and for best- and worst-case scenarios.

> "Nothing ever runs on assumption."

Listen to the "Other Voice." Most of what bumps plans off track are small things that usually have a forewarning that's ignored because of their smallness. We've all experienced a situation where a fleeting premonition jumps in and out of our consciousness in a split second, giving advance warning of a potentially hazardous outcome. Well, that's our "Other Voice." The one that helps us rather than taunts us like The Voice discussed in Chapter 3 that tries to talk us out of everything good in life. Our Other Voice is frequently dismissed as being insignificant because of its size, its irrelevance to present circumstances, or a belief that "Life will take care of it" or that the strength of our assets will neutralize it.

The impact of ignoring such "small" insights can be life altering. One day in my early twenties I was riding a dirt bike when a premonition popped into my mind, telling me that if I didn't slow down I was going to crash and get hurt. I ignored the warning and a few seconds later found myself lying on the ground, wincing in pain and with an injured foot, vividly recalling the crystal-clear warning I had been given. Had I not dismissed the warning, I wouldn't have had to have a skin graft on my foot or hobble around on crutches for a month. Warnings speak softly. Listen to them, because when heeded they can save you tremendous grief and be of extraordinary benefit.

Small problems grow big quickly. Never dismiss small or seemingly innocuous problems because they balloon very quickly to staggering proportion when not resolved, and they never go away until they are resolved. Roger de Coster, one of the great legends in motocross told me that he always looked at small things as though they would become astronomically large if not resolved in their infancy. He said he was always perplexed that others seemed to have the opposite view, asking why, if something was so small, they should bother with it at all. Well, the proof's in the pudding, as they say, and that's the reason he became an icon in his field.

Do it your way. The only thing relevant to any plan is that it's successfully completed. How the plan gets done has no significance as long as it's achieved with the highest ethics and respect for all. The only "best way" to execute your plan is to use your personal execution style and methodology. Many successful businesses have moved away from the traditional management style of dictating how outcomes are achieved to the more effective means of letting those executing the plans decide. Once you've found your preferred way to execute your plans, stick steadfastly with the methodology as it will consistently deliver your goals.

Be organized. Plans always stay on track and advance more quickly when they are highly organized. Keeping an exact inventory of supplies and materials and reordering supplies in advance of running out always keep your plan moving forward efficiently to completion. When you reorder supplies, always allow extra time for their arrival because it's not uncommon for shipped items to arrive after their anticipated delivery date. Always have a well-organized system for storing your supplies so they're readily accessible when you need them. Disorganized supply storage can create frustration and lost time, both detrimental to any plan.

Continually refine your plan-executing capacity. In today's competitive world, staying on top of your game demands that you continually improve your capacity to execute your plan. Take the time to investigate the success methodologies of both the most successful people in your field and the younger up-and-comers. Those who have been around the block a few times have proven track records and highly refined implementation strategies that have been tested by time and proven successful on the playing field. "New kids on the block" have fresh minds, boundless enthusiasm for excellence, intimate knowledge of contemporary technology, and passion for what they do. Since their innovations will make them the pillars of the next generation of successful people, their methodologies deserve serious consideration.

Always follow the "better way." Regardless of how perfect your plan may be, changes will have to be made along its course for it to reach its goal. Whenever your plan starts to veer off course, always give the new direction serious consideration, as it can often be a "better way" to reach a better outcome. Resist the tendency to push the panic button because you fear your original plan is deviating from its original course or that its demise is imminent. Rarely is that the case, and it's more likely that your trepidation and fear, not the deviation, will cause your plan to implode. When confronted with this type of circumstance, always give yourself and your plan the courtesy of stepping back from taking any action until you can objectively and fairly assess the new direction. You might be surprised to find it's a better route to success.

> "Whenever your plan starts to veer off course, always give the new direction serious consideration, as it can often be a 'better way' to reach a better outcome."

Struggle Is Your Friend

No plan ever goes from start to finish completely without incident. Most plans that achieve spectacular outcomes stumble many times en route but reach completion because those executing them have the resolve to surmount whatever obstacles arise. Times of trial are an essential rite of passage from which no one is exempt. We've all endured them, and most have understood that they provide opportunities to access a deeper sense of purpose and allow our hidden talents to surface, helping us to become the best people we can be and to achieve the greatest success possible. Having proven strategies to keep your plans moving forward toward success during times of challenge is essential. During tough times these strategies are often all that keeps you going.

Just keep moving. Everybody at some point in their life gets backed into a life predicament that appears to have no way out. The only option available at those times is to formulate and execute the best plan possible that leads to resolution. First, do your homework to get the facts regarding how best to resolve your predicament, then construct and execute your plan to do so. Once your plan is in motion, implicitly trust that it will get you beyond your crisis and just keep putting one foot in front of the other executing the plan's steps to keep it moving toward completion. I did that for a year and a half while I recovered from mercury poisoning, and then one day, for no apparent reason, I got better. Why that day? Because everything I had been doing to get well finally reached the critical mass necessary to create the change my body required to function at a much higher level. The take-home is: never give up and just keep moving forward because the next step you take may be your salvation.

That also happened to Lance Armstrong during his fifth Tour de France. For the first two weeks he had difficulty finding his racing form and rhythm. He was doing everything correctly, yet he couldn't produce the performance his race preparation warranted. Despite the challenge, however, Lance remained committed to continuing doing what he had historically done during every previous Tour victory, knowing it had brought him top racing form in the past. Then, suddenly, during the final mountain races, he regained his form and pressed on to win his fifth, record-tying Tour victory.

Never break protocol. Maintaining strict protocol while executing your plans becomes more and more essential the more successful and complicated your life becomes. Your successes can occur only as fast as your protocols allow them to happen. The faster plans happen, the more chance that error from breach of protocol will happen. Once you've developed your personal protocols to execute your plans efficiently, never break them.

A patient once called my office to ask if his sister, who was scheduled to leave on vacation the next day, could see me that day to evaluate her shoulder. No appointments were available, but I told him to have his sister come in near the end of the day and I'd see her as a courtesy to him. She got to the office quite early, so I broke protocol, something I rarely do, and had my assistant put her into the examination room—as opposed to a treatment room, which was office policy—with a hot pack on her shoulder. When I finished treating my last regular patient, however, I decided I would drive home and go for a bicycle ride. About twenty minutes after leaving the office I panicked, realizing that my friend's sister was still (I hoped) in the examination room lying face down. I abruptly turned around and sped back to my office, unlocked the door, and entered the darkened suite. Much to my relief she was still lying face down, fast asleep on the table where I'd left her, so I gently awakened, evaluated, and treated her. She had a great vacation and sent me a very nice thank-you card for taking such good care of her and making her vacation possible. The point is when you have a proven operational structure in place and deviate from it, especially in times of intense activity, the window for introducing error becomes wide open. Do everything possible to stick with your proven success protocols at all times, and if they do skew off course, always return to them as quickly as possible.

Finish the job. Increased fatigue can alter how you think and act by significantly reducing your mental and physical resistance and increasing your vulnerability to things people say and do, which can easily drive your state of mind into a downward spiral. At times during your plan's execution, you may find yourself more fatigued than normal, yet you must still complete a step or take advantage of an unanticipated plan-enhancing opportunity before you get to a natural stopping point. Signs and symptoms you're in that zone are when you feel isolated from your normal life rhythm, disconnected from those you're close to, irritable from being overextended, or hungrier than normal because your physical and mental energy reserves are compromised. Whenever you start to experience any of these symptoms, it's imperative that you immediately begin conserving as much energy as possible by not responding to people, places, and things so you can finish the tasks at hand. And then, once they're completed, take the necessary time to fully recover. Only resume your plan when your vitality and clarity of thought have returned.

There's always enough energy to get the job done. Most of us have encountered circumstances that required us to stay up most, if not all, of the night to address them, yet we still had to get up the next morning to resume our normal activities. It is interesting to note that the following day you may find you've got all the energy and clarity necessary to complete your daily responsibilities, as if you'd gotten a great night's sleep. The mechanisms behind this phenomenon aren't fully understood, but what's important is that you know, regardless of the circumstances, that there's always enough energy to get the job done in critical situations, especially situations involving the welfare of others. I once had an early evening flight delayed until 3:30 AM the following morning and arrived at my destination to present a two-day seminar one hour before it was scheduled to start. Though slightly tired I vowed to myself that I would do everything necessary to honor my obligation to the audience and give them an extraordinary learning experience. I felt great doing the seminar despite having had no sleep. There's always enough energy to get through a crisis.

> "There's always enough energy to get through a crisis."

Trust that. It will always be true for you. On the other side of the crisis, though, the energy and sleep debt must be repaid. Always take the time to catch up on your sleep and restore your energy as quickly as possible because sleep deprivation, even if for one night, diminishes immunity and increases the risk of illness.

Keeping Your Plan Moving Forward

Plans are like chores. When the correct energy and time are devoted to them, they get done. Pacing and energy conservation are key elements to your plan's success. Too much energy expenditure leads to burnout, poor choice making, illness, and loss of enthusiasm. Several easy and effective ways are available, however, to conserve energy and make your plan execution easier and more efficient.

Maintain momentum. It's much easier to carry your plan's momentum than to create it. Taking short, frequent minibreaks will carry that momentum better than taking infrequent long breaks. Long breaks interrupt your continuity of thought and momentum, which then must be re-collected to get the plan moving again. The longer it takes to get your plan revved up and on track again, the less chance that it will get done.

Quit before you're tired. A strong tendency exists for motivated, successful people to work too much overtime under normal, noncrisis, work circumstances. Many times the compulsion comes from the belief that a plan will be completed more quickly if more hours are devoted to it over fewer days. That's usually not the case, however, as too many prolonged hours ultimately deplete energy and immune system reserves, leading to poor judgment, illness, or burnout. The ideal time to quit for the day is always before the first signs of fatigue show. Once fatigue shows, the line has already been crossed, making proper recovery both more essential and more difficult to achieve. As a rule, when in doubt as to whether or not to rest, rest. It's better to rest and survive the day and return the next day with a full energy reserve than to complete a day totally exhausted.

> "The longer it takes to get your plan revved up and on track again, the less chance that it will get done."

Dipping too far into your energy and immune reserves by exhausting your-self one day only threatens the following day's productivity.

Use your energy wisely. You only have a finite store of energy to devote to your plan, so use it wisely. Whenever you hit an impasse and aren't sure how to proceed, take a step back to conserve your energy and resume your plan only when you can see the appropriate direction it should take. Little leads to disastrous outcomes faster than doing something just because there's time to do it, rather than because it specifically needs to get done. When you're not clear what to do, do nothing, conserving your energy as much as possible until the direction is made clear. Once you're clear about what to do, proceed at full speed with your plan execution. Such construc-tive delays often provide the time for better plan adaptation and faster, bet-ter plan outcomes.

Prevent human error. Without question, human error is the single-largest and most preventable cause of plan delay. Preventing human error begins with having well-qualified, properly trained, highly motivated, and cor-rectly recruited people, including yourself, implementing your plan. Always recruit the best people you can find to help you execute your plan. Less qual-ified people who are often easier to find and more affordable ultimately cost more in the long run. Their unnecessary errors can disrupt your plan's con-tinuity and require considerable resources to rectify. Only self-motivated people with great communication skills should be involved in your plan. One passive–aggressive slacker can easily derail the whole process by doing or saying the wrong thing at the wrong time, disrupting your team's commit-ment to top plan execution. You'll know such people by their credo: "Don't just do something, stand there." It's best to let them go as soon as they're identified, since most never change despite their assurances.

Remain composed. At times even great plans must be temporarily suspended due to unanticipated events. Plan delays should never be considered a bad thing, since many of the best results come from plans that have been modified by unforeseen circumstances. Plan suspension can, however, be extremely detrimental if it is interpreted as an imminent harbinger of plan termination—especially when the facts don't support that conclusion. Such misassumption can disrupt your plan execution by paralyzing your thoughts and emotions, thereby prompting detrimentally impulsive actions and indecision. Effective methods of maintaining your composure during a plan's holding pattern period include taking a recovery hiatus from working to recharge your mind and body, acquiring a skill needed for a future project, catching up on unfinished business, or even starting another plan. Struggling for answers always compounds the problem.

Sometimes, however, halting a plan creates such an extreme fear overreaction in a person that normal composure strategies aren't effective. If this ever happens to you, it's imperative for you to halt the chain reaction immediately by withdrawing from the crisis epicenter to break the vicious fear cycle. If it isn't broken it can spill over into other areas of your life and drag it into the gutter. Some people never recover from this and never attempt ambitious goals again. Often the best way to break the cycle and shift an overstimulated, tense mind to a composed one is to do some full-body physical activity that doesn't require any thought. Twenty to thirty minutes of easy cycling, walking, shopping, or gardening all do this. Once the steam's been taken out of the overreaction and the mind's activity has returned to normal, the other resolution strategies can be implemented.

Remove obsolete steps. Sometimes, steps in your plan make your plan more complex and difficult than necessary. To keep your plan moving forward, remove or replace any obsolete step the instant it's uncovered, because the longer it's there the greater the risk that it will disrupt your entire plan.

Preventing Plan Self-Sabotage

Strange as it seems, you can cause the demise of your own plans. We've all seen people be their own worst enemy by bungling opportunities offered to them on a silver platter that could have been of great benefit had they taken advantage of the situation. Every decision you make produces an outcome, regardless of whether it's desired or not. Just because something seems right is no guarantee that the outcome will happen or be beneficial. Expected results only manifest if what you do matches what has to happen to produce your intended result. Several tactics can help prevent self-sabotage.

Watch what you ask for. A statement often heard from people with lives and businesses that are becoming busier and more complex from their successes is that they sometimes wish their phone would stop ringing. They think if that would happen that they would not be so busy and thus would be able to catch up and live a more controlled and tranquil life. Prophetically, most of the time what they wish for does come true and their phone does stop ringing. Predictably, because their life screeches to a halt or their business plummets, they hope and pray their phone will start ringing again, resuming its normal activity, which, again, is exactly what happens. What you unconsciously want to happen most often does, so before hoping for anything, make sure it's what you really want.

Execute the basics. A classic act of self-sabotage is trying to make up for what you think you've lost by trying to get it all back at once. This is seen with athletes who believe they are behind in their training and decide, usually from fear, to "catch up" and get it all back in a few days time by training extra long and hard. Unfortunately, this ends up in injury or illness virtually every time, putting them farther behind than had they just stayed on their training program from the beginning. This is exactly the same as life. Most times when the motivation behind a plan is solely about self-benefit, or is based in fear and not about successfully executing the plan to completion, it ends in failure. Whenever your plans take a downturn, promptly return to your basic plan creation and execution strategies to get them heading in the correct direction again. Never try to "catch up" by cramming more tasks than reasonable into a given time period. Just start where you are and most often you will complete your plan on schedule.

Resist impulsive decisions. Willfulness and fear are human emotions that can be extremely detrimental to your plan's success. I once heard a commercial fisherman in Alaska say that the two worst things you could do when

> "Never try to 'catch up' by cramming more tasks than reasonable into a given time period."

fishing the treacherous Alaskan waters was to get greedy or desperate. Both motivations prompt impulsive decisions that are blinded by too much self-interest and usually end in disaster. No one is exempt from this reality. Whenever the impulse arises to react out of pure self-interest or greed or to assuage a fear, it's always prudent to take a step back and resist the impulse to act. Such actions have an extremely high failure rate. Only make decisions with a level head and clear mind.

Let the answer come to you. Many times the overwhelming impulse to fill the vacuum of indecision, inaction, or empty time creates so much anxiety that a person compulsively ends up doing something, anything, just to fill the void. If you don't know what to do and feel as if you're going to crawl out of your skin unless you do something, first back away and do nothing; then accept that you don't know what to do and know that you'd like to find an answer. That desire sets the intention within your subconscious to provide the solution. The answer itself may also be to do nothing. If so, be comfortable with it because you got the answer you sought. Never act until you're certain what to do.

Perhaps my most profound experience at the Tours de France occurred just prior to the opening ceremonies of my fifth Tour with Lance and the team. I was told by one of the staff that Lance wanted to see me in the team bus. Once inside, he told me one of his hips felt a little out of sorts, enough to affect his normal walking pattern. That was a bit disconcerting on the evening before the Tour was to begin, but something I'd dealt with many times in the past. I had approximately twenty minutes to resolve the issue before the team riders had to leave the bus for the opening ceremonies. So, I went to work addressing all the usual causes for his symptoms.

After several minutes of work, I had him stand up and walk around the bus because I knew if he could walk then he was ready to race. Though he walked much better, it wasn't up to my satisfaction. I continued working on the problem a few more times with some improvement, but didn't completely resolve the issue up to the standard necessary to put in a top effort during the Tour's opening day. At that point I only had enough time for one more shot at resolution. As I started back to work I realized I had done everything my training taught me to do; yet, in the scant few seconds I had left I was at a loss as to how to completely resolve the problem. Being painfully aware of my inability and the necessity for a solution, I took a sobering deep breath and completely surrendered to my lack of solution and my intense need and desire to have one. And, during that brief moment of surrender, for whatever reason, when I was gently maneuvering Lance's leg I felt a "clunk" as his hip slid back into proper alignment. He got up and walked perfectly, and I knew, then, he was ready to race. He went on to win the Tour. The lesson is clear. The solutions are always there, we only need let them come to us.

Regularly Review and Modify Your Plan

The only certainty in life is change, which occurs every second of your life, moving you closer to or farther away from achieving your goals. If positive change isn't happening in your life on a regular basis, your life is far from being optimized and needs to change. Reviewing and correcting your plan's overall objective and the steps to get there are fundamental to keeping your life on the winning track to fulfillment and success.

Review your plan daily. Each day, first thing, review your general and specific plans for that day to confirm that they are exactly as you intend. I've known some very talented people who never grew into their talent because they didn't spend the time each day to review and modify their plans in a systematic manner. Without a review, they wasted half their day just trying to figure out what their plan was, or where they were in a preexisting plan, if they had one, let alone what the next step was or how to accomplish it. Their day would quickly evaporate, leaving perhaps one productive hour out of eight since the rest were spent trying to figure out where they were and what they should be doing.

If your plan doesn't match your desired outcome, immediately modify it to bring it in line with your expectations. The more quickly you complete those amendments, the sooner your redirected efforts will begin to produce constructive results.

Consult with your crew. Whether executing your plan by yourself or with others, having weekly meetings to discuss everything related to your plan will keep it moving forward most efficiently. The best time to meet to set the plan for the following week is Friday morning. This allows everybody to start at a strong pace on Monday morning. If meetings are held on Monday, by the time all the recommendations have been discussed and implemented it's already Tuesday, so you end up with a four-day workweek, which adds up to one lost workweek per month. If meetings are held on Friday afternoon, nobody pays any attention to them because their minds are already on the weekend. Friday morning is the ideal time.

Change your plan often. Successful plans change, and should change, often. If you find yourself making constant, regular, small changes to your plan to keep it pointed toward the most beneficial outcome, it's a sign that your plan's on track to reach its goal on time. Small upgrades to plans on a regular basis create bigger and better outcomes that occur with less effort than large, sweeping changes. Plans that don't adapt rapidly enough to meet the ever-changing demands of today's warp-speed world become obsolete quickly. Also, sterile plans devoid of change tend to become torturous exercises in rote technical execution rather than joyous, creative experiences representing the best human ingenuity has to offer. Frequent change will keep you vital and focused.

Avoid confusion. When a well-constructed plan is moving toward completion at peak efficiency, confusion is always only a moment away. All it takes is one small twist of fortune to turn a great plan upside down, and that could be an error from which it might never recover. Confusion easily derails great plans and, ironically, is usually completely preventable. Common causes of confusion result from poor plan execution, trying to execute too many steps simultaneously, trying to force the process too quickly, or failing to keep adequate records. Only work on one plan step at a time, commencing the next only when the previous one's been fully completed. Trying to do too many steps simultaneously creates chaos within your plan, making it impossible to complete any step fully. Such chaos stalls your plan and produces frustration and disharmony among those working on it. Executing each of the plan's steps fully, and in order, enables plan completion to happen efficiently and quickly.

TURN IT UP! TIPS

1. Every successful plan succeeds because of its clarity and certainty about who's doing what, when, and how. Nothing ever runs on assumption. Always communicate openly and concisely with others to make sure there's no ambiguity about who's doing what, when, and how.

2. To complete your plan on time make continued adjustments to it so it continuously becomes a better product and maintains its momentum to completion.

3. By creating a plan step-completion timeline table that illustrates in sequence each of your plan's steps and includes completion dates, you will dramatically enhance your ability to finish your plan on time with the least interference and loss of time.

4. Prior to launching a plan that involves others' participation it is wise to have a brief meeting with all concerned to review your plan's implementation strategy. This will put minds at ease and ensure the best mind-set possible to successfully launch your plan.

5. Never wait until you feel like beginning your plan to get it started because you probably never will. Just commit to a time and date and start it. We all have days when we don't feel like working on our plan, but that day may just turn out to be the one when the new innovation is born.

TURN IT UP! TIPS (CONT'D)

6. Having contingency plans for everything that can go right and wrong with your plans is a must. Always expect the unexpected and have alternate plans for the best- and worst-case scenarios, so if they happen you're prepared for them.

7. Always evaluate the prudence of subtle warning signs that suggest your plan is headed for trouble. Listen to them, because when heeded and acted on, they can save you tremendous grief.

8. To remain at the peak of your plan execution, take the time to investigate the success methodologies of the most successful people as well as the younger up-and-comers who have completed plans similar to yours. Both novice and expert perspectives provide valuable insights that can help you reach your goals.

9. Whenever your plan starts to veer off course, always give the new direction serious consideration, as it can often be a "better way" to reach a better outcome.

10. If your plan starts to unravel, yet you have complete confidence in it, never give up on it. Just keep moving forward, completing one step after another, because the next step you take may be the one that puts it back on its perfect course.

11. To carry your plan's momentum forward at peak efficiency, remove or replace any obsolete step the instant it's uncovered, because the longer it's there the greater the risk that it will disrupt your entire plan.

12. Make sure that what you intend your plans to achieve is exactly what you really want them to. Your intentions most often produce what you want, so prior to hoping for anything, be sure it's what you really want.

13. If you feel as if you're behind in your plan, never try to "catch up" by stuffing additional tasks into time slots that don't exist. Just begin where you are and most often you will complete your plan on schedule.

11

Healthy Habits and Healthy Environments

To lose one's health renders science null, art inglorious, strength unavailing, wealth useless, and eloquence powerless.

—Herophilos

Your habits, living and working spaces, and broader physical environment are the backdrop upon which your life unfolds. Although these are perhaps not as sexy and conspicuous as the highlights of your day because of their discreetness, they profoundly influence the texture and success of your life. Habits, living spaces, and surroundings are analogous to a house foundation. A solid, stable house foundation gives the house predictable, long-term viability, protecting its structure and function during natural events so it can provide it inhabitants the sanctuary to recover from the stresses and strains of daily life and build successful futures. When your habits, living and working spaces, and physical environments align with your talents and goals, they become the rock-solid foundation upon which your life is built. Thus achieving your goals becomes its own life habit, living space, and environment.

Healthy Habits

Your habits are the actions you most often elicit in response to a given set of circumstances. Your habitual behaviors are generally patterns of reaction formed early in life that fully embed into your daily behaviors through countless repetitions. Most of your habits are unconscious actions that occur without any conscious initiative on your part. When a situation arises, you instantly respond with preprogrammed behavior without thinking. In an ideal world, you'd have the most beneficial responses preloaded into your brain, ready to respond to every moment's circumstances. Unfortunately, that technology isn't presently available, so you have to groove your new patterns and repattern your undesirable old patterns the old-fashioned way: by consciously practicing your desired responses through deliberate repetition until they become an automatic part of your daily response pattern.

"Your habits are extremely accurate predictors of how you'll perform in life and what your future will be."

Habits are passively acquired early in life through osmosis by others examples and words and can be very difficult and time-consuming to change once firmly established. Your habits are extremely accurate predictors of how you'll perform in life and what your future will be. They determine what actions you will take and how successfully you will execute them.

Your habits only serve you well when they enable you to generate and maintain peak positive forward momentum, cultivate your talents, and promote your successes. If they can't stand up to the strain of your daily life or they prevent you from expressing your greatest talents, they require modification so you can perform continuously at your best. Your successes are proportional to the extent you triumph over life's daily challenges by keeping your plans alive and on course to completion. This is the fundamental reason you must constantly expose yourself to both everyday life and other people.

Daily exposure to life's real experiences puts you face to face with exactly what your habits are and how they impact you and others while accurately forecasting your future. Deliberately observing, evaluating, and analyzing your habits, as seen through the eyes of how you respond to life, is very different from merely believing you have a specific response pattern that hasn't been tested on life's firing line. People who believe they *are* something just because they *think* it and *aren't* in actions severely compromise their best life experience by living in a dreamland where anybody can be anything at any time. However, how you behave each moment during the heat of battle in the trenches of moment-by-moment life—where you interact with people, places, and things—is the true indicator of who you really are. Who you are is an action, not a thought, and only when you understand this is it possible for you to make decisions about how you can modify your habits to live the extraordinary life of which you're capable.

Your key to habit change is to do exactly what was done to acquire the original habit. First, decide what you want your habitual behavior to be. Next, deliberately, with conscious intention, do the desired behavior correctly, repeatedly, and often enough in real-life situations for it to become a permanent, unconscious response pattern. Change is an action-based phenomenon. Given enough time and repetition, new habits can be acquired that catapult you toward more life stability and success.

Proven Success-Generating Habits

Habits that lead to successful, passionate lives are as varied as the number of people on the planet. However, several specific universal habits will assist you in living a more fulfilling and successful life.

Laugh daily. Lord Byron said, "Always laugh when you can. It is cheap medicine." It's impossible to laugh and be in a bad mood, fearful, confused, unmotivated, or under any other influence that stifles passionate productivity. Life's best moments, creative ideas, insights, and fellowship always occur when the mind is open and receptive. Nothing opens a stagnant brain and body faster than a good laugh. Build laughing into your life so your mind and body remain vital and attentive. This will make success easier to come by with greater frequency. Don't let a day go by without spending time laughing with someone or at something. Watch movies, DVDs, and videos that make you smile. You'll have more success when you do.

Get enough sleep. You need adequate sleep to reach your goals. Tens of millions of people have been diagnosed with insomnia, not to mention the countless millions living with undiagnosed sleep disorders. When deprived of sleep, your body quickly loses its health reserve, which leads to illness or injury that quickly grinds any plan, regardless of how good, to a standstill. It's during sleep that your brain and body cells repair and rebuild themselves and your energy reserves are replenished. When poor sleep prevents your full recovery each day, the functions of your brain and body decline, reducing your productivity, increasing mental errors, and eventually producing burnout, injury, or illness. A further downside to poor sleep is an increase in pro-aging free radicals.

Sleep requirements are individualized, with most people requiring an average of six to eight hours per night. Getting good sleep can be facilitated in several ways:

1. **Stretch your body for five to ten minutes in the evening.** Stretching takes tension out of your muscles, allowing you to relax and get to sleep faster, then remain asleep and arise fresher in the morning. Refer to the following section on stretching for a detailed description of its benefits, techniques, and guidelines.

2. **Set your bedroom's temperature so you fall asleep and stay asleep.** Cooler temperatures facilitate sleep best. Find the best temperature for you and stick with it.

3. **Don't sleep with pets.** Pets can wake you up several times a night, which produces sleep deprivation.

4. **Discontinue use of electrical devices such as computers early in the evening.** They can stimulate the body and make you tense, making it difficult to get to sleep.

5. **Eat early.** Being full creates discomfort and can prevent you from falling and staying asleep. Try to finish dinner a few hours before you get to sleep, especially on work nights.

6. **Restrict liquid consumption in the evening.** By doing this, you don't have to get up and go to the bathroom during the night.

7. **Sleep earthed.** Preliminary research on a new technology, called Earthing™, reveals that reconnecting with the electrons and natural frequencies on the surface of the earth can improve energy, enhance recovery, relieve muscle tension, reduce stress, and restore biological rhythms. For more information and for ways to incorporate Earthing™ in your life, visit www.jeffspencer.com.

Stretch daily. Regular stretching gives you the mental and physical flexibility to think and perform better. Flexible minds solve problems more quickly, envision greater possibilities, create better plans, and forever strive for a better tomorrow. Pliable bodies are more resistant to injury, generate more strength, and have better endurance to be more productive. Stretching also teaches you the mental skill of reaching a little further in life. Each time you stretch mentally, you build your talents, become a better risk taker, and do something unique that builds your confidence in your ability to have an expansive, vital, and gratifying life.

The following flexibility program is offered to help you improve and maintain the quality of your life. To get the most out of your stretching program, follow these guidelines.

1. **Stretch in the evening.** The best time to stretch is in the evening after dinner. Throughout the day your muscles shorten and carry more tension. Ideally, you should go to sleep with your muscles elongated and fully relaxed, ensuring that you'll get to sleep quickly and arise completely refreshed the following day.

2. **Dress comfortably.** Always dress in loose-fitting clothing that allows you to move efficiently without limitation. Also, dress appropriately for the temperature.

3. **Warm up.** Prior to stretching, do a few minutes of brisk walking, jogging, floor exercise, or cardio machines to get your muscles warmed up and pliable before stretching. This allows the most stretching with the least risk of muscle injury.

4. **Never overstretch.** Forcing your muscles to stretch too far invites injury. Never stretch beyond your muscle's first point of tightness. That point occurs when you feel a very slight resistance in the muscle being stretched. Further stretch produces undesirable strain, leading to more tension and injury.

5. **Breathe when stretching.** Before starting each stretch, gently inhale through your nose as your abdomen moves forward, expanding your rib cage outward from your spine, exactly as was instructed in the abdominal breathing exercise in the Controlling the Fear Impulse section in Chapter 3. As you gently exhale through your mouth, move to and stop at the first point of muscle tightness and hold for five seconds. Then, inhale again as you return to your starting position. Repeat the inhale-exhale-stretch sequence four more times, each time stretching a little farther to next point of tightness, before moving on to your next stretch.

The following stretches are recommended, will take less than five minutes to do, and will relax your muscles to accelerate your daily recovery and make you less injury prone. Each stretch, following the preceding breathing guidelines, should take only thirty seconds. If you're in a time crunch, stretch each muscle for only ten seconds. Again, never overstretch or be in a hurry to stretch. Relax and enjoy the experience.

1. **Buttocks stretch.** Sitting with legs crossed, slowly lower your elbows to the floor until you feel first stretch in your buttocks (Figure 11.1).

Figure 11.1

2. **Chest stretch.** Lying face up on the floor with knees bent, interlock the fingers of both hands and place your hands on your forehead. Slowly lower your elbows to the floor while feeling a stretch in your chest (Figure 11.2).

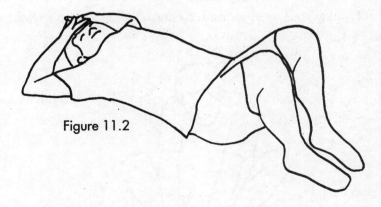

Figure 11.2

3. **Tensor stretch.** Lie face up with arms flat and away from your body. Cross one leg over the other at the knee. Lower your legs to the side of the top leg to feel the stretch on the outside thigh of the downside leg (Figure 11.3). Repeat with other leg.

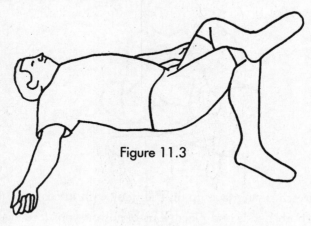

Figure 11.3

4. **Groin stretch.** Sitting with the soles of your feet as close together as possible, preferably touching, grab the ends of your feet with both hands and gently draw your torso forward, feeling a subtle stretch in your groin (Figure 11.4).

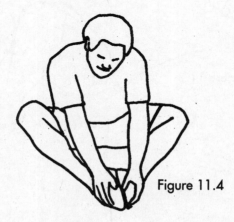

Figure 11.4

5. **Hip flexor stretch.** Place one foot on a chair or stool, with your knee and hip bent at a 90-degree angle. Keeping your back perfectly vertical without poking your head forward, slowly bend the raised knee until you feel a first stretch in the muscles on the opposite leg of the upper front thigh or lower pelvis (Figure 11.5). Repeat with other leg.

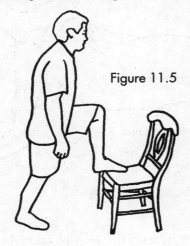

Figure 11.5

6. **Lower back stretch.** While kneeling with arms outstretched, sit back toward your heels until you feel a slight stretch in your lower back (Figure 11.6).

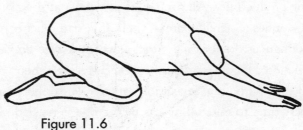

Figure 11.6

7. **Mid-back stretch.** Using the same position as for the low-back stretch but starting with both knees farther back so you can lower your chest to the floor, gently start to draw your buttocks backward until you feel a gentle stretch in your underarms. At that point, lower your chest toward the floor while suspending your back in a reverse arch so you feel a decompression in your mid-back spine (Figure 11.7).

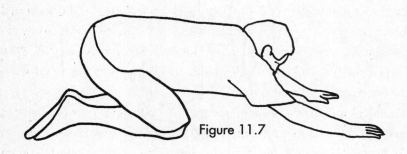

Figure 11.7

Recharge regularly. Taking frequent breaks throughout the day is an essential ingredient for success, because your mind and body can only function at peak output for so long before you need a breather to recalibrate and recharge them. Doing too much of anything for too long leads to physical fatigue, brain fade, and mental errors. Taking periodic breaks is essential to optimizing productivity. All top performers have at their practice and performance venues designated areas where they can relax between rehearsals and performances. Performing artists have backstage dressing rooms, athletes have motor homes, and business executives use their private offices. A few minutes of purposeful relaxation can greatly extend your productivity.

The best time to take a break is before one is needed. At the slightest hint that you're losing traction on anything, stop and take a break. When used effectively, breaks smooth out energy expenditure and mental pacing, leading to optimal daily productivity and minimal mental errors. Breaks may vary from a few minutes to as much as twenty minutes depending on circumstances. No amount of break time should ever be considered ineffective. As you learn your break pattern, you can then antici- pate and take them before you need them. That way you're always ahead of the game.

"The best time to take a break is before one is needed."

Natural break times are midmorning and mid- afternoon, with the most critical break of the day being the one in midafternoon. Cortisol, the hormone that keeps you alert and active, has a normal midafternoon decline, resulting in a slight decrease in energy and mental acuity. Taking a break between 2:00 PM and 4:00 PM is the best time for a quick recharge that will set the tone for a pro- ductive remainder of the day.

The ideal midafternoon recharge includes adequate nutrition, rest, and stretching. These three elements will give your mind and body the energy, focus, and resiliency needed to finish up the day on the highest productiv- ity note.

For peak midafternoon energy and brainpower, employ this powerful mininutrition protocol:

1. Small snack of metabolic-friendly foods (see Chapter 12)
2. 500 grams of buffered Vitamin C
3. 200 milligrams of magnesium glycinate
4. One capsule of adrenal extract
5. One capsule of ginseng

To finish your break, do the following stretches to revitalize you further and remove the tension from your body so you can begin working again at your best. Do each of the stretches for thirty seconds.

1. **Doorway stretch.** Place each hand at shoulder height on the doorway frame. Slowly lean your body forward so you feel a gentle stretch in your chest muscles. Hold this position, and as your muscles relax move farther forward to the next tissue barrier for thirty seconds (Figure 11.8).

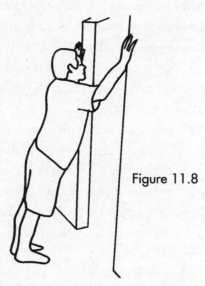

Figure 11.8

2. **File cabinet stretch.** With your arms outstretched, place your hands palm down on top of a filing cabinet, table, bench, or object of similar height. While exhaling, slowly lower your head and chest toward the floor without flexing or extending your head, allowing your mid-back to extend like a suspension bridge so you feel a decompression in your mid-back and spine. At the point of initial tightness, hold the position for a few seconds and, as the muscles relax and the spine decompresses, gradually lower to the next decompression barrier. Do this for thirty seconds (Figure 11.9).

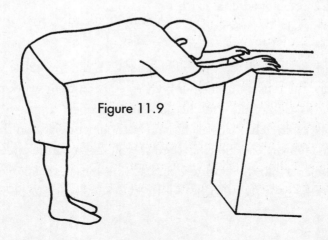

Figure 11.9

3. **Brugger's stretch.** Drop your arms, turn your hands palm out, spread your fingers, and exhale gently as if you were making a candle flicker. Repeat four times. (Figure 11.10).

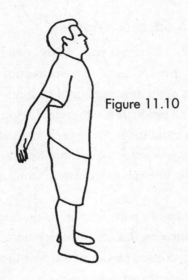

Figure 11.10

To keep yourself fresh and take postural strain out of your body throughout your workday, do these three simple stretches once every twenty minutes. This will keep you performing at your best.

Healthy Environments

The environments you work and live in profoundly affect your capacity to perform. Unfortunately, today's world is not as pristine as it once was. With the advent of synthetic materials over the last several decades, environmental and indoor pollution have risen to the point that they now pose a significant challenge to our immune systems, health, and productivity. This escalation is evidenced by the exponential growth in immune-deficiency conditions—allergies, asthma, and respiratory illness, as well as a new class of illness, called environmental illness—that have become a part of our mainstream. Reducing your exposure to pollutants by creating the cleanest and healthiest possible work and living environments will keep you performing at your best. You can clean your environment and reduce your exposure to environmental pollution in several ways.

Breathe Better to Succeed More

Air provides the oxygen your body needs to generate energy. Unfortunately, as the contents of construction and home furnishing products have been shifted from natural to synthetic materials the use of toxic indoor cleaning products has increased. Home construction methods have become tighter and indoor air has become vastly more polluted than outdoor air, leaving less oxygen available for you to create energy, while also increasing your energy and nutrient consumption to detoxify the pollutants.

Signs and symptoms of poor indoor air quality include an increase in allergies, clouded thinking, loss of concentration, poor memory, increased sickness, sinusitis, decreased productivity, poor digestion, poor disposition, fatigue, itchy eyes, sore throat, and nausea.

The good news is the availability of many easy and cost-effective ways to improve your indoor air quality so you can perform at your best. Certain individuals with increased sensitivities, however, will require a more detailed investigation and remediation program than presented here; to address their specific needs, such individuals should consult environmental health professionals and designers and contractors working with green and nontoxic materials. The following are some of the ways to optimize your work and living environments.

1. **Relocate all indoor chemicals.** Move all solvents, cleaning fluids, insecticides, and paints to a properly confined and ventilated storage area outside your living space.

2. **Eliminate car interior pollution.** New cars have chemical smells from the toxic off-gassing of the synthetic materials and artificial scents used in their production. Even the "leather" smell new cars have comes from artificial odor products designed to make the car smell new. To minimize these

vapors, don't use artificial air fresheners. Instead, use a vehicle air filter that plugs into your vehicle's nine-volt power adapter. Visit the website www.aehf.com for a variety of air-filtering products.

3. **Clean your car's air conditioning and heating systems.** These are notorious mold generators and can send a blast of unhealthy mold into your car interior each time they are used. Running the air conditioning periodically will help keep mold from forming within the system.

4. **Use an air purifier.** Using an air purifier in your home and office will keep air contaminants to a minimum. Medical-grade air filters are suggested because of their quality and effectiveness. Visit the www.aehf.com website for more information.

5. **Use an air ionizer.** Air ionizers generate negatively charged particles—negative ions—that grab onto and neutralize contaminated air particles. Negative ions also boost your energy. These silent devices should be run continuously.

6. **Use a warm humidifier.** Dry air from arid climates, air conditioners, and heaters, dries out your nasal passages, sinuses, and lungs, making you more susceptible to infection. If the air you work or live in is dry, consider using a warm humidifier to achieve the correct health-promoting air moisture balance. Always properly maintain and clean humidifiers since they can generate mold if not properly serviced.

7. **Clean air ducts.** Central heating and air conditioning ducts should be cleaned periodically because dust and mold can lodge there and then contaminate rooms when either system is running.

8. **Clean horizontal surfaces.** Tabletops, desktops, and all horizontal surfaces are massive dust collectors and should be wiped down frequently with a moist cloth.

9. **Open windows.** Open windows frequently to let rooms breathe and exchange bad air for good. Today's construction methods create airtight rooms that trap stagnant air.

10. **Decorate with some Boston ferns.** Keeping Boston ferns indoors helps cleanse room air and gives you energy, as they absorb carbon dioxide

and emit oxygen back into the room. This type of fern fares best with producing less mold and fewer allergens.

11. **Be wise about pets.** Many people react to pet dander and hair. If you are such a person, it's best to keep pets outside your living space, as every allergic reaction takes energy and challenges your immune system. Pets also can track pesticides and other outdoor contaminants into the house, which you then touch and breathe.

12. **Take off your shoes.** Everybody needs to check his or her shoes at the door before entering a home. Like pets, shoes track in pesticides and contaminants.

13. **Dry-clean carpets.** Steam cleaning carpets leaves moisture in the carpet, which promotes mold growth. Mold is a hazardous indoor pollutant, as most forms cause allergies and others are toxic. Every allergic reaction increases pro-aging and illness-creating free radicals. Dry-clean your carpets with nontoxic products.

14. **Dispose of waste paper daily.** The inks used in printing can be toxic and often aren't completely dry when you receive printed material. New magazines usually emit the pungent odor of incompletely cured ink. Some paper goods, such as cardboard, have pesticides embedded in them, along with cancer-causing formaldehyde. Paper goods also decompose, sending small, unhealthy, breathable particles into the air.

15. **Remove or—even better—discontinue using powdered laundry soaps.** Many people react very strongly to powdered laundry soaps, which emit microgranules that produce significant reactions in susceptible people when inhaled.

16. **Run bathroom fans and squeegee surfaces.** After showering or taking a bath, squeegee the shower doors and turn on bathroom fans to remove excess condensation and water, allowing the room to dry out and thus preventing mold growth.

17. **Eliminate artificial scents.** Laundry fabric softeners and electronic scent emitters discharge artificial chemical scents that can activate allergies and make susceptible people nauseous. Use natural products whenever possible.

18. **Don't sleep or relax in spaces that house printers and paper shredders.** Printers and paper shredders produce and broadcast minute paper particles containing chemicals from inks and dyes into the air we breathe.

19. **Ventilate your space well.** If working or living in proximity to heaters or appliances that burn natural gas, oil, propane, or wood, make sure that no equipment leaks and that proper air ventilation is taking place. All combustible materials emit vapors that can be harmful. Choose electric appliances over gas whenever possible.

Upgrade Your Working and Living Space

As you become more successful and your success momentum builds, it's inevitable that your work and personal spaces will be updated to remain consistent with your current needs to keep creating success. Healthy upgrading practices will help you optimize your future successes by promoting better health, creating more energy, and enabling you to think better.

1. **Nontoxic paint.** Most paints are toxic. Both water-based and enamel paints contain fungicides, bactericides, and other toxic ingredients that are breathed during and after painting. Nontoxic paints are available and should be used so that your energy can be drawn upon to create your successes, not diverted to detoxification. Find out more by visiting www.afmsafecoat.com.

2. **Carpets.** Most new carpets are made of synthetic materials that give off tremendous amounts of toxic fumes. Nontoxic carpets made of wool and cotton are available, but some people are allergic to these materials. All carpets collect dust, debris, and mold that can contribute to your total health load and create ill health. Tile and nonlaminate hardwood floors are best.

3. **Wood products.** Many wood products are wood laminates made of thin wood sheets glued together with toxic glues. Plywood, most wood cabinets, and office supply "wood" furniture are composed of wood laminates that give off toxic vapors, adding to poor indoor air quality. Metal cabinets and furniture are best because no glues or laminates are used in their construction. Older wood products that no longer produce any off-gassing are also acceptable.

4. Full-spectrum lighting. Most artificial light doesn't emit the full, health-producing spectrum of light frequencies given off by sunshine. To see and feel your best, full-spectrum light bulbs are best because they are most compatible with human biology. This can be extremely important for those who live in cloudy, gray climates and suffer from seasonal affective disorder (SAD), a light-deprived condition. SAD occurs when insufficient light intensity produces changes in brain chemistry, making people extremely depressed—often with intense sugar cravings.

SIGNS AND SYMPTOMS OF AN UNHEALTHY ENVIRONMENT AND HOW TO FIX IT

Regardless of how intelligent you are, how great your plans might be, or how motivated you are to reach your goals, if you're working, living, and driving in unhealthy environments your mental and physical faculties will be compromised, making your aspirations less achievable. Once you know and understand the signs and symptoms of an unhealthy environment, you can implement remediation measures to keep yourself performing at your best. Use the following charts to help you identify and remedy these unhealthy environments.

Signs of an Unhealthy Environment	Symptoms of an Unhealthy Environment
Water spots, warped wood from water intrusion, standing water	Sinus congestion, pressure, breathing difficulty, asthma
Chemical smells	Depression
Chemicals in bottles	Scratchy eyes
Gas appliances	Unexplainable physical symptoms such as digestive upset, flulike symptoms, tingling
Electrical outlets, appliances	Headache
Wood-burning heating appliances	Concentration difficulty, brain fog

SIGNS AND SYMPTOMS OF AN UNHEALTHY ENVIRONMENT AND HOW TO FIX IT (CONT'D)

Signs of an Unhealthy Environment	Symptoms of an Unhealthy Environment
Soot around heating, ventilation, and air conditioning (HVAC) vents	Tiredness, fatigue
Stagnant, stale air	Skin rash
Water condensation on walls, windows	Nausea
Visible mold	Insomnia

Causes of an Unhealthy Environment

Budding plants	Dirty air ducts (mold, dust)	Wood-laminate cabinetry
Mold	Water leaks (mold)	Cleaning chemicals
Dust	Toxic chemical fumes	Bug sprays
Animal dander	New carpet	Uncured ink
Airborne paper particles	Toxic fumes from fresh paint	Natural, propane gas leaks

How to Fix Your Most Familiar Environments

There are several economical and effective changes that can easily be made to the environments you find yourself in most often. The minimal effort to initiate these measures is worth the increased productivity, health, and longevity they provide.

1. **Home.** Replacing toxic home products with nontoxic ones is the easiest step in creating a healthier home environment. Common home products that often contain toxic substances include cleaning products and pesticides. Most of the major natural food chain markets carry a selection of nontoxic alternatives for these products. To find a more comprehensive list of nontoxic home items visit www.aehf.com, or conduct an Internet

search for nontoxic products. For circumstances where nontoxic options aren't available, all products should be removed and stored outside of the home in closed cabinets. For full protection wear gloves, full coverage clothing, and a rubber mask respirator with disposable cartridges when using the products.

2. **Bedroom.** Creating a healthy bedroom can be done by improving bedroom air quality and reducing exposure to electromagnetic fields. Improving air can be done by running an air purifier daily, vacuuming and dry-cleaning carpets with nontoxic cleaner, regularly cleaning heating and air conditioning ducts, and opening windows to increase fresh air flow. Reducing exposure to electromagnetic fields is accomplished by reducing the number of electrical appliances in the bedroom, and, if possible, plugging all electrical devices into one power strip to be unplugged when going to bed, and using a battery-powered alarm clock.

3. **Workspace.** The workspace is the most difficult location to make healthy because of the office equipment. Start by improving the workspace air quality by implementing the suggestions offered for healthy bedroom air in the previous paragraph. Next, minimize dust in your workspace by frequently dusting with a damp cloth placing particular emphasis on horizontal surfaces. Place dust-collecting items as far back on your desk as possible and locate the desk as far from copy machines, paper shredders, and paper storage areas as possible, as they continuously emit unhealthy odors and particles.

4. **Vehicle.** To improve the health environment of your vehicle's interior, use an auto air purifier and eliminate the use of chemical-laden artificial scent air fresheners. Regular carpet and car mat vacuuming and frequent dusting of the interior with a moist rag will significantly reduce your car's interior dust. To prevent mold growth, periodically run the heating and air condition systems and repair any trunk water damage. To minimize bad exhaust emissions, correct all exhaust system leaks.

Interact with Healthy People, Places, and Things

Interacting with the right people, places, and things at the right times can make your life passionate and success easy. Conversely, the wrong people, places, and things at the wrong times can put the best of lives into a major tailspin. Controlling your exposure to these influences is a vital success skill to master. When done well, you can consistently manifest your best intentions and potentials. If not, your life is ruled by the external events and the wishes, demands, and dictates of others, which makes creating personal success extremely difficult. The following guidelines will help you control your environment and allow you to fortify your relationships with people, places, and things, building your success capacity and your continuing ability to manifest your best talents.

1. **Surround yourself with like-minded people.** Successful lives are lived in the company of others who contribute to and encourage your successes rather than detract from them. Associate with those groups and people whom you like.

2. **Contact people you value who have enriched your life.** It takes two to tango, and great relationships are privileges that require cultivation. When you think of someone, call or e-mail to touch base. In today's world, a call or e-mail without asking for something is much appreciated and speaks volumes about the sincerity of the relationship.

3. **Surround yourself with material objects that bring you joy, happiness, and appreciation,** especially those things you love to see upon awakening. A special painting, garden, music, object, or view all wag people's tails in different ways. Feeling empowered by your environment pays great dividends in motivation and enthusiasm. Your best investment is in your personal belief and empowerment. Anything that inspires empowerment and appreciation is worth having.

4. **Invest every second of every day in whatever way you see fit.** Devote time only to those things that serve your talents, passion, and humanity, to the fullest. In today's top-heavy communication world, it's impossible to be

all things to all people. Only answer those e-mails and calls that are relevant to your highest calling. Let the others go. Otherwise you'll spend all day deleting pop-ups and junk e-mails, without ever advancing your life.

5. **Listen to music that makes your soul sing.** In every culture, music plays a central role in every ritual and celebration. It should do the same for you. It's hard to be anything but enthusiastic while listening to your favorite music. Do it often.

6. **Resolve or eliminate unhealthy relationships.** When experiencing difficulty in relationships, do whatever is necessary to resolve or eliminate them in a prudent, swift manner so that you can proceed with your life as quickly as possible. Never hang onto something that isn't meant to be. If there's no future in something or someone, let go of the rope as soon as the hope for reconciliation is gone. Trying to resurrect a dead horse is futile—and only prolongs the pain.

7. **Let go of having to know why something needs to be done.** The only thing you need to know is that something does need to be done—and you are the one to do it. Trust the process and get it done. Often the "why" behind a correct action is only fully revealed at a later time. Don't delay an action that you know needs to be done even if the *why* isn't presently apparent.

TURN IT UP! TIPS

1. Spend time interacting with people so you can accurately identify exactly what your habits are, view the efficacy of any habit changes you've made, and see how your habits impact yourself and others. This information will inform you as to what steps can be made to improve your habits.

2. To change a habit, first, decide what you want your new habit to be. Next, deliberately repeat the desired behavior often enough for it to become a permanent, unconscious life response pattern. This can take considerable time for it to become a long-standing habit, so be patient.

TURN IT UP! TIPS (CONT'D)

3. Important healthy habits that are relatively easy to implement, even in this rush-rush world, are frequent laughing, getting enough sleep, stretching, relaxing, and exercising. When incorporated into your schedule, they will significantly enhance your life.

4. To improve your energy reduce your exposure to pollutants by creating the cleanest and healthiest work and living environments possible by using air purifiers, nontoxic cleaning agents, and regular dusting schedules.

5. If you notice an increase in allergies, clouded thinking, loss of concentration, poor memory, increased sickness, sinusitis, decreased productivity, poor digestion, poor disposition, fatigue, itchy eyes, sore throat, and nausea, a thorough home and/or workspace toxicity assessment is warranted.

6. Spend regular time with those people who enrich your life and encourage your success. Such relationships are an important factor in your personal success program.

7. Surround yourself with tangible things that put beauty into your life and bring you joy. Paintings, sculpture, ceramics, photos, plants, and architectural elements can add a new dimension to your life. It's better to have few things that you truly love than several you're lukewarm about.

8. Being around incompatible people, places, and things can quickly put you into a downward emotional tailspin. When you find yourself in such circumstances kindly excuse yourself as quickly as possible.

9. Don't let a day go by without humor. Humor and wit are the universal antidotes to anything.

12

Training to Win

That cause is strong which has,
not a multitude, but one strong person behind it.

—J. R. Lowell

Winning at your game is only possible if you have the mental and physical strength, endurance, flexibility, and agility to plan and execute your plans. Few things are more tragic than seeing a motivated person and a great plan fail halfway to completion from lack of mental and physical stamina. Yet that happens all the time.

Developing the Physical Capacity to Achieve Your Goals

To construct and execute your plans and manifest your highest ambitions, your brain and body must work together in complete harmony, each matching the other's functional capacity. When your body is working at peak capacity, so is your brain, and the best way to generate and maintain a lifetime of peak mental and physical performance is to follow a sensible and implementable diet and exercise program. Several proven strategies can help you attain and maintain the health needed to live a productive lifestyle and reach your goals.

Every nutrition and fitness measure you incorporate into your life must support your ambitions without disrupting other areas of your life. Highly detailed and extensive health-building routines can be extremely appealing, as they hold the promise of extraordinary results in minimal time. Most often, however, they quickly become overwhelming, disruptive, and ultimately destructive to a natural and reasonable pace that would, otherwise, produce consistent success. Small additions and modifications to nutrition and fitness routines always produce superior results over the long term. It's imperative to never make too many life modifications too quickly.

"When your body is working at peak capacity, so is your brain."

Since everyone has a unique biochemistry, there is no perfect "one size fits all" diet or fitness program that works universally for everybody. The recommendations provided in this chapter give generalized, easy-to-implement health and fitness suggestions that are within most people's capabilities and have proven to promote successful lifestyles without turning lives upside down. Individual needs differ from person to person, so modifications may be necessary beyond the scope of the information provided here. In such instances you are encouraged to find appropriately qualified people to help you with those refinements.

Never try to be perfect with your health management program. Being perfect isn't possible in this or any other domain, and trying to be often leads instead to program abandonment from failure to reach an unobtainable goal. Always follow the 90 percent rule and never stress about it if you break your diet and exercise programs 10 percent of the time. Our 10 percent fiddle factor makes long-term diet and workout programs sustainable.

Always be cognizant that *you* are the one who creates your success, not your diet or your fitness program. If you're not self-motivated to create a success, a perfect diet will never do it for you. Never empower any food or exercise to do for you what you must do for yourself. I've seen people become so obsessive with their nutrition and fitness regimes that they place their entire confidence in those programs to do for them what they should be doing for themselves. When I won the Olympic trials, my fiercest rival, the pre-event favorite, fell apart when his race-winning "secret" grape juice was forgotten at his hotel. Predictably, he crumbled and failed to make the team. How ridiculous is that!

Eliminate Harmful Molecules

Ideally, life should be a perennial string of successes from start to finish. Unfortunately, however, chronic illness is a primary reason that doesn't occur. Medical science points the finger at free-radical-based inflammation as the precipitating event behind all degenerative diseases, including rheumatoid arthritis, diabetes, cancer, lupus, irritable bowel syndrome, and multiple sclerosis. Poor diet, stress, and overexercising create an excess of free radicals that, in turn, accelerate aging and mental decline.

Free radicals are unstable molecules, missing an electron, that are produced by both an overactive immune system in response to any physical or mental stress or just by normal metabolic activities such as breathing. Your body neutralizes free radicals with free electrons from various sources, including antioxidant-rich dietary foods, antioxidant supplements, the sun, and earth's surface—or from your healthy cells.

An insufficient supply of free electrons in your body to stabilize harmful free radicals increases your risk of degenerative disease. When your body doesn't have enough free electrons available to neutralize free radicals, the free radicals steal electrons from your healthy cells. The healthy cells are then injured, generating an immune response that creates further inflammation. Eventually, this creates a self-perpetuating inflammatory loop that injures tissue, leads to chronic degenerative illness, and makes long-term success an afterthought.

Free-radical damage can be minimized with diet. Eating antioxidant-rich foods, including grains, garlic, seafood, strawberries, blueberries, spinach, nuts, seeds, avocados, beans, pomegranates, curry, and ginger will quench free radicals. The antioxidant vitamins E and C and fish oils also donate free electrons to neutralize the deadly effect of free radicals. Foods to avoid that promote inflammation are saturated animal fat and egg yolks, as well as safflower, sunflower, corn, and vegetable oils.

> "Eating antioxidant-rich foods, including grains, garlic, seafood, strawberries, blueberries, spinach, nuts, seeds, avocados, beans, pomegranates, curry, and ginger will quench free radicals."

Ten Nutrition Steps to Better Thinking and Productivity

Good nutrition gives your mind and body nutrients to think, feel, act, and look better. Healthy food is fundamental to your becoming a better achiever because it accelerates tissue repair, building tissue and generating energy to keep your body running at its best. Just a few simple changes can dramatically enhance your capacity to perform. Large, sweeping, complicated, exhaustive changes in nutrition habits are usually unsustainable because of the disruption they bring to an existing lifestyle and the mental burden they impose. So, it's always best to start with subtle modifications first and then make additional changes once they have been firmly established within your daily routines. As always, follow the 90 percent rule.

By implementing the ten basic nutrition tenets listed here, you can build a better brain, feel better, and generate the energy to reach your goals without feeling strapped into a dietary straightjacket.

1. **Restrict calories.** The only scientifically proven means to increase longevity is to maintain a calorie-restricted diet. Reducing dietary calories makes more energy available to create successes, since the simple act of digesting food consumes a large portion of the body's energy. Eating less also helps create and maintain optimal body composition so you look and feel better. Better composition also takes physical stress off the joints and requires less energy to move the extra mass around. Reducing body fat also

reduces the accumulation of nutrient- and energy-robbing toxins, which are stored in fat. In addition, reduced calories are associated with decreased risk of heart disease, cancer, and stroke. Most people do well eating 1,800 to 2,000 calories a day, which equals three modest-size, nutrient-dense meals.

2. **Drink before you eat.** Hunger and thirst both produce the same sensation. If you eat when you should be drinking, you will gain weight, dehydrate, and consume more energy from increased digestion. To tell the difference between hunger and thirst, drink eight ounces of water fifteen to twenty minutes before eating: if you're still hungry then, you need to eat; if not, you needed water, not food. Making this a regular premeal practice will promote a consistent energy level throughout the day and help control body composition. Since the brain is 80 percent water, it's imperative that it always be hydrated so your thinking-and problem-solving skills can function at peak capacity. Drinking six to eight cups of water each day is suggested.

3. **Eat before you're hungry.** Waiting too long to eat often leads to an energy crash that interrupts your productivity flow and leads to your devouring whatever food is conveniently available to stabilize your energy. Most convenience foods (those from boxes and cans) are made from highly processed, nutrient-void, calorie-rich, and preservative-laced ingredients. Such foods never create the energy the body and brain need to perform at their best. Also, because they're devoid of nutrients, convenience foods steal nutrients from your nutrient reserve for digestion, thus consuming copious amounts of nutrients that could be used more constructively. To avoid energy blackouts, eat quality food *before* you get hungry. It takes much less time to keep your energy up than to get it back once your energy lags. Always have a nutrient-rich snack or two within reach at all times, especially if you're going to be in situations with high potential for interrupting your schedule. This way, if you're thrown off schedule, you've got food with you to keep your energy up so you can perform your best until you can have a regular meal.

> "It takes much less time to keep your energy up than to get it back once your energy lags."

4. Eat right for your metabolism. Metabolism is the process by which your body creates energy to run its biologic functions. Food is the primary fuel for this process, but not everyone's body uses exactly the same food to generate optimal energy. In his groundbreaking book *Nutrition and Your Mind*, George Watson shared his research, which revealed that diet profoundly affects how people think and act. When their diets matched their metabolisms, they performed at their best physically and mentally.

Clinical research following Watson's and others' metabolic diet models has shown that to generate optimal energy the body prefers either a "grazer" diet of fruit, grains, vegetables, and limited light protein or a "high density" diet of protein, vegetables, moderate fat, and limited carbohydrates. Grazer-type individuals, who can go long periods of time between meals without an energy crash, feel physically and mentally drained by heavy, high-density, protein and fat foods and will feel much better eating lighter, less dense food. Conversely, high-density types have more energy; think better after eating dense foods such as steak, salmon, dairy, and vegetables; and feel best when they eat frequently. High-density types can experience severe energy crashes after eating too many carbohydrates, especially refined grains and sweets.

To confirm whether you're a grazer or high-density metabolic type, follow the grazer diet for a day or two. If you feel better and have more energy, that's the diet for you. Conversely, if you feel sluggish, tired, and constantly hungry, you're a high-density type and need to switch to the high-density diet.

5. Eat organic food whenever possible. Ingesting pesticides and additives from conventional foods produces pro-aging free radicals that damage the tissue in your brain and nervous system, create brain fog, stifle energy production, and consume tremendous amounts of nutrients, oxygen, and energy to detoxify the pesticides. Detoxification significantly stresses the liver, kidneys, lungs, and digestive tract, which steals energy you could better use for reaching your goals and living a better life.

6. **Eat fresh-catch, nonfarm-raised fish two to three times a week.** This will build you a better brain and create more mental energy for you. Fish is the ultimate brain and energy food. It contains the fatty acid DHA, which improves memory, prevents degenerative brain diseases such as Alzheimer's, improves cell communication, inhibits inflammation, and is a free-radical-neutralizing antioxidant. In general, avoid large fish such as shark, swordfish, and canned tuna because they contain elevated concentrations of mercury, which is toxic to the nerves and brain.

7. **Enjoy diet diversity.** To perform at your best, your diet must give you all the nutrients to generate the energy to create and complete tasks, grow strong, maintain health, and repair your cells from daily wear and tear. A wide assortment of foods that favor your metabolism will promote that. Eating too many of the same foods too often can compromise your getting all the nutrients you need to create and maintain health and increases the risk that you'll develop energy-zapping delayed food allergies. Delayed allergy means that the symptoms produced by the reactive food can occur hours or days after ingesting the food unlike hyperimmune allergic reactions, which produce immediate allergic affects as seen, for instance, by a bee sting. Symptoms of delayed food allergy include fatigue, light-headedness, and nausea. The most common delayed allergy foods are wheat, corn, soy, peanuts, dairy, and citrus fruits. If you experience any of the symptoms associated with delayed food allergies, remove the suspected foods from your diet and see your doctor; your natural vitality will most likely return in time.

8. **Take nutritional supplements.** It's impossible to have the brain and body power to live a vital life in today's world without taking nutritional supplements. Today's food doesn't have the nutrient value it once did and, considering the nutrient-robbing effects of stress and processed food and pollution, diet alone won't supply your body with adequate nutrients to perform at your best. Supplements should never be taken as a substitute for a sound diet. Specific supplements when combined with a proper diet, will, however, help neutralize the harmful effects of free radicals, support energy

production and recovery, and promote optimal health so your mind and body can perform at their best.

Supplement recommendations (see the Three-Phase Brain and Body Nutritional Supplement Program section later in this chapter) involve three phases. Phase 1 is an essential core supplement program that is the minimum that is necessary to support most peoples' basic supplementation requirements. Phase 2 is more extensive and addresses most of the other nutrients needed to become—and remain—a consistent top performer. Phase 3 is the icing on the cake, providing other important, but optional, nutrients for health. Since these phases are generalized and everybody's biochemistry is individualized, these guidelines may require fine tuning to insure the best fit between person and supplements. Always consult with a qualified healthcare professional to determine your individualized supplement needs. Following are a few guidelines to help optimize your supplement program.

- First and foremost, only implement the phases that work for your goals and lifestyle. Never exceed what's realistic for you. If only doing the Phase 1 program works for you, do only the Phase 1 program. As previously stated, your success is based on your entire success program by working the Turn It Up! formula presented in the book, not by a few supplements that weren't taken. Never forget the cyclist who failed to make the Olympic team because he forgot his grape juice! Start by implementing the Phase 1 program first. Once it's firmly established in your daily life, Phases 2 and 3 can be initiated.

- Implement each phase only as fast as your lifestyle and interest permit. Never try to do too much too quickly. When in doubt, always take more time.

- Don't worry about not taking your supplements when circumstances don't allow it. Follow the 90 percent rule and never, ever worry about not taking them. Taking them regularly over time is what's important, and missing them once in a while is not harmful.

- After a while, if you don't feel like you're receiving any further benefits from your supplements and have reached a plateau, it usually means your body has found the best supplement combination for itself and is performing at a very high level. This signals that your supplement program is right for you. If that occurs, just keep taking your supplements at that level.

THREE-PHASE BRAIN AND BODY NUTRITIONAL SUPPLEMENT PROGRAM

Phase 1

This supplement phase is very easily implemented and provides the core nutrients your body requires to support optimal health, which your diet may not be completely providing.

- **Multivitamin-mineral supplement.** A multivitamin-mineral supplement with breakfast and dinner is a nutrient insurance policy that provides essential nutrients your diet may lack.

- **Buffered vitamin C.** 500 milligrams of buffered vitamin C three times a day with meals builds potent immunity, provides mind-body free-radical protection, and builds strong body tissue.

- **Vitamin E.** 400 international units of vitamin E with breakfast and dinner will support brain-body free-radical neutralization, help prevent heart disease and stroke, and accelerate wound healing.

Phase 2

Adding these supplements to your core Phase 1 program will take your brain and body supplement support program to a much higher level.

- **Magnesium.** Most people are deficient in magnesium. Consumption of 100 milligrams of magnesium with breakfast and dinner will support the essential enzyme processes required for your body and brain to be at their best.

THREE-PHASE BRAIN AND BODY
NUTRITIONAL SUPPLEMENT PROGRAM (CONTD)

Phase 2 (cont'd)

- **Ginkgo biloba.** Taken with breakfast, 500 milligrams of this brain antioxidant will improve memory, as well as brain-cell-membrane pliability, to improve thinking speed and accuracy, reduce stress, and prevent strokes.

- **Alpha-lipoic acid.** Taken with breakfast and dinner, 50 milligrams will promote cell antioxidant protection; detoxify the brain and body tissues from heavy metals; increase mind-body energy by supporting optimal blood sugar transport; and improve memory.

- **Acetyl-l-carnitine.** At breakfast, 500 milligrams supports antioxidant free-radical control, lets fat into the cell to promote fat burning for energy and body composition, and increases memory.

- **Coenzyme Q_{10}** When taken once at breakfast and once at dinner, 100 milligrams of this supplement increases oxygen-based energy production, serves as an antioxidant, increases the potent antioxidant glutathione, improves memory and brain function, and protects the cell-energy production center (mitochondria).

- **Fish oils.** Taken with breakfast, 2 to 3 grams reduce inflammation and support and repair cell and mitochondrial membranes, creating energy and improving memory.

Phase 3

Probiotics and B vitamins are optional supplements. Supplement-committed individuals can add them to the Phase 2 program if desired.

- Probiotics. Taking one capsule of probiotics (good digestive-tract bacteria) thirty minutes before breakfast and one before bed will improve digestion, increase energy, and reduce sickness.

- B-complex. One B-complex capsule with breakfast and dinner increases energy, repairs cell DNA, and improves DNA synthesis.

9. **Snack your way to success.** Keeping energy at sustained levels throughout the day keeps your plans moving along steadily to completion. Many people experience a midafternoon energy bog that often stalls momentum. To transition through that nonproductive lull, power snacking is recommended. The best sustained-energy snacks contain a balance of protein, carbohydrates, and fats. Snacks should be modest in size and packed full of nutrients to provide sustained brain-body energy. The following are snack suggestions that meet those requirements:

- *Protein shake.* A protein shake will increase your serotonin and energy level, keeping you feeling your best throughout the rest of your day. Place 15 grams of rice protein powder in a blender and add one banana, one cup frozen strawberries or blueberries, one teaspoon of lecithin, 1 tablespoon of molasses or 1 tablespoon grade-B maple syrup, and a quarter teaspoon of liquid minerals. Blend and enjoy!

- *Nuts and seeds.* Nuts and seeds contain the antioxidant vitamin E; fiber to promote digestion; and fat, protein, and modest carbohydrates for sustained energy. A small handful can do wonders in a pinch between meals to keep your energy at or near peak levels. The best nuts include almonds, walnuts, and Brazil nuts. Preferred seeds are pumpkin, sunflower, and sesame.

- *Whole-grain crackers with nut butter, seed butter, or avocado spread.* This combination provides carbohydrates, fat, and protein. One or two of these make a perfect snack.

- *Low-fat yogurt with almonds.* Six ounces of plain low-fat yogurt sweetened with grade-B maple syrup and half a handful of almonds make a great snack.

- *Hard-boiled eggs filled with hummus.* Two hard-boiled egg white halves filled with hummus provide great sustained-energy and brain-power, especially in the midafternoon.

- *Cottage cheese with almonds and apple.* Mix six ounces of low-fat cottage cheese with several small apple slices and chopped almonds to make this flavorful between-meals treat.

10. **Maintain a healthy body weight.** Having a healthy body composition promotes and conserves energy, improves physical capacity, and supports a highly vital lifestyle. The following are several strategies proven to help you develop and maintain a healthy body composition.

- *High-quality protein.* Eat a serving of high-quality protein at breakfast, lunch, and dinner. High-quality protein is more easily and more thoroughly digested and absorbed than lesser grades, so less is needed. It also creates sustained energy, good moods, and terrific recovery from daily stress and strain. Good sources include poultry, fish, and tofu.

- *Fresh-caught coldwater fish.* Have fresh-caught coldwater fish three times a week for its fabulous protein and beneficial omega-3 fatty acids. Great sources include halibut, salmon, mackerel, sardines, tuna (avoid canned tuna when possible because it has a high mercury content), and cod.

- *Free-range chicken eggs.* Eat two to four omega-3, free-range, hormone- and antibiotic-free chicken eggs each week for their brain-enhancing good fats and mood-enhancing features.

- *Whole grains.* Eat one serving of whole grain per meal. Whole grains contain fiber, vitamin E, and complex carbohydrates. The best sources include brown rice, millet, and quinoa. These gluten-free grains eliminate the risk of a gluten sensitivity reaction.

- *Fruits and vegetables.* Having one or two pieces of fruit and vegetables per meal provides antioxidant protection, fiber, minerals, and vitamins to your diet. These promote digestive-tract health, energy production, and immune support. Great sources of these foods are strawberries, blueberries, avocado, kale, spinach, broccoli, and alfalfa sprouts.

- *Seeds.* Eating two tablespoons of seeds a day provides fiber, oils, and antioxidants. The best seeds are flax, sunflower, and pumpkin.

You'll know your diet, snack, and supplement program is working when you have steady energy throughout an entire day, aren't constantly hungry, have high optimism, better mental acuity, digest well, and are sick less often.

Ten Benefits from Developing a Great Physical Capacity

From the outside, every success looks easy. Few see the incredible commitment and effort required to develop the skills and create and execute the plan it really takes to do it. To achieve your goals consistently requires that you have the physical capacity to create your plan, execute your plan's steps, and solve the myriad of problems that come up with every plan. Developing your physical capacity makes you a consistent winner in many ways. The following are ten of them.

1. **Building a high-performance brain.** Exercise creates a better brain by generating new brain cells, making more connections between brain cells for better communication, building more muscles to maintain ideal blood sugar levels, and enabling the brain to think better by increasing the amount of oxygen available in the blood to nourish the brain and support better brain aging.

2. **Less illness.** Appropriate physical fitness builds a stronger and more effective immune system, keeping you healthier longer.

3. **More optimism.** Healthy, fit people leading productive lives tend to be more optimistic than those with ill health.

4. **Greater energy.** Regular fitness activities build a better body engine, providing more energy for mind and body to accomplish what you want.

5. **More productivity.** Health, fitness, and a productive life go hand in hand. Productivity is directly proportional to appropriate physical capacity, with the greatest successes coming from the healthiest people.

6. **Better aging.** The greater your physical capacity, the better your body and brain age. Fit people are sick less often and have less disease than the unfit.

7. **Better recovery.** Your body and mind must deal each day with stress and strain. Living a healthy lifestyle and being physically fit help your mind and body recover faster and more completely from day to day, keeping you always ready to meet the opportunities and challenges of your day.

8. **Better body composition.** Regular physical activity builds a better body with leaner tissue mass so you can look, feel, and act your best.

9. **Decreased blood pressure and cholesterol.** Exercise promotes better cardiovascular health, leading to decreased risk of heart disease and stroke by controlling blood pressure and cholesterol.

10. **Increased self-esteem.** Fit people have a better sense of self-worth, which gives them greater confidence because they feel and look better.

Ten Ways to Build Your Physical Capacity

Building the physical capacity to become and remain a consistently top performer requires the synergy of several complementary factors. Each factor shares similar importance in creating the fitness and health necessary to live a highly productive and successful life.

1. **Regularity.** Consistency is the name of the game when it comes to building the fitness required to attain success. Compared to intermittent exercise, small amounts of exercise regularly, produce superior results. No amount of exercise should be considered irrelevant, as fifteen to twenty minutes here and there add up to significant fitness advances over time. As a general rule, exercising four to five days a week for forty-five to sixty minutes will create the fitness to execute your success plans.

2. **Personalized fitness.** Everybody's fitness needs are unique to their individual body, mind, age, and circumstances. The best and most lasting fitness gains come from having a personalized plan. The guidelines provided in this chapter will take most people there, but the option remains to find someone who can help you with, or construct for you, a personal fitness program, if that's an avenue you wish to pursue.

3. **Less is always better.** Too much vigorous exercise too often leads to body breakdown, illness, and injury. When in doubt as to whether you are exercising too much or too hard, it's always best to cut an exercise session short or out. Never push yourself by exercising to the point that it makes you excessively tired, sore, or prolongs your recovery. Each fitness session should make you feel more empowered and energized, never listless or dull.

4. **Smarter is better.** Unfortunately, the "No Pain, No Gain" mentality

of recent decades produced untold injuries, sickness, and burnout for exercisers who pushed themselves over their physical limit too often. Today's success-oriented fitness is driven by intelligent program design that follows the body's physical needs rather than pushing beyond its limits. Always exercise within your limits. Never exercise too hard or too often.

> "No amount of exercise should be considered irrelevant."

5. **Variation.** The mind and body thrive on variation. Constantly changing the tempo, sequence, and intensity of your fitness program heightens your response to exercise, thereby building a better brain and body.

6. **Appropriate intensity.** Too much exercise intensity can overstress your body and generate excess free radicals, which harm the body through oxidative stress. Your exercise should never be so hard that you can't maintain a conversation with someone while doing it. Excess intensity can also lead to overtraining, producing plan-derailing illness and injury. Remember, you're training to be a consistent success in all you do, not to win an Olympic gold medal. Your workouts should be thirty to sixty minutes long. A few minutes either way is acceptable, but if your workouts exceed that too often, they're too long, which increases your risk of injury, illness, or burnout. Whenever in doubt, do less.

7. **Breathing.** Breath is your mind's metronome and should always be incorporated into your exercise so your mind and body synchronize to get the most benefit from your training while generating the least stress. Gently inhale when lifting a weight or other object toward you, and exhale on the return to the starting position. If pushing a weight away from you, exhale on the push and inhale on the return. Always let your breath set the pace for your movement.

8. **Recovery.** Exercise challenges your body, but fitness gains are made during your recovery when your body is built back up to a higher level. You should only exercise at light to moderate intensity to allow for proper recovery. Knowing when to take an unscheduled day off is crucial. Once in a while your mind and body just aren't going to want to exercise or do

regular daily activity. When that infrequent occurrence happens, don't even think of exercising or doing your normal daily routine. Back away from everything and take a mental-health day: your body and mind need rest and change. Continuing to do regular routines in such circumstances most often ends in disaster, especially if one becomes extremely willful and attempts to force something to happen. Backing away is probably the hardest thing for anybody to do. The Voice often tempts you at such times, telling you, "You're giving up too soon," that "You don't want it bad enough," or "Somebody else is going to gain an advantage if you let go." This, of course, is complete garbage attempting to bait you into destructive actions. Recognize the game, back away from the brink of disaster, and regroup by doing something completely different from normal.

9. **Balance.** Every successful fitness program incorporates elements of strength, flexibility, and endurance. These elements, when incorporated into a workout in correct proportion, always lead to better fitness benefits than if only one element is the focus.

10. **Sequencing.** Sequencing the elements of an exercise program is a primary determinant of its success. Ideally, a workout should contain a warm-up, then transition, strength, decompression, and cool-down phases, in that order.

The Winner's Workout

The winner's workout is a time-efficient physical fitness plan, consisting of the five elements in sequence mentioned in the preceding paragraph. It is designed to exercise all your major physical areas to develop the greatest amount of overall fitness in the least time so you can have the health and fitness to advance your success ambitions. More extensive workouts are certainly possible, but the objective of your fitness routine within the context of *Turn It Up!* is to build the fitness required to help you achieve your goals without imposing on your life. Since the workout

"Knowing when to take an unscheduled day off is crucial."

can be done at home, it will save you time going to and from the gym that you can use to build other areas of your success program. Most of the exercises provide the resistance by using your body weight and gravity, which has the advantage of using the most muscles to execute the exercises leading to efficient gains in fitness, weight loss, and muscle toning simultaneously. You can do the winner's workout four to six days a week.

1. **Warm-up.** Your workout begins by gently warming up your body so you can do the best workout possible with the least risk of injury. To achieve this begin with ten minutes of easy cardiovascular exercise. This can be done by pedaling on a stationary bicycle or elliptical machine, walking, or other aerobic activity at a pace that allows you to maintain a very comfortable conversation. After approximately ten minutes, your body should feel slightly warm and you should be perspiring very slightly. When this occurs it indicates that your circulation is flowing at the appropriate rate and your muscles are nice and pliable, allowing you to get the most out of your workout while minimizing the risk of injury.

2. **Transitional phase.** Three transitional exercises—the woodchopper, straight leg raise, and free squat—are done to further warm up your muscles to prepare them for the exercises to be done in your workout's strength phase. Do these three exercises in order without rest between. Do each exercise ten times, and repeat the three-exercise sequence three times.

- *Woodchopper.* The woodchopper exercise actively exercises all your postural muscles while stretching your muscles that tend to become tight from your normal activities of daily living.

  Setup. Stand with your feet shoulder-width apart with fingers interlocked and your hands overhead with elbows slightly bent. Look straight ahead while keeping your torso perpendicular to the floor (Figure 12.1a).

  Execution. Begin by letting your arms naturally arc and lower forward toward the floor as you bend your knees into a squatting position, so your interlocked hands swing between your legs, keeping your back flat and vertical while never bending forward at the waist. Keep your head up and your face looking straight ahead

(Figure 12.1b). From the lowered position, swing your arms upward, as you straighten your legs and return to the starting position (Figure 12.1a). Repeat this ten times, and then begin the next exercise, the straight leg raise, without resting.

Figure 12.1a

Figure 12.1b

- **Straight leg raise.** The straight leg raise warms up your lower torso muscles that unite your upper and lower body as a single functional unit so you can move as a synchronized whole. Synchronized movement spares the low back of excess strain.

  Setup. While lying face up on the floor with legs straight out, gently tighten your abdominal and lower back muscles slightly while pressing your palms into the floor looking straight up at the ceiling (Figure 12.2a).

  Execution. Gently inhale as you vertically lift up your legs together as far as you can comfortably go without arching your back or neck (Figure 12.2b). At the zenith of your leg lift, slowly lower your legs down to the starting position (Figure 12.2a) while gently exhaling through your mouth and never allowing your back to arch. Repeat the straight leg raise ten times without rest before moving on to the free squat.

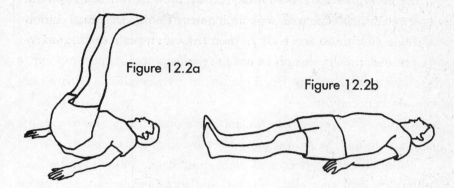

Figure 12.2a

Figure 12.2b

• **Free squat.** The free squat exercises virtually all of your lower-body muscles simultaneously. It is the foundation upon which full body strength is built.

   Setup. Stand facing forward with arms at your sides and feet shoulder-width apart (Figure 12.3a).

   Execution. Lower your buttocks toward the floor no farther than 90 degrees while looking straight ahead, keeping your back flat, torso vertical, and feet flat on the floor while never bending at the waist. At the bottom of your squat, return to the starting position (Figure 12.3a) without bending forward at the waist (Figure 12.3b). Repeat the squat ten times and then repeat the three-exercise sequence two more times.

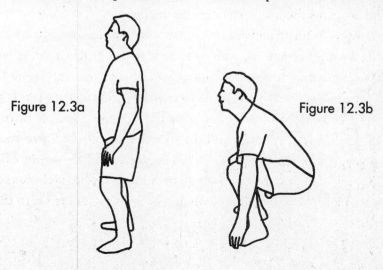

Figure 12.3a

Figure 12.3b

3. **Strength phase.** This strength phase of your workout increases strength and muscle tone without building significant muscle mass. It helps you develop your mind and body to push through times requiring intense focus. The exercises in this phase are the push-up, incline push-up, lunge upright row, and chair dip. Do three sets of ten repetitions with a one-minute rest between sets.

• *Push-up.* The push-up is the most important upper-body exercise because it uses the most upper-body muscles of any exercise.

   Setup. Face the floor and place your hands directly under your shoulders with your elbows locked and shoulder blades spread apart. Keep your mid-back flat and your head on the same plane as your torso so your head doesn't lower toward the floor, which would strain your neck (Figure 12.4a).

   Execution. Slowly bend your elbows and lower your chest toward the floor without letting your shoulder blades come together, your lower back arch, or your neck extend (Figure 12.4b). When your face is four to eight inches from the floor, press into the floor with your hands pushing you away from the floor to your starting position (Figure 12.4a). Repeat ten times. You may prefer to do the push-up kneeling, which is entirely acceptable, if it accommodates your strength level more appropriately.

Figure 12.4a   Figure 12.4b

- **Incline push-up.** The incline push-up increases chest and shoulder flexibility while increasing their strength. It also teaches you the skill of moving your arms against resistance without straining your shoulders and neck. This skill helps you to lift, carry, and move objects without placing excess stress on your neck, which can lead to headaches, neck and shoulder stiffness, and other discomfort and pain.

  Setup. Place you hands on the edge of a stationary table or bench that will support your body weight when you push yourself away from it. As with the push-up, keep your mid-back flat and your head on the same plane as your torso so your head doesn't lower toward the floor, which could strain your neck (Figure 12.5a).

  Execution. Slowly lower your torso toward the table or bench while maintaining your setup position until your chest is four to eight inches from the table or bench, without letting your neck arch or your shoulders come together (Figure 12.5b). At that point, press your hands into the table and push yourself back to the starting position (Figure 12.5a). Repeat ten times.

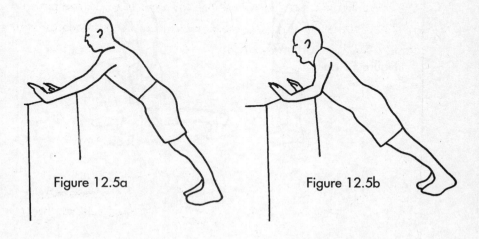

Figure 12.5a

Figure 12.5b

- **Lunge.** The lunge helps you develop the strength and coordination to bend, lift, and reach without straining your lower back, hips, or pelvis.

  Setup. Stand vertically with hands comfortably at your sides. Now, straighten your posture slightly by pressing your feet into the floor and facing straight ahead (Figure 12.6a).

  Execution. Take a long step forward with one foot, plant your heel and bend your knee forward until your back knee almost touches the floor and you are balancing on the ball of your back foot. Make sure the foreword knee does not go over your toes. Your front leg should now be bent to 90 degrees (Figure 12.6b). Pushing through the heel of the front foot and without bending at the waist, stand up, and bring your leg back to starting position (Figure 12.6a). The emphasis should be on the front quadricep. Repeat the lunge ten times.

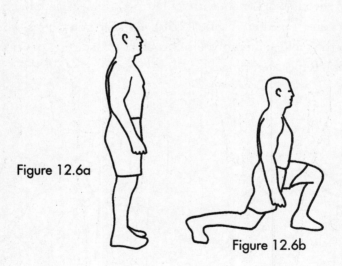

Figure 12.6a

Figure 12.6b

• *Upright row.* The upright row will elevate your shoulders and improve your posture. Postural strain consumes needless energy and strains the small muscles and joints of the neck and shoulders.

Setup. Holding either soup cans or dumbbells, stand with your feet shoulder width apart with palms facing your legs and torso vertical with head drawn toward the ceiling (Figure 12.7a).

Execution. Keeping your hands close to your torso, draw your hands up toward your chin with elbows held high so when they reach chin level your elbows are slightly higher than your chin (Figure 12.7b). Return your hands to the starting position (Figure 12.7a). Repeat the upright row ten times.

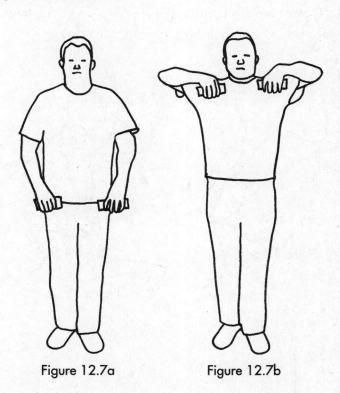

Figure 12.7a   Figure 12.7b

• **Chair dip.** The chair dip develops the postural muscles of the rear
upper arm, rear shoulder, and sides of the chest.

   Setup. Find a chair with armrests that will support your weight as
you raise and lower yourself up and down doing the exercise. Lock
your elbows and place your hands on the armrests, with back straight,
feet flat on the floor, and legs stretched in front of you (Figure 12.8a).

   Execution. Slowly lower yourself toward the chair by bending your
elbows without arching your neck or back (Figure 12.8b). When your
elbows have bent approximately 45 to 60 degrees, press yourself up to
the starting position (Figure 12.8a). Repeat the exercise ten times.

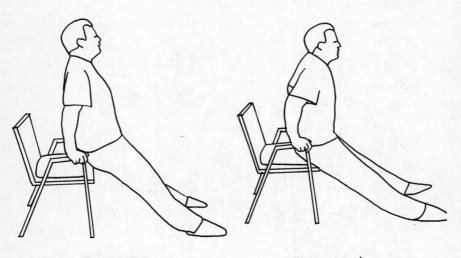

Figure 12.8a   Figure 12.8b

4. **Decompression phase.** When your muscles are working their hardest during the strength phase of your workout, they generate significant tension that causes them to shorten, bunch up, and distort the body toward poor posture. To unwind and take tension out of your body and restore its best symmetry, the decompression phase coordinates and strengthens your pelvis and shoulder blades, creating central posture stabilization. The exercises in this phase are the medicine ball torso twist and dead bug abdominals. Do three ten-repetition sets per exercise, alternating between the two without resting.

- *Medicine ball torso twist.* The medicine ball torso twist will build strong side abdominal muscles and allow you to conserve more energy and move with minimal strain in your body.

  Setup. Lie on your back, face up, while holding a light medicine ball directly above your face with both hands. Now lift the left knee off the ground so the thigh is vertical to the ground with the knee bent at a right angle (Figure 12.9a). Next, gently tense your stomach and low-back muscles without allowing your lower back to arch.

  Execution. Now lift the right knee off the floor to a right angle, and, with elbows locked and keeping tension in your stomach and low-back muscles, lower the medicine ball six to ten times to left side while lowering your knees two inches to the right (Figure 12.9b). You will feel tension in your side abdominal muscles when you do this. Then reverse positions with the knees slightly to the left while lowering the medicine ball six to ten times to the right keeping tension in your low back and abdominals to feel the opposite abdominal muscles work.

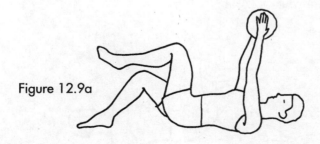

Figure 12.9a

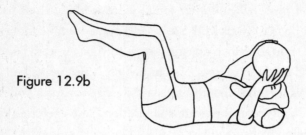

Figure 12.9b

- *Dead bug abdominals.* The dead bug exercise will build your middle abdominal muscles to support your low back and allow you to move, lift, bend, and reduce your risk for low-back strain.

    Setup. Lie on your back, face up, while holding a light medicine ball above your head. Next, tighten your low-back and abdominal muscles so they contract against and support your spine. Then draw one knee off the floor while keeping your stomach and low-back muscles tense until the thigh is vertical (Figure 12.10).

    Execution. Alternately lift each foot off the floor, bringing the thigh to vertical as if you're marching on your back. Do this ten times with each foot.

5. **Cooldown.** The cooldown is the time for your body to wind down from your workout as you slowly transition back to baseline metabolism and posture. The cooldown consists of repeating your warm-up activity of easy stationary bicycle, elliptical, or other aerobic activity for an additional ten minutes. At the end of the ten minutes your body should feel energized and loose from your workout.

Figure 12.10

TURN IT UP! TIPS

1. The easiest way to generate and maintain the energy to live a high-performance lifestyle is to follow a sensible diet and exercise program. Never exercise too hard, too often, or become compulsive about your diet. Find balance between diet and exercise.

2. Small changes to your diet and exercise routines produce the best results over the long term. Avoid making too many life modifications too quickly.

3. Be mindful that you're the one that creates prosperity in life, not your diet or exercise program. Food or exercise alone will not to do for you what you must do for yourself.

4. Harmful molecules called free-radicals accelerate aging. Eating antioxidant-rich foods, including grains, vegetables, and fruit, will help neutralize free radicals.

5. To feel better and generate more energy restrict your calories, drink a cup of water twenty minutes before eating, eat before you're hungry, eat metabolically friendly organic foods, and consume fresh-catch fish.

6. To build a better body and brain take a multivitamin/mineral supplement along with vitamins C and E, magnesium, alpha-lipoic acid, Coenzyme Q_{10}, and omega-3 fish oils.

7. Every nutrition and fitness measure you incorporate into your life must support your health without disrupting your life. Only implement those beneficial changes that can easily merge with those elements that produce success in your life.

8. Always follow the 90 percent rule and never stress about it if you break your diet and exercise programs 10 percent of the time. The 10 percent fiddle factor makes your long-term diet and workout programs sustainable.

CONCLUSION

Twelve Steps to Perpetual Success

*Behold the turtle. He makes progress
only when he sticks his neck out.*

—James Conant

ost of us can recall in vivid detail the indescribable elation felt when we produced our first significant success. Few events in our lives will ever carry that intense sense of validation, pride, and relief that says to us, "Yes, you can do it; yes, your thoughts and actions do count and yes, you do make a difference in this world."

That experience, unfortunately, seems to be fleeting at best, barely giving us time to savor it before life's mundane challenges *immediately* begin to percolate back into our lives, crowding out some of the joy and enthusiasm our success gave us. It hardly seems fair that success should take so much deliberate care and attention to create and that the joy of success so quickly evaporates from life's daily challenges. Never fear, though—with the consistent application of the success model presented in *Turn It Up!*, a life of continual success is readily available!

By far the biggest dilemma all winners face the instant they begin to regularly attain their goals is to find the methodology that perpetuates their success. Ask any top performer, and virtually all will tell you the same thing:

255

its one thing to make it to the top but entirely another to stay there. For example, countless musicians dream of having a hit song that reaches the top of the charts. A few do, but most don't, and only a scant few of those who do ever have a second hit. In the music business, perennial mega-success groups, such as the Rolling Stones and U2, have the Midas touch, an uncanny ability to keep churning out hit after hit while their "one-hit wonder" counterparts top the charts only once, then quickly vanish seldom to be heard from again. The mega-success performers remain so by steadfastly adhering to proven strategies that have created and kept their success machine humming along at peak efficiency year after year.

"Ask any top performer, and virtually all will tell you the same thing: its one thing to make it to the top but entirely another to stay there."

Perpetual success is the exception rather than the rule, but it needn't be. Ideally, life should, and can, be one long, uninterrupted sequence of goals achieved. The following twelve strategies, many of which are discussed elsewhere in this book, have proven themselves to be the infrastructure upon which successful lives are perpetuated. When diligently applied, success eventually can become its own rewarding habit.

1. **Maintain your health.** Health is the foundation upon which your perpetual success is built. Without health, achievement over the long haul is impossible because you won't have the energy to create and perform the tasks necessary to complete your plans consistently and efficiently. Paradoxically, though, once you begin to experience success on a regular basis, success itself can be the very thing that can compromise health. The more success you have, the more opportunities occur and the more critical the selection process becomes as to which ones you will pursue, which ones you won't, and what you'll do with the ones you have on schedule that will be superseded by more important ones that come along. Time, energy, and resource constraints make it impossible to undertake all opportunities. In fact, the choice-making process itself can make you sick

from the massive stress it can create when you have to decide how to allocate your time when there's not enough time to allocate to everything. When you add this to the increased distractions and time consumption from endless phone calls, e-mails, meetings, travel, social obligations, and other common responsibilities associated with success, it becomes a first-class recipe for burnout and illness.

As these circumstances further impose on your time and energy they can, and most often do, forcefully squeeze out of your life existing elements that keep it balanced and you healthy but for which there's no longer any time. When most people begin to feel the time constriction new obligations bring, usually the first things to be let go of to accommodate them are health-generating and health-maintaining practices. Unfortunately, the moment health-promoting routines begin to lose the slightest traction, health begins to deteriorate, until illness occurs. Shortly thereafter, the first symptoms of ill health manifest. Ironically, once sickness occurs it takes significantly more time, energy, and resources to reacquire lost health than it did to create and perpetuate good health originally.

To regain your health once you're sick, you must immediately reinstitute the health management program you followed prior to your illness and obtain the best professional care to get well as quickly as possible. In the final analysis, when you get sick you may end up losing everything you have gained from giving up your original health management program in the first place and then some. In essence, you may have spent much, or all, of your time and effort for nothing. So, always build your success around your health, never vice versa.

"Build your success around your health, never vice versa."

Several steps must be taken to preserve your health once you've achieved harmony between productivity and recovery. The first step is to proactively see a health-and-wellness professional periodically for evaluation to make sure your musculoskeletal system is functioning optimally, and to check in on your vitamin, mineral, hormonal, and neurotransmitter levels. Any deficiencies identified can be resolved in time, so that your body and mind resume performing at their best. Regular wellness visits to a wellness-trained chiropractor, acupuncturist, or physiatrist (a doctor who specializes in rehabilitation medicine) for evaluation and care of postural and structural strains is also suggested. Soft-tissue techniques including manipulation, massage, and soft-tissue therapy can work wonders when specifically tailored to your individual needs, especially, when combined with regular exercise, vacations, fellowship with people who enrich your life, and engaging in recreational activities you love to do. It's also prudent to have yearly medical physicals that include blood tests to rule out other causes of ill health.

2. **Keep evolving.** The dinosaur went extinct because it couldn't adapt quickly enough to a changing climate. It's exactly the same for you. As long as you have the skills to respond to the demands of each moment, you'll remain successful. If you don't, someone who does will muscle his or her way in front of you and capitalize on *your* opportunity. Realize that you will never "arrive" at a point where you're exempt from acquiring new skills and information to remain successful. To stay at the top of your game, remain a student of your discipline by investing time and effort to stay abreast of new innovations. All successful people and businesses do this. They proactively spend tremendous amounts of time and money researching and developing creative means of maintaining their competitive advantage over their competitors. If what they're doing at any point is no longer a viable means to remain a forerunner in their industry, they scrap it in favor of something that is.

> "Remain a student of your discipline by investing time and effort to stay abreast of new innovations that keep you at the top of your game."

To further facilitate your success capability spend time with fresh and brilliant minds in your field, read publications and blogs, and attend programs that keep you a leader in your endeavors. The best time to build your proficiency is before your life begins to produce symptomatic signs that it's becoming obsolete. Being proactive is the name of the game in today's high-paced world. Your mind needs—and thrives on—the constant stimulation of innovation and change. So does your career.

3. **Be brilliant at the basics.** All successful people regularly practice the basic fundamentals that took them to the top of their discipline. These may seem boring, elementary, numbingly repetitious, and lackluster, yet they are the foundations upon which all success is built. Great musicians practice daily the same scales they learned in their first music lessons. That's the very thing most singers do before stepping on stage. They spend time backstage with their voice coach, singing voice scales following a keyboard. Sound boring? It is. Why do they do it? Because they know that's the only way they can sing their best. It's the same with the great golfers. They spend countless hours at the driving range, honing and adapting their golf strokes. The great performers know their success is in the hidden details of the fundamental skills that built their careers.

It's extremely common to see newly—or battle-weary—successful people first slowly drift away from the basics that made them successful and then slide back into their old habits. Frequently, the reasons people dispense with their basics include getting lazy from mistakenly thinking they've transcended the basics; getting greedy and trying to cram more productivity into their already overstuffed lives; and becoming distracted by too many opportunities, excess flattery, others' criticisms, or dealing with others' incompetence. Diligently practice your own personal "musical scale" basics daily to keep your fundamental skills razor sharp, because your future successes depend on them. The best time to practice is in the morning before you start your day. That way they'll get done. The longer you wait each day to practice them, the less likely it is that you will.

4. **Keep moving forward.** Success is never self-perpetuating. It requires a daily infusion of energy to gather and carry its momentum into the future. Every successful person knows they're only as good as their last success. Past successes are not a guarantee of future ones. All you have control over in creating your

future is to keep your plans moving forward by devoting time to them day by day. Each time an action advances your plans to completion, you're one step closer to a better future. The only way you get to tomorrow is through today's actions. Now is where tomorrow is built. Make now count by keeping your vision and commitment on the execution of your plans so you'll have a better tomorrow. Review and refine your plans daily so that each action taken points precisely toward completion. Productive change is good and encouraged.

> "Now is where tomorrow is built."

5. **Keep refining your team.** It's not possible to create a successful life without the help and partnership of others. Multiple talents and skills are needed to take full advantage of life's circumstance, and no one possesses the capacity to do it all alone. A very successful client of mine told me that the hardest and most valuable lesson he's learned in business is to "hire up." He hired the best people he could find in lieu of the cheapest. He said each of the business associates he's hired through his "hire up" policy have consistently exceeded their salary in product sales many, many times over. The assets that have made them so valuable are their skills and motivation to get their jobs done correctly the first time, on schedule, and without the help of others. Another important statement he made is that the most expensive decisions he's made are those that didn't produce the desired results or get the job done on schedule the first time. To build the best team possible, always confirm that your team's members are compatible and motivated to achieve your goals, not theirs, that they are compensated appropriately, that they are trained well, and that you have an accountability system to confirm that they're doing their jobs as agreed.

You also have another team in life that requires your daily commitment, and that's your personal team that supports you in your private life. Always cherish, acknowledge, and cultivate your relationships with those who contribute to your life in meaningful ways. People never get thanked enough for their contributions. These loyal partners in life are priceless. When properly acknowledged, they will do anything to support you.

6. **Let go of the rope.** To keep your successful life rolling along, it's imperative to make sure your plans are properly staffed, are executed in the best environment possible, and have the necessary materials, supplies, and equipment to get the job done correctly the first time. If any of these areas aren't fully compatible with your plans, you must convert unacceptable ones to those that meet your criteria or replace them with ones that do. Every plan element must keep pace with every other element so that each plan advances continuously toward an on-time completion.

In that vein, everyone working on your plan must keep pace with everyone else in completing their tasks and remaining in agreement on the project's steps and goals from start to finish. If any disparity exists among people or their allegiance to your plan, your plan will proceed only as fast as the slowest person and the least loyal person allow. Every success is an evolutionary process composed of several very specific steps with varying degrees of difficulty. The more steps and the more difficult those steps are, the greater the risk of personnel incompatibility. With even the slightest hint of incompatibility, the chances of your plan stalling increase exponentially. If incompatibility does arise, immediately modify any circumstances so your plan's integrity is maintained and no momentum is lost. Delayed change creates additional losses that can be impossible to regain. When change becomes imminent, make it swiftly and decisively. Postponing the inevitable only amplifies and prolongs the suffering. The pain of hanging on to something that has no future is much greater than the temporary pain of letting go.

7. **Never skip steps.** The fastest way to extend the time required to complete a plan is to attempt to complete it more quickly by implementing an untested shortcut. This is especially true if this means eliminating essential steps that are already in place. Skipping steps is an extremely risky proposition and will inevitably trip you up, ultimately making your work to rectify it and get your plan back on track extremely more difficult. The only time you should ever consider breaking protocol is if you find a better way to achieve your goals that has proven itself through previous implementation.

Taking the steady, predictable route to plan completion also helps you conserve tremendous amounts of mental and physical energy. Worry and uncertainty about a risky outcome can scramble brains and consume vital physical energy, quickly compounding any difficulties. Usually, sticking with a well-thought-out plan is the way to go.

8. **Maintain a razor-sharp mind.** For you to reach your goals continually, your mental reaction time, decision-making astuteness, mental endurance, and knowledge base must constantly be at their best. Your brain, like your body, needs constant stimulation and balanced rest to maintain peak function. It's well known by neuroscientists that regular mental challenge and stimulation improve and maintain your brain function and structure. Easy ways to stimulate your brain are to read material that requires mental dexterity and synthesis of information; engage in stimulating dialogue with others; research topics of interest to you; make meals that require following a complex recipe; play Scrabble, chess, or other strategy games; and listen to books and other source materials on audio media. You should, however, only do these mental activities when you're mentally up to it. If your mind is a little fuzzy or your brain is dull from too much thinking, you need rest more than additional tasks to complete. Once your natural mental vitality returns, resume your brain-stimulation activities.

9. **Boost your skills.** You can never have enough skills. Each skill you have takes you a step closer to gaining your personal and financial independence. The more skills you have, the faster and more competently you can seize and convert your opportunities into goals achieved. The best time to build your skills is before they're needed—as well as when you have the time to acquire them. A perfect time to add to the skills you'll need for future success is whenever your life slows down and a natural lull in momentum occurs. Always prioritize acquisition of new skills. Start with the most important skill that suits the time you have available for it. Never try to learn a skill if you don't have the time to learn it fully, even if it requires several days. Learning it start to finish without prolonged interruption inscribes it in your mind and body, which makes reinforcement

through repetition significantly easier. If you start to learn a skill, then stop and set it aside for a few days, weeks, or months, you disrupt the continuity of the acquisition process and consume massive amounts of time regaining momentum once you resume. Never hesitate to acquire additional information or attributes because they're the best investment you can make

> "The best time to build your skills is before they're needed."

in your future, as your best investment is in yourself. You are the force that makes your life, and your skills get you there. Nothing else will.

10. **Never get greedy.** Success can be extremely paradoxical, becoming either the best or worst of all worlds. The dark side of success is that it can create greed that can become the biggest reason for your future failures. The demise of all seemingly invincible empires, businesses, and people most often occurs when their successes spark an insatiable hunger for achieving bigger, greater, and more grandiose—and most often overly self-serving—successes. With rare exception, every empire ultimately collapses from resource dilution by pursuing too many ambitions simultaneously, or from excess resource consumption that is required to maintain the infrastructure and overhead needed to support existing services. Before undertaking any new project, always take stock of your time and resources to make sure both are in adequate supply to complete your task without placing any hardship on your reserves. Also, you must, as part of your normal success protocol, make sure you have enough reserve, plus some extra, to capitalize on any unanticipated challenge or beneficial opportunity that may come along. Doing so will prepare you for any eventuality, ensuring that you'll most often come out a winner.

11. **Remain on the offensive.** There are two basic ways to approach life: offensively or defensively. The most successful players in the game of life pursue their dreams offensively. There is only one option for them. They proactively pursue and engage life, rather than waiting, watching, and reacting to it. Living offensively means making decisions about what's to be gained, never on what could be lost. Nobody has ever prospered in life by

continuously reacting to other people, places, or things like a puppet on a string. Lance Armstrong didn't win seven consecutive Tours de France by waiting for his competitors to impose their will on him. He proactively did everything possible to be in top shape at the start of each Tour to set the tone of the event by offensively controlling the race along with his trusted teammates from the first to last stage. If you believe something can happen, and you've got the skills, and your plan indicates that you can achieve it, pursue it because all the elements pointing to success are there.

> "Living offensively means making decisions about what's to be gained, never on what could be lost."

12. **Remain spontaneous.** Most people experience intermittent, random levels of average success throughout their lives but just can't seem to make the pivotal breakthrough that takes them to a higher level of success. The most common reason people fail to make the leap to a more consistent and advanced success level is that their mind-set dramatically shifts when they start to experience regular success. People are often so over-joyed about their initial success that they just keep doing what they did to achieve it without really thinking much about how they actually did it, and they continue to succeed in the process. However, once they consciously realize it's possible to have a successful lifestyle and how good that lifestyle could be, they often abandon the carefree spirit that created their original successes. Instead they adopt the success kiss-of-death philosophy of trying to ensure a successful life by controlling and manipulating every action so tightly and perfectly that they stifle their success momentum and creativity. This then throws their confidence and trust in their ability to achieve their aspirations into the toilet. To avoid this all-too-common success-implosion scenario, always approach every opportunity for success with the same enthusiasm, ambition, and vitality as you did when you first started producing your wins.

In summary, by following the rules discussed in *Turn It Up!* and by placing your trust in your proven track record, your preparation, and your plan, you will consistently produce successful outcomes. Once this is done enough times, the success lifestyle you know is possible can happen.

Turn It Up! is about developing a winning formula that has consistently proven to support people in achieving their goals and making their dreams come true. The fact is, you're born a winner with all the talents and drives to make it happen. You have the innate capacity to lead an extraordinary life of passion, purpose, productivity, and prosperity. The key to unlocking your success potential is to identify your unique talents and follow a proven methodology that enables you to flourish and experience regular, unprecedented success.

Success is a privilege, not an entitlement. Past successes are not a guarantee of future ones. The bridge between past and future achievement is the creation of great plans based on vast uncensored possibility thinking coupled with superb execution. Trusting your life process, your skills, your history as a winner, and your preparation are the pillars that create and maintain a successful life. Fear and The Voice, your constant detractors throughout life, are powerless in the context of the trust you place in yourself and your ability to manifest success. Your faith, matched with the health to sustain a successful lifestyle over a lifetime, creates the string of achieved aspirations that constitutes the legacy you desire and are meant to create.

> "Success is a privilege, not an entitlement."

Each moment gives you an opportunity to be the best you can be. Your best insurance that success will happen is for you to grab the brass ring of opportunity whenever it appears and never look back. You must remain fearless in your commitment to excellence and to developing your gifts. In the end, it's your willingness to embrace unconventional opportunities and methodologies that makes you who you are and determines what successes you will create. Lance Armstrong once said to me, "When you get a second chance, go all the way." Each moment is a second chance to live an extraordinary life. Life's best moments always come from unanticipated directions. When life gives you a chance at the extraordinary, grab it and go all the way. You just might be surprised by what you achieve.

INDEX

Page numbers followed by an *f* indicate figures.